SHE FOUND HER VOICE

To Margaret and Allan
Enjoy reading!

BR McKinnon

THE LIFE OF
NANCY EVANS ROLES,
ARTIST AND ADVOCATE

SHE
FOUND
HER
VOICE

BARBARA MCKINNON

CLEARSIGHT
BOOKS

Raleigh, North Carolina

ISBN hardback: 978-1-945209-38-3
ISBN paperback: 978-1-945209-39-0
ISBN ebook: 978-1-945209-40-6
Library of Congress Control Number: 2023902753
Published by Clear Sight Books, Raleigh, North Carolina
Cover and interior design by Patricia Saxton

*For Mom
and for all who ask the important questions*

TABLE OF CONTENTS

PREFACE

My mother was a remarkable woman. Many children think that of their mothers, but since all who knew mine shared my opinion, that judgment is confirmed. In fact, it always seemed to me there was only one thing she did not do well, and that was to stand up to my father—and perhaps that is not so much a fact as it is the impression of a daughter who was influenced by the feminism of the 1960s.

I knew during my youth that my mother was president of many different groups of women and that she had many friends. The specifics were of no interest to me and only became important when I was in my forties and started to realize how incredibly accomplished my mother was. In the early 1990s, I started writing down the stories I could get her (and other family members) to recount.

She was told by a longtime friend to keep her files—that the importance of the records of her life was not hers to judge but was the responsibility of succeeding generations. She took that advice, and the result was a large number of boxes holding her files, programs, correspondence, and writings.

Soon after our mother's death, I promised my brother and sister that I would organize these artifacts and put them on a computer so the family could all know about her and perhaps find additional insights into her life. I wrote a 270-page narrative record and then sought a copyeditor. I planned on binding the pages and presenting them to my siblings and anyone else I thought might be interested.

A friend agreed to look at the material and, when he had done so, suggested that I decide on a perspective, take out extraneous family material, and rewrite her history for publication. What fun it has been to look more closely at the events of her life and seek out the meanings my mother found and how they impacted what she achieved.

Nancy Evans Roles was a woman of the twentieth century. Her life spanned an explosive revolution in transportation, communication, and technology, two world wars, the Korean and Vietnam eras, and the flowering of the women's and civil rights movements. A lifelong proponent of John Dewey's progressive education pedagogy, she participated in its codification and promulgation. She was an energetic and effective proponent of a cultural transformation that freed many women from positions of dependence and perceived inferiority, and she supported equalizing rights and opportunities for all Americans. A forceful advocate, she produced a body of work that contributed to the progress of justice and wholeness even while functioning within acceptable societal norms and fulfilling her youthful dreams of becoming a wife and mother. She brought a creative lens to life—literally as a talented painter and writer and figuratively in how she viewed the world and inspired others to fulfill their potential.

Twenty-first-century youth face a different revolution, one potentially with even further-reaching consequences. Our cyber world, secular society, gender issues, and extreme political partisanship have left them with few concrete standards by which to establish a legitimate moral compass for themselves. To let Nancy Roles's participation in the evolution of women's history remain unheralded would be to deny the importance of all the twentieth-century women who faced the questions of women's and minorities' rights and made the decisions that have produced a more just society. But it would also deny this next generation an awareness of a particular life history that can serve as an example of how one woman developed her own ethic and found the resources and standards that built a genuine, exceptional, and significant life. It is for these reasons that I have written this volume.

Barbara Evans Roles McKinnon
January 2022

ONE

IDEAS AND PASSIONS

"AS THE FIRST IDEAS ARE CONCEIVED, AND A LINE OR TWO

BECOMES A REALITY FOR A SKETCH TO BE FORMULATED INTO

A MEANINGFUL COMPOSITION, I FIND MY INTEREST AND

AMBITION TO BE AWAKENED." (1935)

We are all makers, doers, thinkers, changers, compilers, and organizers simply by virtue of being alive. When we become conscious creators of our actions and purposefully live into these roles, we become artists. It was from this perspective that Nan Evans wrote in her journal on September 28, 1935, about her plans for the ensuing three months. That fall, at the young age of twenty-seven, she was chaperoning a group of American students in England. Her boss, Dr. Thomas Alexander, the dean of New College, a subset of Teachers College at Columbia University, had arranged for a ticket on a Cunard Line ship and sent her to London by herself. She was tasked with taking charge of a small group of undergraduate students who wanted to be teachers and were involved in a study abroad program sponsored by the college. The previous person in that job had had to leave and Nan was to take her place. Nan was single, quite beautiful, well-liked, and highly intelligent. Dr. Alexander's only admonition to her was that some of her students were older than she was, and she was not to date them.

Nan Evans knew that she was to guide the students in their studies. Her only personal ambition was to learn about London and England's history. A journal entry written while on the ocean liner, however, shows a much broader vision and a sense of personal responsibility for doing a good job. Nan did not intend for the journal to be read by anyone but herself, and her words sound pretentious to our modern ears. Against the backdrop of her life and her emotional fabric, however, they come alive in their prescience. The entry also reflects the underlying and unifying theme of her life—to assemble within herself a comprehensive, coherent philosophy and faith and to produce a worthy work product.

The things I want to do are gradually unfolding before me, and little by little the blank wall that I looked at for the past two weeks, without aim or any real ambitions, is becoming the background for a very large and beautiful and interesting mural. As the first ideas are conceived, and a line or two becomes a reality for a sketch to be formulated into a meaningful composition, or a valuable part of a very large composition, I find my interest and ambition to be awakened and sharpened to a keen edge, one that I hope will be so sensitive to development and progress that the ultimate mural will be a creditable, worthwhile, interesting, and meaningful accomplishment. The way towards this goal will be a series of progressive steps, each a little higher and a little broader than the preceding one. I pray that each one will be constructed, studied critically as to character and foundation and value, and will serve as encouragement and guidance towards the building and surmounting to the next step. The mural has as its theme an integration of valuable and interesting experiences in work and social intercourse—of the group of students and myself portraying our living in England, or rather London, during the next three months. The background has been prepared, and a program of designing mapped out during the past two months. A fuller development of the design, the realization of a worthwhile composition, and the form, depth, and colorfulness of the completed mural remain to be developed. Faith in ourselves and our associates, continuance and habitual work, continual and exhaustive use of our tools, mental and physical health, and sound philosophical reasoning will direct us on to the actual realization of the painting.

Art is the arrangement of different elements to create a whole. It is a spiritual act wherein the creator delves into his or her psyche to discover and uncover a reality awaiting expression. If our art constructs meaning in and for our lives, if our art energizes us and we feel most alive when we are creating, if in our art we are attempting to form connections in our environment and wish to bring a sense of order or comfort out of what appears to be chaos, we have the possibility of producing good art. That was Nan's goal, both in her art and in her life.

In the closing decades of her life, Nan's community identified her as an artist, with an appreciation of the landscapes and portraits she painted. Although her life was not centered on drawing and painting from the mid-1940s to the mid-1960s while she raised her children, she still always viewed her world from an artist's perspective. She had just completed her first two years on the faculty at New College when she wrote the above entry. There she was introduced to the ideas and passions that would shape the rest of her life.

....

Nan first experienced New York City in 1932. Three years into the Depression, the city was just beginning to reinvent itself and forge ahead. The Chrysler Building and the Empire State Building had been opened in 1930 and 1931 respectively, and, by 1932, The New Yorker Hotel, the Waldorf Astoria, and Radio City Music Hall were engaged in attracting business. Shanties with homeless people still abounded, however, particularly from 72nd Street to 110th Street. Columbia University was north of there, starting at 116th Street. If Nan went south, she could not avoid seeing the misery that was between her and the shopping and entertainment. If she went north into Harlem, that same despair prevailed: she was then in an area that had 50 percent unemployment. At one point she commented:

All of us went to ride down on the Point and then across the island through the slum section. What an awful existence those people seem to have. Why is some life so wretched? Is there nothing to do for them? Are we the people to change things, our standards of living? And if so, how?

Perhaps the majority of college-educated individuals have some concern about social issues while in their twenties. Since arriving at New College, however, Nan had been immersed quite intensely in discussing and investigating ways to bring about social progress. Her trip to London and a tour of Germany the previous summer were a part of her absorption into and training in classic progressivism.

The early 1930s were a time of political turmoil, with much of the trend towards and support for Communism finding its focal point at Columbia. Large-scale protests took place on the grounds of the school. New ideas and approaches were greeted there with an open-mindedness that permitted and encouraged experimentation in all disciplines. In the field of education, New College was the epicenter of research and development. John Dewey, one of the seminal educational theorists of the twentieth century and a member of the faculty of Teachers College, was promulgating his concepts there. He was later ranked with educators Rudolf Steiner of Austria and Maria Montessori in Italy. While the approaches of these academicians were different, their pedagogy was quite similar: a child learns to be a whole person by how education is presented to them. Learning should not be a pouring of information into the child's head; it should be a process wherein the child interacts creatively with the environment—in its entire natural, communal, and experiential aspects. Learning should be a multifaceted activity that gives a child a chance to grow holistically.

Dewey argued that the curriculum should be relevant to students' lives. He suggested that, due to urbanization, "home" had shifted from being a rural, farm-based "workshop" where children learned many life lessons to being primarily a dwelling place. The teaching of previously home-based studies—such as how to be part of a functional business that provided the communal livelihood—had shifted from the parents to the schools. Thus, the approach to education had to change.

In succeeding years, Montessori's writings and her system became much better known than either Dewey's or Steiner's, and many schools based on her theories continue to educate students today. But in 1932, at Columbia, it was Dewey's ideas that held sway.

Dr. Alexander, Nan's boss, was an early supporter of Dewey, and it was he who established New College, acting as its director during most of its existence. Alexander had joined the Columbia University faculty in 1924 when his good friend, William Fletcher Russell, the dean of Teachers College, asked him to become the associate director of the International Institute as their expert on German education. Alexander's organizational ability, his love of education, his pragmatism, his belief that education was a lifelong learning experience, and, in particular, his connection to and agreement with John Dewey's ideas induced in him a desire to reform the way teachers were trained. He felt that while teachers had to know their subject matter, such was only the beginning. They also needed to know their students—their backgrounds, talents, and stage of development. Only then could the teacher engage the student in activities that involved the direct personal experience and the problem-solving that would engender growth. Alexander appealed to his friend, Dean Russell, for permission to begin an experiment. That experiment was New College.

The school was created primarily to develop and promote Dewey's pedagogy. Through the concepts articulated and developed by Nan, Alexander's other undergraduate faculty members, and the assisting Teachers College faculty, however, the New College curriculum also pioneered both the idea of mandatory foreign study in an undergraduate program and the idea that teachers should experience the lives of others. Both concepts were included in the syllabus, the latter through an obligatory "period of industry" during which the teachers-in-training had to go out and get a job for a time.

Dr. Alexander was also influenced by Dr. George Counts, who had joined the Teachers College faculty in 1927. Counts's theory was that teachers should be trained to educate for political purposes, a concept called "social reconstruction." He argued that teaching was always a political act, whether or not teachers were aware of their prejudices and viewpoints. This teacher bias, he believed, always impacted the students' worldviews. Issues of social justice, therefore, were inherently a part of all forms of education. Thus, a critique of society and motivation towards future action to promote social progress should be consciously taught.

Dr. Alexander and his faculty asked questions that incorporated both men's views: What is the best way to prepare teachers? Who should teach? What do teachers need to know to facilitate their students' growth? The curriculum they devised was based on seminars that directed the would-be teachers to teach themselves what they needed. The outline included fieldwork in the community, internships in industry, foreign travel to broaden their perspective, connection to nature through participation in creating a farm community, and student teaching. This holistic method involved the faculty's creation of "units" for education, intensive one-on-one critiques, and the development of personal relationships between the faculty, the teachers-in-training, and the students they were to teach.

Dr. Clarence Linton, a member of the faculty, once said that New College was looking for "individuals with high intellectual endowment, high scholastic attainment, high social and economic status, superior personal qualities, good health and good character" in both faculty and students. Nan certainly met those criteria. When later in life she took the Stanford-Binet intelligence test as a favor to her daughter, her score exceeded the scale's limits.

Nan arrived at New College with the abilities and open-minded attitude necessary to participate in this radical and experiential adventure. For women to engage in these revolutionary activities, however, had become acceptable only in the previous decade. Fortunately, Nan had had the advantage of being raised by a woman on whom all the responsibility for a family rested, and this departure from the norm, while a negative in many ways, provided Nan with a model for independent thinking in a world just recently according women any rights at all.

At that time, Nan quite possibly was only partially aware of the extreme nature of the situation in which she found herself. She actually wanted to be in New York because she wanted to study art. Joining the faculty at New College was the means by which she could accomplish that goal. She did not enjoy being a teacher; only sporadically during the decade she taught did she feel she had a good day in the classroom. There were moments of enthusiasm and hopefulness:

> *Enjoyed reading Smith's* Parties & Politics. *When I become interested in reading such I always have such seemingly impossible desires, to be ambitious, to be brilliant, to really teach a regular class in history and make it terribly interesting. Imagine!*

However, those moments were rare. Her true love was art. She frequently wished that she were in a financial position to stay true to that love. Her indoctrination into the progressive ideas at New College, however, did inculcate in her a genuine desire to nurture and advance those policies that would increase the potential of children. The goal of the Dewey pedagogy was to integrate all aspects of life, fitting the pieces together to form a healthy life that was satisfying to the individual and of benefit both to that person and to society. From the perspective of the budding artist, this integration made sense. Promoting education, whether for children or adults, would later become one of Nan's major foci as a community leader.

Nan was in New York at the invitation of Dr. Alexander. There was a synchronicity about the events that eventuated in his offer that causes one to pause. She had been teaching at Needham B. Broughton High School in Raleigh, North Carolina, a school that was trying out John Dewey's ideas. Had all of Nan's life led towards her arrival in New York to become part of the progressive movement that would underpin all her later public activities and would both further and delay her study of art? Are we all led to whom we become? Choices lead to consequences, and consequences result in choices. Nan's history prior to Alexander's offer indicates her ability and availability to take the chances that the move entailed.

TWO

FOUNDING FAMILIES

"SHE USED TO TELL ME STORIES

ABOUT HER EXPERIENCES." (1989)

The turn to the 1900s began a century that would see multiple cataclysmic events, a century of radical change, with those living through it challenged to respond to the barrage. Nan was proactive and open to possibilities partly because her heritage was of a family with a long history of involvement and prominence in eastern North Carolina.

THE EVANSES

Greenville has had its place in the history of North Carolina recorded ably by historians, notably by Hugh Lefler, whose wife, Bet, became one of Nan's closest lifelong friends. However, *Chronicles of Pitt County, North Carolina*, compiled by the Greenville Historical Society in 1982, relates the specific details about the town, its inhabitants, and its surround. From these chronicles comes information about the Evans family:

From the rugged green mountains of Wales to the sandy shores of the New World on to the rich soils of the North Carolina coastal plains, the Evans clan has grown and prospered. Each individual Evans family is one of the links in the long chain dating back to the 11th century when the Evans name began. (p. 296)

In the mid-1700s, a Richard Evans married a woman named Susannah Coutanche. Her father, Michael Coutanche, was a successful builder in Bath, North Carolina. He had purchased a large parcel of land west and somewhat south of Bath earlier and, upon Susannah's marriage, he deeded part of this land over to the couple. Thus began the Evans family history in what was to become Pitt County.

Richard was living in New Bern, North Carolina, at the time of his marriage and was a member of the colonial assembly. He introduced a bill to create Pitt County shortly after he acquired the western parcel, and it became law in 1760. Later, Richard was instrumental in creating the town of Greenville, the eventual county seat of Pitt County, "on his land, wherein space should be available for a courthouse, a church, prison and stocks." Unfortunately, he died before he could complete and sign the required documentation. Eventually, a new assembly passed an amendment to the bill that would create a town initially called Martinborough (named after a royal governor of the time). This made it possible for Richard's widow, Susannah, to complete the required paperwork and the town was founded in 1774. Originally a 100-acre tract cut from the Evans property, Martinborough was platted into lots of one-half acre each and the streets and the government were designed. In 1787, the town fathers renamed the small community Greenesville in honor of Nathanael Greene, a hero in the Revolutionary War, and it was later shortened to Greenville. The main street is still named for Richard Evans, and the first half-acre lot was sold to an Evans. A Charles Forbes, prominent in the political affairs of the time and whose descendants married into the Evans family several times, was the treasurer in the sale of these lots. In addition, there is a Cotanche Street, presumably named after Susannah Coutanche

Evans. Nan and her siblings were aware that Evans Street was named after their family—and that several other named streets were connected to relatives—but they thought that was normal and did not make them any different from other people.

Nan's Grandfather Evans bought his original acres in 1860 from an A. A. Forbes. He acquired a second tract in 1863 through a trustee arrangement to care for the daughter of J. J. Forbes, and in 1867 and 1868, he bought a third and fourth tract. Neither more nor less elaborate than the surrounding farms, the Evans acreage was one of six parcels that had been part of the Forbes land grant in colonial times. As the landowner of record during the Civil War, this William Evans was responsible for maintaining the road that bordered his property, known locally as Tarboro Road since it went from Greenville to the hamlet of Tarboro, and the Greenville supervisors paid him a fee to perform this task. Grandmother Susan Caroline Cornelia Forbes Evans deeded the land to her four children in 1880 after her husband's death. The property was divided, and Nan's father, Will, eventually inherited about a third.

THE BROWNS

The family of Nan's mother, Nannie Brown Evans, had arrived even earlier. Originally from England, the Browns first settled in Jamestown, Virginia, in the 1600s. Then, in the early 1700s, one of them moved south. The family records include a copy of a land grant dated June 26, 1762, given to John Brown of Pitt County by Earl Granville, Viscount Carteret, and Baron Carteret of Hawnes.

Nan's great-grandfather, John Reddin Brown, was a descendant of the John Brown who received the land. He married Martha (Patsy) Stancill, and they had nine children. One of them, John Stancill William Brown (Nan's grandfather), enjoyed a large holding that began on the north side of the Tar River just opposite the Evans property on the south side. This Brown married Rebecca (Becky) Fleming, connecting yet another of the early families. When Becky was married, her father gave her a personal slave and quite a bit of personal property. She drove herself from her birthplace to her new home with all her earthly belongings. The Civil War broke out shortly afterwards. The Browns had slaves, so "JSW" joined the Confederate army, and Becky was left to manage the farm. Nan recounted later:

> She used to tell me stories about her experiences. Several times when the Yankees came through, she said, they stole everything in both the smokehouse and the house. She learned to hide everything whenever there was a hint that the Yankees were coming through again.

Nan's grandfather fought in the Battle of Gettysburg, where he was wounded in the knee and taken prisoner. He was released from prison in 1863, wounded again at the Battle of the Wilderness, and lived to reach Appomattox. While in the Confederate Army, he became so hungry that he ate the bark of trees. Of the one hundred men who left with him from Pitt County, he was one of only three who returned alive. In all, 2,000 men from Pitt County answered the Confederate call.

Nan's genetic inheritance included, thus, the Evanses, the Browns, the Forbeses, the Flemings, and the Stancills, all of whom were among the early settlers of Greenville. Again from *Chronicles of Pitt County*:

> Almost all the early families of Pitt Co., with Greenville as its capital, are descendants of colonial settlers, many of whom were second sons of the nobility of England, Ireland, Scotland, Wales and France.

Nan pored over the chronicles when they were published and chuckled at the mistakes made, since she had learned her history at her Aunt Martha Forbes Stancill's knee as a child—when the family Bible was still in existence. She knew by heart the genealogy of most of her relatives. In 1993, she wrote to a cousin in Raleigh, "I might challenge you to find even *one* of the original Greenville families with whom you are *not* related." This genetic heritage of having descended from community leaders, in addition to the birthright of a large and interdependent family grouping, was quite probably a significant factor in instilling in the young Nan a sense not only of community but also of ambition.

....

Greenville was a typical small Southern town surrounded by farms. It had been overrun and raided by Union forces several times during the Civil War, and Reconstruction had brought a carpetbagging government to add to the misery of post-war poverty. By the close of the war, Greenville's population had dwindled to less than 1,000 (a good percentage of whom were related to Nan in some way), and cotton was king.

In the mid-1880s, however, Nan's uncle, Leon Evans, with neighbors (and relatives) Theopolis ("Offie") Stancill, Gus Evans, and Jacob Joyner, became interested in a change from that precarious fiber. Tobacco had been grown in Pitt County as early as the late 1700s, but with the Revolution and the decline in the British markets, the crop's production had contracted precipitously. One summer evening, Leon and his friends met with A. A. Forbes (another relation) at his farm three miles outside Greenville and discussed the possibility of growing tobacco again. A particular strain had been successfully farmed in Kentucky, and Ben Warren Brown over in Nash County (North Carolina) had produced a commercial crop. The group decided to go over and see. While there, they not only learned as much as they could about the process but also met A. H. "Gus" Critcher. This gentleman eventually moved to Greenville to help the men get started, where he subsequently met and married Leon's sister, Lillian. The men built four curing barns and in 1886 produced Greenville's first commercial tobacco crop.

Turn-of-the-century Greenville was beginning to recover momentum and was on the cusp of revitalization. Farmers and small businesses in the state were impacted most by the advent of three forces that significantly changed Greenville's history: tobacco, transportation, and education.

The first force—tobacco, Leon Evans's undertaking—grew to be a key industry in North Carolina. The first tobacco warehouse in Greenville was built in 1891. By the third decade of the twentieth century, Greenville had become the state's largest center for the distribution of tobacco.

The growth in the tobacco industry was aided by the second force: improvement in transportation methods. Plank roads had been chartered as early as 1851 in North Carolina. They were constructed of vertical logs covered with horizontal planks, and their purpose was to keep heavy loads from getting stuck in the mud. At the time of Nan's birth, there was just one plank road in Greenville, which ran from there to Raleigh. Although it was a toll road, it was an improvement over the dirt and corduroy roads that had been providing Greenville its pathways, and it presaged the coming of better thoroughfares.

In 1908, the wooden bridge across the Tar River was replaced with a steel one. Further, the Washington Branch Railroad going through Greenville was established in 1892, and the first telephone exchange was opened in 1896, with nearly 100 subscribers. A still-extant photographic postcard from the 1900–1920 period depicts Evans Street as a wide dirt roadway with wooden curb boards separating the dirt road from the dirt sidewalk. The houses shown are commodious and elegant, testifying to the newly developed wealth of the town, even though the infrastructure had not yet caught up.

Transportation via the Tar River had also become an economic force. Steamboats offering passenger travel, mail service, and conveyance of freight were common by 1896.

The third catalyst for change experienced by the small community was its leaders' recognition that for the town to thrive, its youth needed a sound education. While academies existed for the affluent and a free school had opened in Greenville in 1840, most education before the Civil War was voluntary and at the parents' discretion. In 1905, just three years before Nan was born, the North Carolina General Assembly enacted a compulsory school law, and in 1907, it chartered the East Carolina Teachers Training School in Greenville. (Within twelve years, in time to accommodate Nan and her sister, the school became a four-year degree-granting institution and was renamed East Carolina Teachers College, or ECTC. It is now East Carolina University.) In 1903, the city had already voted for a school tax and decreed that schools, however small or large, would be "graded."

In 1903, Greenville had forty stores, six warehouses, six "tobacco factories," six trains, a blind/door/sash factory, a knitting mill, a grist mill, six churches, twelve barrooms, and a public library. This town and the farms surrounding it were the environments that encompassed Nan's world as a child. Like most children, she accepted that which made up the circumstances of her life without question. Having an inquiring mind, high intelligence, and a background that promotes action rather than passivity is probably always grounded in the situation in which one grows up. The dynamics of Greenville's communal life, her extended family (with all the ramifications of its challenges as well as its support), and a healthy exposure to the freedom of country life cultivated in Nan a discerning nature.

....

Nan's father, Will Evans, married Nannie Brown in 1901 and moved his twenty-four-year-old bride—he was twenty-eight—into the family home with his mother, Susan Caroline Cornelia Forbes Evans. Whatever the young bride's thoughts about this, her mother-in-law and her husband expected her to run a well-ordered and immaculate house. In later years Nannie commented to Nan that if company came, the minute they departed her mother-in-law would insist that all the surfaces they had touched—even the doorknobs— be wiped down. This obsession with cleanliness, Nannie said, "drove her nuts." Keeping a house free of germs, however, was essential to survival. Wire screens for the windows and doors were available only for the rich, and refrigerators for the home were not produced until after 1913. Food had to be kept cold in boxes with compartments for ice, and when there was no ice available, what was eaten had to be salted, dried, canned, or consumed fresh. Disease-carrying insects and spoiled food were constant sources of concern.

Nannie Elizabeth Evans, called Nan, was born on September 5, 1908. It was a home birth, as were all at that time, as the first hospital in Greenville was not opened until 1923. Later, Nan did paintings that indicate her birthplace was a small wooden structure of perhaps four or five rooms with a brick fireplace. It had been built most probably in the late 1860s by her grandfather. The first house on the property had been a sixteen-by-twenty-foot homestead, abandoned almost immediately and used during Nan's childhood as a storage shed. She later described her home as having a front porch with two doors, one open to the front room and one to the dining room. On the back of the house was another porch with one entry into the house. A shed on the left and a kitchen on the right were attached to this rear porch. Over the dining room there was a loft. At some point, Nan's father moved a structure his own father had built from across the road to beside the house, and this structure added a parlor and another bedroom. Farmhouses in that period were built more for utility than appearance and were sized appropriately for the family's needs. Their house was not a showplace; nor was it a shack. It was the home of a young farmer and his family.

Nan had an older brother, Bill, born in 1904, and a sister, Mattie, born in 1906. Her parents' first child died of colitis before he was one year old, but the three surviving children were healthy and seemed to have had no serious medical issues until after high school. Nan was told as a young adult that she had a heart murmur, but she never had any issue with her heart until she was in her eighties, and she was a person with abundant health and energy throughout much of her life. In fact, she had such strong straight teeth that she didn't have a cavity until she was in her seventies—and she always believed that the dentist poked and poked until he created one because he simply couldn't believe how healthy her mouth was.

By the time Nan was born, her father's 133-plus-acre farm was as much a going concern as any tobacco farm could be, given the dependence on weather inherent in the enterprise. Tobacco had become the primary crop on most of the surrounding farms, although each farm had a produce garden of some size (as did many of the homes in Greenville itself) and her father still raised some cotton. Nan attributed her earliest memory of her father to somewhere around the age of three or four, though she was unsure whether it was a real memory or a story told to her many times.

There was a cotton field right outside our house and we hired people to pick the cotton when it was ready to be harvested. Sometimes, my older brother and sister would pick a little bag and get something for it. One time, when my dad was going to town, apparently I begged for something too. He gave me a sugar bag that said "5 pounds" on it and told me to fill it and he'd bring me something. I did, and he brought me a big bag of candy.

Mattie retained that same memory, but, in her mind, the prize was a bag of bananas, which she remembers her father bringing home from town every Saturday.

Nan recounted later:

The oak grove in front of our house on the farm was very beautiful, and I remember my father coming down the drive from the Tarboro Road to the house and emerging from the grove. I know from being told that he had a personality that everyone loved. He was very talented and should have been a doctor. He always set bones, lanced boils, and generally treated the sick. Everyone around came to my dad to get treated, and they would always get well. He was very kind and generous; too kind, my mother sometimes said.

While at least two doctors were practicing in Greenville, the exigencies of time, travel, and cost would always factor in the decisions about to whom to turn for minor medical issues. In that area of the county, Will was that individual.

Life in the Evans home was built around industry, a strong Christian faith, and relationships with their extended family and neighbors. The years from 1908 to 1912 were unexceptional. The rhythm of their lives was based on a six-day workweek and a Sabbath rest. Once a month, the family would climb aboard a one-horse buggy in their Sunday best, go across the river to join the Brown family for services at Mt. Pleasant Christian Church, and then visit Grandmother Brown. The Brown family had given land for the church to be built in 1870, and John Reddin Brown and a Stancill were the first elders. Nan's aunt, Lucy Brown (Worthington), was listed on the original roll and Nan's maternal grandmother, "Becky" Fleming (Brown), was a Sunday school teacher in the 1870s. Nannie's brother, Peter, lived with their mother in the homeplace near the church. He had a side business of winemaking along with his farming operation, and he supplied the wine for the weekly communion whenever the more usual grape juice had been forgotten. Nannie Brown Evans would remain a member of this church throughout her life and is buried in its graveyard.

Mt. Pleasant was a Disciples of Christ church. Their particular slant on Christianity was loosely evangelical. Nan absorbed its fundamental teachings as her birthright: reliance on biblical authority, insistence on personal conversion, and suspicion of any formal worship that depended on written and memorized rituals. They confessed "no creed but Christ" and asked only one question of anyone wishing full fellowship: "Do you believe that Jesus Christ is the Son of God and accept him as your personal savior?" A total immersion baptism would follow a "Yes" response. Nannie sang in the choir, and Nan sat with her.

> Of course, sometimes I would put my head in her lap and go to sleep. At that time, a lot of the preachers preached about hellfire and damnation. I always wondered why they always had to talk about that.

Many preachers then were circuit riders, traveling from church to church, being paid by the congregation and staying with a local family in each town. A preacher came to Mt. Pleasant once a month; the family would make the trip that Sunday and stay nearer home on the other three Sundays. Uncle Leon Evans was the superintendent of the Methodist Church that met in the Forbes schoolhouse a mile down the road, and the family was expected to be there when they were not across the river. This alternate denomination offered additional theological training to young Nan. Methodism was founded on the idea that the holiness of one's life depended upon action rather than thought. There was, thus, a method to living a devout life to be learned and followed. This denomination also encouraged the idea that one could only grow in faith through participation in a community of people who held similar beliefs. Perhaps its most significant contribution, however, was its hymnody. Charles Wesley, brother of Methodism's founder, John Wesley, wrote some of the most beloved hymns of the Christian faith, including "Hark! The Herald Angels Sing" and "Christ the Lord Is Risen Today." Some people today think that the theology of this church has been delivered more through Charles Wesley's hymns than through any of its observances and practices. The child Nan was comfortable in both denominations and would, much later in life, belong to first one and then the other.

THREE

THE EARLY YEARS

"ALL MY MEMORIES OF BEING AT

THE STANCILLS' ARE PURE JOY." (1989)

In most households, discipline in the early decades of the twentieth century was strict, and the "spare the rod and spoil the child" philosophy was current. It was an application of the Proverbs verse that says, "The one who withholds [or spares] the rod is one who hates his son." The Evanses were people who read and studied their Bible and would undoubtedly have ascribed to that philosophy. Nan grew up with switches (made from the branches of saplings) always available when infractions of her mother's rules occurred.

Their father also took part in any punishments to be dealt out to the children. The first time Nan's brother, Bill, remembered being whipped was when he and a neighborhood boy were playing in the tobacco-curing barn and caved in the furnace:

> He really laid it on. The only other time that I remember getting a whipping from Papa was when he did so at Mama's insistence. At the time of that whipping, there was a County Fair in Greenville. All of us were there, and

so were my Uncle Offie Stancill and his family. Uncle Offie's boys and I got lost in the crowd. And, late in the afternoon, we walked from town to my Uncle Offie's house, about three miles from Greenville. When our parents could not find us at the fairgrounds, Mama and Papa made the trip out to Uncle Offie's house and found the three of us sitting on Uncle Offie's front porch steps. I mean Mama got mad! That night, Mama sat on one side of the fireplace in our house and Papa on the other side, and I sat between them. Time after time that night she would switch me and hand me over to Papa, who would then whip me. Finally, Papa said to Mama that I had had enough, and that ended the whipping.

Despite the harsh discipline, the general memory of the Evans siblings in those early years was of a very happy time of their lives. It was a short time as well. Things were to change in 1912, and Nan's true memories began shortly after that. As Bill later recounted the events later:

Now in the fall of 1912 Papa was building a tenant house on his farm. He cut the timber on his property, but they were sawed into lumber at a sawmill, which was located on the Whitehurst farm. The sawmill was probably about a mile down the road from where we lived. Papa used his wagon and team to haul the lumber from the sawmill to where he was building the tenant house. And, in December of that year, Papa became sick with what was then called the grippe, and then with pneumonia, and Papa died. Mama, sometime later, told me that we three children spent the night on which Papa died at Uncle Offie's. On the afternoon of the next day, Papa was buried in the old Evans graveyard.

All three children understood that their father's death was due to an infection he caught at the sawyer's farm. The newspaper clipping, with a date of December 6, 1912, written on the bottom, says:

Mr. W. J. Evans Dead—Friday night Mr. W. J. Evans died at his home about four miles west of Greenville. He had been sick only a little over a week, being first taken with a chill the day before Thanksgiving, which developed into pneumonia. Mr. Evans was about 40 years of age and was an industrious farmer and good citizen. He leaves a wife and 3 children and is also survived by one brother, Mr. L. F. Evans, and one sister, Mrs. A. H. Critcher.

Nannie Brown Evans was thirty-five when her husband died. She was left with three children, aged eight, six, and four, and a tobacco farm. Will Evans had left no will, so under North Carolina law the children inherited his property, even though, since they were minors, Nannie was in charge.

While being in the country at that time was safer than it would be later, a lone woman was expected to have some male presence on the property. The black couples who lived and worked there did not qualify in the community's understanding. Within the family there was just one male available, a nephew, Frank Worthington. He was living in Ayden, North Carolina, and newly married; he and his wife agreed to come live with the family and work the farm. Unfortunately, Frank apparently did not know enough about farming. Nannie had counted on the money from a successful crop to sustain her family, and Frank was unable to achieve that success. She then had hard decisions to make. At the same time she was grieving, she had to go forward expeditiously, and Frank Worthington's failure to make any profit from the land convinced her that she could not stay where she was.

....

For young Nan, 1913 passed without much change in her life. Her father's death was a blow for the family, but Nan was only four years old, and death to a person of that age generally means only that the deceased isn't there anymore. Any grieving she did was most probably a response to the demeanor of those around her. If there is a community of support—and in Nan's case there was a considerable one—the absence is probably not the gaping hole it would be for someone older. She recalled:

> I spent a lot of my time about then with my Aunt Martha (Forbes Evans) and Uncle Leon. Their son, Hugh, had a pony that I loved and, even after we moved to Greenville, I would go out to Hugh's for the weekend and ride the pony. I loved Aunt Martha so much, and I stayed with her so much, that I sometimes called her Mama. Aunt Martha used to tease my mother, telling her that she was jealous. Aunt Martha was one of those people that everyone loved. I never knew anyone who didn't. She was very kind and had a very attractive personality.

Family always surrounded Nannie and her children, and the relationships were close. Nannie's sister, Mattie Brown Stancill, lived just down the road on the Falkland Highway. She was married to Theopolis J. (Offie) Stancill. The interrelationships between the Stancills, the Forbeses, the Evanses, and the Browns were extensive by 1912, and Offie was more than Nannie's brother-in-law; he also was from the same family as Nannie's grandmother, Patsy Stancill Brown. Intermarriage among Greenville's founding families was a frequent occurrence; apparently there was only one Evans brother, Richard, who married outside the family grouping.

Mattie Brown Stancill opened her home to Nannie and the children. She and Offie had nine children—Leland (the eldest), Wilfred, Claxton, John, Offie, J. Russell, Verna Lee, Lela Brown, and Robert—but their hearts were big. This move was the only practical choice Nannie could make, and even though the four of them had to stay in one room, she accepted the help. She rented out the farm and moved her children from their birthplace.

This relocation had varying effects on them. For Nannie, there was the challenge of providing for and raising three children on her own, and the move gave her time to sort out her options. It was an easy transition for Bill, who fit right in with the Stancill boys. Mattie was closest in age to Verna Lee, but they were still several years apart, so they did not develop a close relationship. As a result,

Mattie spent much of her time alone and was unhappy. The opposite was true for Nan: she and Lela Brown became best friends, and being included in a large family seemed wondrous to her:

> I often thought it was unusual and wonderful that Uncle Offie would invite us in. . . . All my memories of being at the Stancills' are pure joy. . . . The Stancills' home was large and beautiful. Originally, it had a great big porch in front with a white banister all around. One of the showplaces actually. There was a big hall that ran down the center. On the front left side was the parlor, and it was fixed up for company. Back of the parlor was a bedroom. On the other side was a large bedroom that covered the whole side of the house. This bedroom, which was Uncle Offie's and Aunt Mattie's, had a fireplace in it, and after dinner the whole family sat around it while studying or talking. Upstairs were two large bedrooms on the left-hand side and one big room on the right that was the bedroom for the seven boys. Then, at the back of the house upstairs, there was a narrow room over the back porch. There was another wing that ran off downstairs from the back porch. It had a big dining room with a table large enough to seat fifteen. Behind the dining room was a big kitchen and pantry. On the back porch, behind Uncle Offie's bedroom, was the basin for washing up. In the side yard there was a pack house, where the cured tobacco was stored.

On the other side of the house was a sandbox that Nan used to enjoy:

> I remember building cars in the sand with Lela Brown (we'd pack the sand with water so we could sit on it) and imagining that I was driving across the United States in a car by myself.

Even at that young age, Nan's wanderlust and thirst for adventure were a part of her makeup.

In the backyard was the smokehouse. We had hogs, which
were kept in a pen down near the river, but we never ate
bacon. It was considered food for the poor people. We
always had ham, a smokehouse full of it. In the back corner was the "back house," where you went to the toilet.
Behind the kitchen was a huge grape arbor, all different
kinds of grapes: James, black, red, scuppernong. There
was one grape called a fox grape that was special, a small
white grape that was very sweet and very good. When I
was long about five or six, Lela Brown and I saw some up
a tree and we went up the tree to get them. As it turned
out, the tree was covered with a poison ivy vine and we
had to stay out of school for almost six months because
we got infected from top to bottom. Our mothers took us
to the doctors, but they couldn't cure it. Then one day a
black woman on the place told Mama to buy some cop-
peras in the form of the ore from the drug store. She said
to take some of that and put it in a saucer with water. It
would turn the water green, she said. Mama was then to
put us on a table and cover us with the water. She was to
do that both in the morning and at night. Mama did as
the woman said, and it cured us in a hurry.

Nan may have exaggerated the length of time she suffered since
one day to a child can seem like forever. Still, images from childhood
frequently leave strong impressions and Nan's memory of that
event remained vivid, as did her ability to recall details about the
Stancill homestead.

The Stancill farm was large. There was a fenced-in field for
the horses and mules, with a big barn for the saddles, bug-
gies, and the surrey. Behind that was a field devoted to produce. Across the road were acres of tobacco and, nearer
the house, six barns had been erected for curing the crop.

Offie Stancill ran an extensive operation. In addition to his own
large family and Nannie's, several other families, both black and

white employees, lived somewhere on the property. He was one of the first in the area to have a car. He had a Haynes, then a Packard, then a Ford. "After a time, the boys stripped down the Ford and painted it red. That was very appealing to me," Nan recalled.

With the number of residents at the Stancills' home, the arrangement needed strict discipline to work. This was not a problem for the Evans family because they were used to being obedient, but being there was not an easy life. No one on the farm was idle, and children were not exempt from the constant work that must be done. The term "work ethic" would have raised eyebrows since there was no ethical question involved—there was simply necessity and the assumption of each individual's contribution. There were copious fruit trees that had to be harvested, and the younger children gathered and peeled produce for canning alongside their elders: "It was a place that had everything you could think of to eat."

Nan had her job in the laundry:

> In the right back corner was a very deep well that always had fresh water. Behind it were three big pots that you built fires under. Aunt Veeney, one of the black tenants living on the place, would come on Monday and boil the clothes; she'd boil them and then hang them. Then on Tuesday she would take them to the back bedroom and all the women would stay in there practically all day and iron. Lela Brown and I had the job of ironing handkerchiefs. Boy, you had to do that just right. The irons were heated on the fire in that room.

Nan also helped out in the fields at harvest time. A mule truck traveled between the rows of tobacco, and the pickers would fill it up. Then the tobacco was taken to the barn where it was put on a stick to dry. Nan and Lela Brown loved to be chosen to drive that truck and would beg for that job.

> You had to pick up the "tree" (the apparatus used to connect the animal and the cart) at the heels of the mule and hook it onto the truck. You'd pick it up right where

the mule could kick you, and the fear that might happen added to the excitement.

The world was thrilling for Nan. Because there were so many older people around, she had the freedom to move among them without a hovering adult, and the farm was a wonderland in its bounty of exciting experiences. Her life was spent primarily outside, where the nascent artist absorbed and was stimulated by nature, with its lineaments, balance, and cohesiveness. There was a timelessness in the progression of the seasons that would later be reflected in her landscapes: the changing of the heavy, mosquito-laden air of summer to the crisp brightness and clarity of autumn; the fragrance of the flowers in blossom and the redolence of ripening fruit; the frozen fragility and starkness of the winter's bare trees. There was also an awareness of aromas—the encumbering scent of tobacco, the pungency of the animals, the sweat of the workers (who probably bathed monthly if at all and likely in the river). There was the feel of new grass between her fingers, the texture of dandelion necklaces, the bouncing of the buggy rides, and the power of the Tar River's current against her young body.

Later in life, particular sounds would always return her heart to those days:

> One of the sounds I can hear again is the nighttime chorus of the bullfrogs in the pond down the road from the Stancills'. Another is the sound of dogs. Uncle Offie had nine hound dogs. At dawn, foxhounds loved to stand out with their heads to the sky and howl. When Uncle Offie went foxhunting, it was with everyone in the neighborhood, and they were exciting sound-and-smell occasions. They became even more exciting as Lela Brown and I grew a bit. On the days that a hunt was to be held, all the men would gather on horseback at Uncle Offie's farm before dawn. When they would come back from the hunt, the horses would be tired out and the men would put us up and teach us to ride. After we learned, we were permitted to take the horses. We couldn't have been more than six or seven.

The adult Nan would find living in New York and London exciting and fascinating, but roaming the countryside held a strong appeal throughout her life. Even after the family moved to Greenville, she would explore nature whenever schools were closed on snow days, beguiled by its constant change and captivating multiplicity.

> I loved it because then I could get wrapped up and go for long walks all by myself. We were right across from the college campus and the woods behind it. When it snowed, we would set up traps with boxes and sticks and put food in them. When we trapped a sparrow, we would take it in and clean it up good and fry it. If I recall, it tasted good. No different than catching and eating quails. We didn't get too many.

It is possible that the lack of funds to do other things contributed to Nan's having time to wander and dream, and thus time to spend collecting images and sketching on her drawing pad. That was definitely true in later periods; nature always grounded her, whatever challenges she was experiencing.

....

The experiences at the Stancills' farm not only helped Nan establish attitudes and preferences, but they also became fond memories that sustained her in difficult times. She related two incidents from that time that illustrate not only her need to investigate the unknown, always part of an artist's motivation, but also her daring and thirst for the new and untried.

She and Lela Brown spent much of their time exploring and taking chances. They loved to swim in the Tar. There was a wide sandbar behind her Uncle Offie's property, and he had built a changing hut for the children on the bank at that location.

> On the other side of the river there was a high bank, and we could dive down and pick up mussel shells at the bottom. The sandbar was wide. One time we were diving

and Lela Brown hit an open shell. We had driven the car down—the red Ford—even though we were very young, probably seven or eight—and when Lela Brown continued bleeding all over the place, we put her in the car and hurried up home. When we got up to the house, she was still bleeding terribly and had to be taken to the doctor. Lela Brown had a bad scar as the result of that adventure, perhaps because we had been forbidden to go that day.

Another time:

Lela Brown and I had many adventures once we learned to ride. There was a cave that we had always heard about that was about three miles up the road from the farm. Grown folks talked about it, but, although we begged, they wouldn't take us to see it. So, one day, we decided to go by ourselves. We rode the horses up the road and went into the cave, roamed all around, and forgot about the time. It suddenly dawned on us that time had passed, and when we came out, we found we were at a different place. We had the dickens of a time trying to find the horses. We finally did and we rode like the devil home. Everyone was at dinner. We went in, expecting to get our heads blown off, but no one said a word. We learned our lesson.

During this time, Nan's sense of community, her work habits, and her faith were formed and became steadfast. Living with a large number of relatives whose lives were inextricably connected to her own meant that not only did she have to learn how to cooperate, but she also had to pull her own weight, however limited. In addition, she necessarily absorbed—and these became ingrained—the rhythms of Sunday rest and the certainties of the faithful committed Christians surrounding her. The duration of the Evans family's stay at the Stancills' was not more than three to four years, and was intermittent even then, but the imprint on her soul was absolute.

Meanwhile, her mother was struggling with the dilemma of what to do. When Nannie was twenty-two, she had gotten a degree in education at Carolina Christian College in Ayden, North Carolina, with the financial help of her brother, John Ivy Brown. When the crisis of Will's death came, Nannie had not only her sister's support but also a college education behind her. Nannie's training as a teacher provided a wage-earning possibility. After eleven years of being a farmer's wife, however, she knew she would have to get recertified. Fortunately, the family again came to the rescue; another sister, Dora, lived just two blocks from the newly opened East Carolina Teachers Training School and was willing to take them in. It was a mixed blessing because Dora was a domineering woman who thought that, because Nannie was younger, her word was to be accepted as law. Still, necessity prevailed, and Nannie got her certificate. She then immediately moved her family back to the Stancills'.

In those days, one had to be elected rather than appointed to the post of teacher, and teachers were paid only for a designated period. Parents took up a collection to pay the teacher more if they desired additional instruction for their offspring. There was a three-room schoolhouse just down the road from the Stancill farm called the Forbes School, and Nannie became its lead teacher (there was one other) in the fall of 1913. The school had no electricity or plumbing. The Stancill boys had to bring water from their well to the school each day, and a dipper was used for drinking; lunch was brought from home, and the heat came from a pot-bellied stove in the middle of the room.

Teachers were given complete control, backed up by the parents, so discipline was not an issue, even with many children of different ages in the small rooms. Were a child to misbehave, Nannie had the right, perhaps even the obligation, to punish the mischief-maker. Teachers also had to teach more than the three Rs: the curriculum included instilling moral values. Short papers written by members of the community were read aloud. They tended to be moralistic and frank: there were warnings for girls not to fall in love with boys who drank and for boys to be aware that it was not right to beat someone of the opposite sex. Nan was too young to be enrolled, but since her mother was the teacher and Bill and Mattie were students there, Nan wandered from one group to another picking up knowledge according to what interested her. Dewey, Steiner, and Montessori would later introduce the idea of teaching a child through having the student interact with subjects that appealed; Nan's first educational experiences simply predated this concept. When Nan finally was enrolled, she was put in the second year, skipping over first grade.

Unfortunately, teachers of that era made very small salaries; in Greenville they averaged from $35 to $45 a month. The Fleming School was across the Tar River, and for the years 1915–1917 Nannie changed jobs and taught the higher grades there. This school served the area where Nannie had been born and raised. It was located about two miles from the Brown home, and the small family stayed with Nan's Grandmother Brown and Uncle Pete and walked the two miles to school each day. According to brother Bill, the Forbes School was an eight-month school and the Fleming School was a six-month school:

> So, for each of those two school years, Mattie and Nan
> and I went to school at Forbes School for one month in
> the fall before moving in with Grandma and Uncle Pete,
> and one month in the spring after moving back to Uncle
> Offie's and Aunt Mattie's.

Did Nannie teach one month at the Forbes School, then go to the Fleming School, and then reverse the move in the spring? Did the Fleming School pay better? Was this choice a way of giving the Stancills a break from having another family living with them? Nan always felt that her mother was extremely strict, and she knew that part of that discipline was because they were living with someone else and had to be well-behaved. Did Nannie experience some stress relief by living with her mother and brother for some part of the year—with fewer people? Nan only remembered walking, or rather running, most of the distance from Grandmother Brown's home to reach the schoolhouse.

> I was so small I had to run to keep up with Mother, Bill,
> and Mattie. On the way, we went by Mt. Pleasant Church

and the home of a Mrs. Teel, who had a billy goat. I was afraid of the goat even though he was behind a fence. Mother was principal at Fleming School. I was in second grade. I remember recess periods and enjoying playing outside. This school was on what was originally the property of Grandmother Rebecca Fleming Brown's father. The big old family house was not very far away. A few times Mother took us to visit her mother's relatives who still lived in it.

The Brown homestead, where Nan's grandmother and Uncle Pete lived in 1915, was a small place even though it had a porch all the way around it. The kitchen had not been a part of the original house but had its own building, constructed before the Civil War. The distance from the main house to this building was about 100 to 150 feet, a separation found in many homes built in the 1700s because of the fire threat. At one end of the kitchen house was a "great big fireplace." A wood-burning cookstove with a flue up through the roof was close to the other end. Grandmother Brown used the wood stove, but she kept utensils hanging next to the fireplace so she could cook there as well.

Sometime before the period when the Evans family stayed there, Uncle Pete built an addition to the main house. He then extended the front porch around one end, roofed a breezeway from the original home to the addition, and connected the front and back porches. The addition became Grandma Brown's kitchen and dining room. The original kitchen was moved to another location on the farm and converted into a tenant house.

What Nan remembered most (besides her fear of the billy goat) was Grandma Brown serving her oatmeal. In addition:

> Grandma Brown had a certain spot on the back porch where she would sit and read her Daily Reflector newspaper. Sometimes she would read to me.

Mattie's only memory of those stays at the Brown house was of her Grandma Brown sitting by the fireplace "dipping snuff." Since the house had only two regular occupants, perhaps the small family did not feel they were imposing quite so much as at the Stancills'. Maybe Nannie felt that, for at least a short period, more breathing space was a personal necessity.

FOUR

INDOMITABLE SPIRIT

"I NEVER WANTED TO BE A TEACHER." (1989)

Nan and Bill were comfortable living at the Stancills', even with the family having to stay in one room, but their mother soon began making plans to bring about her family's independence. Leaving their home place, and then moving from the Stancills' to Dora's, back to the Stancills', and then to the Browns' and back several times within four years had to have left not only Nannie but also the children with a sense of rootlessness, even with all the family living around them. To have her own home and be self-supporting would have been Nannie's priority.

In 1916, with funds from a life insurance policy that Will had taken out and a loan from a building and loan association in Greenville, Nannie paid $600 for a lot in town and began building a house. The land was almost directly in front of her sister Dora's house. Cotton had been farmed there until just the previous year, and then the cotton field had been subdivided for residences; Nannie erected the first house. Her lot faced what was later to become Fourth Street and was just a block over from where the teacher training school was located. When the family moved in during the late spring of 1917, after the Forbes School let out for the summer, there was no plumbing. The plans called for it, and it was eventually installed, but the construction shed behind the house had to be used as a latrine for the first year.

The house was approximately 2,000 square feet, framed and cedar-sided with a porch its entire length. The front door led into a small living room with a fireplace. There were pocket doors on the left leading to the dining room. Behind the dining room was a kitchen, and there was a back bedroom off the small rear porch. Nannie had two bedrooms constructed upstairs, one for her and one for the girls, while Bill slept in the downstairs back room. Eventually there were bathrooms on both floors. One can imagine the relief and the pride Nannie experienced when she and her children moved in, even though there would also be a constant uneasiness regarding finances. (Even when Nannie grew quite old, she wouldn't sell the house, and somehow or other she always made it "home" at least once a year. The house remains standing today with a marker designating it as an historic home.)

Nannie knew she had to supplement her income from the farm—it did not provide much since the Mr. Kennedy who rented the acreage did not use fertilizer and drained the soil's productivity. Teaching had not paid very well either, and she understood it was only a stopgap method for dealing with the immediate future. Her sister Dora was a seamstress and helped Nannie get started in the same work. By "taking in sewing" from girls at the training school, Nannie could supplement her farm income enough to keep the family economically stable. She also crocheted bedspreads out of tobacco twine and sold them. There was even money for the occasional treat: it was a custom of the household to have oranges in the Christmas stockings, and even though these were expensive, the custom was retained religiously. Further, Nannie was very well liked and had many friends around Greenville, particularly among those at the newly named East Carolina Teachers College. It wasn't long before she was asked if she would work there, and for several years she was the assistant to the dean of women.

In Nan's memory:

> We didn't have the money to be social. We were what
> was known as "property poor," but Mama still had a lot
> of friends among people who did have money. She was
> also active at the Eighth Street Christian Church. She
> taught Sunday school as well as participated in other
> events there. Mama was highly respected; I think she was
> probably the most respected woman in Greenville. She
> was quite a character and a wonderful woman. She was
> called on to give a lot of programs and once, I remem-
> ber, she was asked to give a program for a women's group
> and afterwards there was a newspaper write-up on that
> program. The last line of the write-up said: "When Mrs.
> Evans speaks, everybody listens."

Eventually that would be said of Nan too. Having had this role
model for leadership would later stiffen her back when nerves
threatened.

Nannie's internal discipline had to have been strict. She was a
beautiful woman when she was young. This, and her attractive personality, garnered many suitors. Laying some of the responsibilities
on another's shoulders was probably a somewhat constant temptation, but Nannie never remarried even though it was quite common
for widows at that time. Nan later admitted that she and her siblings
were jealous of all who might be serious suitors and found ways to
discourage them. That did not mean they wouldn't take advantage
of some of the privileges of having these men try their luck. Although it was inappropriate to give Nannie gifts, her suitors would
try to connect with the children. One of them gave the family a
Victrola, which for some reason was acceptable, and they enjoyed
the music that the machine afforded for a long time. For Nannie
Brown Evans, life must have seemed to present one challenge after
another, and providing as normal a life as possible in a one-parent
household had to be a priority.

Being "property poor" also meant to her daughter Nan that she
shouldn't invite friends to her home.

Our family was well known. At school I had lots of friends, but no one came home to play after school. Mattie did have a friend who came in, but I didn't have any social life after school with a couple of exceptions. After the Winslows moved to town, their daughter, Effie Mae, and I became friends and they had me over quite a bit.

From time to time, all people read into their experience meanings that may not be correct. For Nan, not having friends come to the house may have been her way of supporting her mother's frugality. It may also have been that her mother kept a tighter rein on her than on Bill and Mattie because Nan was a handful and her mother worried about the effects on her health from constant liveliness.

I was always tiny as I could be, and Mama used to worry whether I would grow up. She would take me to the doctors to see what to do. One of the doctors told Mama to have me drink a quart of milk a day! I remember doing that for a while. It was a lot of milk to drink each day.

Concerns about her children's health, however, did not mean that Nannie backed off from her standards of conduct. The children were expected to be well-mannered, courteous, and "good Christians." Sunday was always a day of rest, beginning with attendance at Sunday school. Afternoons were spent visiting with family. Knowing she was responsible for all the parenting probably made Nannie tend towards a firm regimen, although she had been a strict disciplinarian when her husband was alive as well. Even their carriage and deportment were part of the children's training:

When we were small, she used to fuss at us and say: "Stop sitting on your back. Sit on your bottom."

She made them stand up against the wall for "posture moments," and they had to walk around with books on their heads.
Nan's memories of these years were reflective:

As I recall, Bill, Mattie, and I grew up like most other siblings. We had our chores, helped each other, and argued. Bill was four years older than I, the only boy, and I adored him. As he often said, I was always "in his footsteps." Our relationship was very close until he married. We considered Mattie the outstanding intellectual sibling. She had a very pleasing and outgoing personality and made friends very easily.

Nan always felt that her sister was able to sit down with strangers and get to know them "right away"—better than she could.

The extended family, however, did not always meet with Nan's approval. She thought many of her aunts—nine in all—were bossy, and she didn't get along with her Aunt Dora.

I particularly didn't like it that she was always telling me what to do and complaining to Mama about me.

One day during the period when Nannie was getting her certification and they were living with Dora, young Nan was swinging on a swing hung from a tree when her Aunt Lela's son, J. J., demanded that he be given the swing.

I refused, so he took a stick and hit me on the back, leaving quite a scratch. I ran into the house crying. Aunt Lela and Aunt Dora said it was my fault. I should have given him the swing. When Mother came home, they told her I was scrapping with J. J. and got myself hurt. I got a whipping.

According to Mattie, Nan would get into fights with Aunt Dora throughout her childhood. When Nan didn't get her way or became angry with her aunt, she would get a cup of water, open the screen door and throw the water on the floor. Of course, Dora would tell Nannie every time, and Nan would get whipped with a switch.

....

The move to Greenville started a new chapter in Nan's life. The household was reduced to four people and their interactions must have had heightened impact; she no longer had the almost daily company of her best friend Lela Brown; she had to have become more aware of the straitened financial resources her mother faced; and there were strangers in her immediate vicinity. The move also meant that she faced an entirely new educational environment. Nan entered the city schools, called "model schools," in the fall of 1917 and was placed in the fourth grade. She recalled:

> Our classroom was upstairs, and we had to march out to go to recess, two by two, the girls together and the boys together. There was a place, however, where we went four abreast, two girls on the right and two boys on the left. There was a boy in that class named William Stewart Bost. When we got to the place where we were four abreast, he would be on my left and as we marched out, he would hold my hand. One day he slipped me a note that said, "When we grow up will you please marry me?" It was the first of a lot of marriage proposals.

Mattie related that, whether it was young Mr. Bost or not, Nan did have beaus. This was during the First World War, and the students were encouraged to buy "war stamps" for twenty-five cents apiece. The Evans children did not have that discretionary money, but Nan's beaus always bought hers for her. One of the threads of Nan's life, throughout her entire life, was how much the opposite sex admired her.

Being in a classroom where she was instructed through a standard curriculum and taught by "teachers-in-training" must have felt somewhat strange to Nan. It had previously been necessary to learn only on her own intellectual level, which was significantly above that of most of her classmates. For many intellectually gifted students, finding classwork easy frequently results in the material's not being well learned. These bright students can cram for a test, get a high grade on it, and then do what they want with their time. The material often is not committed to their long-term memory.

Nan found that true later in high school when she had a teacher whose attitudes about classwork differed from hers. The criticism that she did not work hard enough was leveled at her again in college, although in neither instance were her grades affected.

> When I was in high school, every year at the end, you had to take final exams. There were four girls in the class who were always at the top of the class, and when that time came, we were always exempt from the final exams. Once or twice I had to take the English exam because I'm not a very good speller. One time when I finished my exam and started to leave, the teacher called me back and made me sit while she read my exam. On that exam I didn't spell anything incorrectly and she was surprised. My response was that I thought I could spell rather well. Before you entered college in that day, you had to take a spelling test. I passed it. The year when I had to take geometry, I didn't get it at first. I went home and finally Bill told me to sit down and he taught me. He said, "This is the way it is, get it through your head." Once he explained it and I understood the logic, I did well. I eventually taught high school mathematics.

At the same time Nan's horizons became significantly larger as a result of her living in Greenville, she found the scope of education to be more specialized than she had known. Perhaps having more than one type of educational environment as a child, more than one way of acquiring intellectual knowledge, later factored in her ability to entertain the Dewey theories with a positive attitude. She had, in addition, the fodder of encountering town life and being exposed to different personalities and philosophies. Increasing her number of contacts may also have taught her how particular viewpoints can mold and steer opinions, and may have produced a slightly more observant orientation than her previous hurly-burly approach to life, further fostering her artistic perspective. Examination and inquiry are critical to an artist's creative ability.

Nan's education was not confined to school. The home was also a laboratory in which she learned. A man named Tripp rented the farm in 1920, and after the tobacco crop was cured and in the pack house, Nannie bought the crop from him. She moved Bill into one of the upstairs bedrooms and Mattie and Nan into the other, and the downstairs back bedroom became a tobacco-grading room for that fall and winter. Bill related:

> The tobacco that Mama had bought was hauled to town to our house. She graded it during the day and all of us tied it at night into bundles. To grade the tobacco, the first step was to get the leaves supple. On the farm, this was accomplished by taking the tobacco out of doors. In the back room, Mama sprinkled the tobacco with water, packed it down and left it overnight. She graded it the next day. There were, then, five or six different grades, determined by "body" and "color." Each leaf had to be graded and then bunched according to grade. Mama bought cotton string bags and used them as sheets in order to make the bunches. These bunches were then piled onto a wagon and hauled to the warehouse and put into three-and-a-half-foot baskets. The tobacco went on the auction block in those baskets. Mama also graded tobacco from Uncle Offie's farm, and he paid her for that. The tobacco market opened in September, operated until about the first of December, then closed. It reopened about the middle of January and stayed open until about the end of February.

Nannie did everything she could to earn money. The family was never comfortable financially, but she was able to keep herself and her children fed. There was enough money for a wide variety in their diets during the years when the weather was good and the farm income was positive. Other times, while they never went hungry, their diet included cheaper cuts of meat and a more restricted meal plan. At many points during their childhood, Nan's mother would tell all three of her children, "You don't have a father, honey, and there are things you can't do, but remember who you are." Each of them fortunately understood that the "can't do" part of that admonition was simply regarding finances, not any other potentialities. While the responsibility was on Nannie's shoulders, all three children did what they could to help out. Nan's attitude towards work, established at the Stancill farm, became ingrained. Whatever her field of effort, whenever her mother asked anything of her, whatever the job at hand, she did as well as she could. Most of the time she did it better than anyone else.

An additional expense was added to the household in 1921, although it was one that was understood and accepted. Grandmother Brown had started having difficulty taking care of her home and managing it for her son. Uncle Pete approached his sister and asked her to take their mother in. He wanted to find a wife. The downstairs bedroom in which Nannie had graded tobacco became Grandma Brown's room. Uncle Pete had told Nannie that he would give her $400 each month for their mother's upkeep. Unfortunately, that lasted only two months, while Grandma Brown lived another five years. Nan did not speculate later on why her uncle stopped supporting his mother financially, but there must have been some acceptable reason, because the siblings did not become estranged.

It seems to have been a season for family homecomings. The same week Grandmother Brown moved to Fourth Street, Nannie's older brother, John Ivy Brown, who had been away from Greenville for many years, returned home. Since it was John who had funded Nannie's college education, there was no question that she would welcome him. Bill shared his room with his uncle. This was made easier because Bill spent so much time at the Stancills'. When school let out in the spring, Bill would depart from Fourth Street to stay at the Stancills' and work on their farm throughout the summer; then he'd return for school in the fall, contributing to the family the income he'd earned. There was also a period when Uncle Offie's son, Offie Jr., stayed with them in the Fourth Street house because "country folk" couldn't attend Greenville schools without paying tuition. There was no respite from the crowded conditions of Nannie's home, but at least she could content herself with the knowledge that she was the one offering sanctuary rather than receiving it.

At that time, crowded quarters and lack of personal space were not considered such hardships as they are today. The situation, however, must have been draining. At some point, Nannie taught her children the Brown family motto to sustain them when life was hard:

> "Accept the inevitable, rise above it; otherwise, come hell or high water, fight and win. Look up, not down. Look out, not in. The tragedy in the lives of others is greater than your own. Be thankful for your blessings."

Nan never forgot that motto, and she and Mattie would quote it to each other many times during their lives.

World War I ended in 1918, with the Treaty of Versailles taking effect in January 1920. In Greenville, where the population had grown from four thousand to five thousand, such world events scarcely registered for the average high school student, and the years came and went without any significant disruptions to the flow of Nan's life. The school Nan attended was just a couple of years old and had been built by another relative, J. J. Stroud, Aunt Lela's husband. Since there was no twelfth grade at that time, Nan graduated at the age of sixteen. She later felt that she didn't date very much and wasn't particularly social, but her "memory books" from those days and the stories she later shared say otherwise:

> Uncle Willis's nephew, Frank, who lived near us, had been at our school, but by the time I dated him, he was going to West Point. On my street was a family who had a nephew who lived in Ohio and used to come to Greenville a lot. His name was Alan Thomas. I used to date him. He fell in love with me and used to bring me gifts. I still have an amber mirror that was part of a set that he gave me. He was one who I dated.
>
> I also dated Elmer (Chick) Hardee. Alan Thomas knew about Chick and used to say that he had to come down a lot because he was afraid Chick would beat his time. Chick was a good friend of Offie Stancill's. I don't remember where he went to school. We dated for two years (my last two). He was the second person to ask me to marry him. He wanted to marry me when I finished high school.

He wanted to honeymoon in the Carolina mountains in a tent and sleeping bags. One weekend he and a group were going to Washington, North Carolina, to go swimming, and he wanted me to go, but I wouldn't. That day he was on the pier and someone tapped him on the shoulder; he overbalanced and fell in and broke his neck. I visited him in the hospital that, by that time, had been built right behind my house. He was paralyzed from the neck down, and he died after about three months.

Nan pasted a Camel cigarette into her memory book with the notation "The kind Chick used to smoke," and she detailed the gifts Chick had given her:

> *My Kodak, My Little Gold Fish, My Watch, His Sister's Picture, My First Easter Flowers, His Scarf, Candy, My Portable Victrola, And Best of All His Love, His Friendship and a wonderful time.*

Chick's death was the second time a person for whom Nan cared had been taken from her, but the Evans motto helped, and her naturally positive attitude soon reappeared along with her continued involvement at school. The 1922 yearbook had a poem about North Carolina illustrated by Nan. Under her picture in the class of 1925 volume it says, "Here's one of the versatile members of the class. Nannie can draw pictures as well as shoot baskets. And besides that, she's as sweet-tempered as the day is long. An All-round American girl." She is listed as having been involved in the Senior Girls' Club, the Girls' Athletic Association, the Glee Club, and the Operetta; she was also on the basketball team and was the art editor of the yearbook. The senior class prophecy about Nan was that she would become a great artist.

Nan's college selection was predetermined because she could attend East Carolina Teachers College (ECTC) without paying tuition. It was just two blocks from home, and Mattie was already going there. Both girls trained to be teachers. Mattie wanted to be one; she hoped to teach high school mathematics, her best subject and one she loved. On the other hand, Nan did not like what she would be doing.

> I never wanted to be a teacher, but I could go to East Car-
> olina for free and the only other alternative for a woman
> then was to be a nurse—and I wasn't about to be a nurse.

She later became a strong and eloquent advocate for women in their desire to get degrees and work in all professions. Was a part of that endeavor due to the narrowness of her presumed choices when she was sixteen?

She started at ECTC immediately after high school graduation, intending to get her degree in three years. The first two years would give her certification as a teacher, and the last, if her plan worked out, would enable her to get her undergraduate degree. Some of the curriculum was not to her liking, particularly the practice teaching.

> Every time I was practice teaching, the principal would
> come in and sit in the back of the classroom. Then, each
> week, on Friday, there would be an hour session of critique
> by her on the work of all the student teachers. She criti-
> cized everyone but me. I began to think that I was a lousy
> teacher. At the last session I finally asked. She said that I
> was the best student teacher she'd ever seen. She died the
> next week, before turning in the grades, and someone else
> had to assign the grades. This person gave everyone a C,
> and I was very upset. Miss Sally Joyner Davis, who was a
> friend of Mama's and the head of the history department,
> a brilliant woman and well respected in the community,
> was also upset for me. She was a relative of the Hookers
> and told Travis Hooker later that I was the most brilliant
> student she'd ever had; Mrs. Hooker told Mama, who told
> me. Miss Davis also told Mama one day that she would
> like to spank me. When Mama asked why, she said that
> I was a brilliant girl but that I didn't study enough. This
> Sally Joyner Davis was the reason that I got my job in
> Raleigh.

Nan's having been short-changed in the grade she was given brought her to the special attention of Miss Davis, which led to her being in the right place at the right time to become involved in the Dewey experiment.

....

According to Mattie, Greenville was a safe place to live when she and Nan were growing up, and they did not need escorts when they left the neighborhood. Still, groups went places together, either just running around Greenville or to nearby towns—like Washington to picnic and swim, to Southern Pines for a weekend, to Rocky Mount (on which trip they exulted, "The Essex actually didn't break down!"), and to Raleigh. The guys were expected to be—and were—gentlemen. There were many notations of dates and places in Nan's journals. Later she felt that she had worked so hard and been absent from the college scene so much that she didn't have a group of friends from her undergraduate days. Notations in her memory book do not quite back that up—she recorded dates with pals of both sexes throughout that time. Mattie and "Snookie" (her name for Lela Brown) were frequent companions.

In October 1927 Nan was chairman of a party thrown by the junior class for the first-year students.

> We had a masquerade party and the costumes were beau-
> tiful. The hut was decorated in Halloween . . . We enjoyed
> everything and hope that all had a good time. Dancing
> was the main thing—I learned to do the Black Bottom.

The 1928 *Tecoan*, ECTC's yearbook, lists Nan as one of the junior class officers. Another memory book kept during that period has a section in the front for autographs. Most of the many "toasts" named Nan as "the sweetest girl (or pal)" or "all-round gal," and they commented on how much they all "loved" her. There were about the same number of remarks from males as females, but the guys seemed to concentrate more on her physical beauty. One, Hannis Warren, wrote, "I remember the day we met; I will remember the night of my heart's discontent." The same memory book has a printed cutout about "The Senior Class—The Blue Bird." Affixed to it is a poem written by Margaret Patrick:

TO NANNIE EVANS—

There is a girl name Nannie,
Who is very much like Annie.
Her face is bold and fair,
While wavy and light is her hair.
She is like a rose in June,
And a sweet melody in tune,
This fair dame is from my home town,
Her eyes are not blue but brown.
Her cheeks are like the rose,
While awfully white is her nose.
She is very, very sweet,
And makes all the boys say "tweet-tweet."
This modern girl can sing and dance,
When she hears music she begins to prance.
Her merry laugh is of glee,
and a right merry companion makes she.
Her coat is of blue,
While her dress of another hue,
She admires Lindberg very much.
But takes ocean flying as a hunch.
Go there you see is no change for me.

Nan's diploma stated that she completed the two-year professional course of study as "prescribed in this institution" on June 6, 1927. She had planned that the fall of the following year would be her last undergraduate semester:

I should have finished at East Carolina in 1928 at Christmas because all my required work was finished. The previous summer, however, I was one of four people asked to do a special program at the college—a "scarf" dance, which was scheduled in between the main entertainments for the evening (four of us from gym were picked). It had a lot of modern-type dance and some kind of clogging, which I was pretty good at. It just so happened that a member of the board of education in Raleigh, a Mrs. Lacy, was visiting the college that night. Right after my performance I got a note from the history teacher, Sally Joyner Davis, saying she wanted to see me. Miss Davis was the most recognized teacher at the college. When she came backstage, she brought this Mrs. Lacy with her. We chatted for a while. Then Mrs. Lacy asked me how far along I was and, after I told her, asked me if I would like to leave college and teach in Raleigh, then come back and finish my electives the following summer. I thought she was joking. I answered yes, then went home and told the family. They just laughed. But Mrs. Lacy had said that I would have a contract before the week was out and I did. She contacted Miss Mildred English, who was the assistant superintendent of the Raleigh schools, and told her to send me a contract, which Miss English did. I went to Raleigh that fall and taught, then came back and did the summer sessions and graduated in 1929 instead of 1928.

It was a busy time for Nan, but Mattie retreated from activities during her sophomore year, as she began to lose her hearing. By her senior year, she knew she couldn't keep up and begged her mother to let her drop out. Although the college president, Dr. Wright, urged Nannie to make Mattie finish, Nannie yielded to Mattie's wishes. Nan recalled:

When it first happened, I remember our going to Raleigh every single week to try to get something done about her deafness and spending a great deal of money. Nothing seemed to help. I think the loss may have been the result of a strep throat infection. It seems to me that my brother,

Bill, lost his hearing that way as well, but he didn't become deaf until after he was married. Mattie had the highest intelligence of the three of us.

Mattie later confessed that from age eighteen to twenty-seven, she felt left out of everything and felt Nan had stepped into the shoes she'd envisioned for herself. Later, at Nan's suggestion, Mattie eventually went to Virginia and attended Richmond Business College. Nan, who was teaching school by then, paid her tuition.

Bill was away at the University of North Carolina during these years, and the money he made from working on the Stancill farm was needed for his tuition. With Nan and Bill gone, Nannie and Mattie were in the home alone. Nannie remodeled the house; she built two more bedrooms on the second floor and rented them out. Her first renters were college girls, and then she rented to people she knew or the children of people she knew. She received income from this venture from then on until she died.

According to Bill, the money used for the renovations came from the sale of a back lot adjacent to the house, and Nannie and Mattie lived in the four-room downstairs area. Nannie's decision to enlarge her house proved to be a good one. Mattie left Greenville and moved to Raleigh in the early 1940s. The children were no longer at home, but Nannie was not by herself since people were living upstairs. This situation allowed her children to pursue their independent lives without concern for their mother's safety. It was also important because Bill married a woman who wanted nothing to do with the family, and from that time until his wife's death in 1972, the family was kept at a distance. His only connection was that he managed the farm, which did entail trips to Greenville and seeing his mother, so he was not entirely out of touch.

The year 1926 brought about another of those milestone events in a family's life that are cast forever in memory. It was a summer day in the South, and young men's tempers flared. On this occasion, two of the Stancill boys, Leland and Wilfred, were shot and killed. Leland had rented a garage from his Aunt Mag, and he got into an argument over its use with Edward, Aunt Mag's son from her second marriage. A cousin who witnessed the tragedy took the blame, although he was not the perpetrator. Whatever the rights of the affair, for Nan it meant the loss of two very dear cousins.

A series of Stancill tragedies followed this event: Leland's wife later killed herself by driving off a bridge; both their son, Leland Jr., and his aunt, Verna Lee, hanged themselves; Robert was thrown from a horse and badly injured; and John, a nephew, got drunk at a party and ran his car into a tree. Nan always felt very close to all the Stancills—Lela Brown was her best friend in childhood and continued to be a close friend throughout their lives. These events of the late 1920s and early 1930s didn't directly impact the course of Nan's life, but the emotional hits had to have influenced her. They may have contributed to her desire to both find a sustaining philosophy and to find a mate who could anchor her safely. Tragedies have a way of encouraging in us the tendency to look deeply at who we are and what we want in life. During that period, the members of the Evans family must have repeated the family motto regularly.

FIVE

THE YEARS IN RALEIGH

"THE PROGRESSIVE SYSTEM DEWEY USED CAME INTO DISREPUTE

LATER BECAUSE TEACHERS DIDN'T KNOW HOW TO DO IT RIGHT

AND IT TOOK A LOT OF WORK. I DID IT RIGHT." (1989)

Nan taught in the Raleigh public schools from 1928 to 1933 and, at the same time, attended North Carolina State University to pursue a master's degree. Her first two weeks in Raleigh were spent at the local YWCA. Unfortunately, the Y had a curfew that Nan didn't know about and she had to climb in the window at 1 a.m. one night because the door was locked. The matron, who was lying in wait, was livid. According to Nan, who had repeatedly rung the bell, the offense was slight and the matron would have saved them both a lot of bother had she just answered the door. Nan could see only the logic; the almost twenty-year-old did not feel she had done anything wrong. Perhaps she also felt that her new life granted her a new liberty and she wanted to test its boundaries.

Fortunately, the Mrs. Lacy who had approached Nan at East Carolina with the job offer stayed in touch.

> Mrs. Lacy told me not to worry about a place to stay. She
> sent me to stay with a Mrs. Briggs, in a huge home. Mrs.

Briggs sat in a chair most of the day. She was elderly and
almost totally deaf. She had one of those big horns that she
held in her ear in order to hear. She was a prominent lady
in Raleigh. I would go in and see her and talk with her when
I got home from school almost every afternoon. Apparently
she was very fond of me. She was always mighty good to me.

Nan later said that Mrs. Briggs was "a ray of sunshine, and her
heart overflowed with love and generosity for humanity." After her
experience at the Y, Nan also carefully let Mrs. Briggs know her plans.

While I was living at Mrs. Briggs's, I met a Harry Parker,
whom I dated for a long time. Everyone said that although
he was not handsome (they thought he was ugly) he was
as neat as a pin. He was a nice fellow. We went together
almost three years, though I had other dates every so often. The only reason we broke up had to do with his job.
He was an accountant and his company sent him up to
Greensboro for six months. While he was gone, I started
dating one of the professors at North Carolina State University in Raleigh who was in charge of the horticultural
department. Someone told Harry, and he started dating
someone up in Greensboro. The professor was very nice.
I went with him for quite a while. He wanted to get married, but I didn't. In his case, he was just a little bit too
proper to suit me. I was out with a friend one night and
she said she wanted to date him. I told her to go ahead,
and she eventually married him.

The record of events in Nan's memory book indicates that she was
extremely busy.

She also found time for travel, her thirst for adventure undimmed.
Back in 1926, "Ole Aunt Bett," Nan's great aunt on her father's side,
had died. Bett had had lifetime occupancy of her father's property,
and her death meant that the farm was to be sold. As a result, each
of the three Evans children received a small inheritance, so the
children had, probably for the first time, some discretionary funds.

One summer, while Nan was still at East Carolina, Miss Davis had recommended that she travel to both the eastern and western parts of North Carolina. Nan's inheritance from Aunt Bett probably made this idea feasible, because her celebration of her twenty-first year included her making a trip to the western North Carolina mountains. Her friend Bet Piner was in favor of the plan, and an expedition was undertaken in the summer of 1930. Nan, Bet, Lela Brown, Mattie, and someone named Ann went. What Nan remembered most was that they wore shorts, only recently acceptable attire for women. Until the ratification of the Nineteenth Amendment in 1920, "appropriate" women's behavior had been strictly limited. During the following decade, however, societal attitudes began to change. It was a time of shorter skirts and silk stockings, dropped-waist dresses and cloche hats, long beaded necklaces and feather boas, slender cigarette holders and bobbed hair.

Undertaking a trip with women without a male escort was a part of Nan's blossoming desire to experience the freedom the new era promoted. "A wild trip with Five Women – Exploring the country; Bumming our way and living like gypsies – Boy – What Fun." She made another trip that summer as well, with Bill, Mattie, and Bet. They went to Canada, then to New York City and Norfolk, Virginia, on the way back. Nan loved to travel, and 1931 saw her in Pinehurst, Morehead, and Oxford, North Carolina; Charleston, South Carolina; and Virginia Beach, Virginia. She also visited Richmond, Virginia, for the sesquicentennial celebration at Yorktown, and she made several other trips to Virginia, one of which was to attend her friend Bet's wedding to Hugh Lefler—"the most beautiful and sacred of weddings."

So much was happening in her country, and she wanted to taste its richness. It was the era of the automobile industry's large-scale development and the invention of a profusion of electrical appliances. It was a time when the advent of motion pictures and of radios in homes increased popular focus on celebrities and their extravagances and follies. Even through the Depression, young people seemed to have a desire to break with tradition, break out of their background environment, and race towards the new and untried. It was a time in which Nan could bloom.

One visit to Virginia Beach resulted in a relationship with a man named Leo. He sent Nan a letter from the SS *Westernland* on his way to London in which he commented on a conversation he'd had with a fellow passenger. There is every indication that he was smitten:

> I told him all about you, but of course I don't have the ability to describe you as wonderfully as you really are; nevertheless, he told me that I was very lucky to know such an unusual young lady. Of course, I knew this long beforehand. There are lots of things that can be done all during the day, and night too; but what I like to do is to sit and sit and sit for hours and hours and dream of my precious little Nan.

The fact that she kept this letter among her things for over sixty years argues either that Leo meant something to her beyond a flirtation or that she valued being the recipient of such an accolade and used it to prop herself up when she was depressed. According to her calendar from that time, she also experienced her first plane ride and her first time on the Atlantic Ocean. She had become a young woman to a large degree on her own, and her life seemed to be opening up towards new horizons.

Nan led a lively social life in Raleigh. There is a *News & Observer* clipping from that time that states:

> Miss Evans Hostess—Miss Nan Evans entertained at bridge Friday evening at the home of Dr. and Mrs. J. A. Robertson on Park Drive. The residence was beautifully decorated with Christmas colors, and bridge and dancing were enjoyed during the evening. The high score card prize was awarded to Dr. Hugh Lefler and the low score fell to Miss Georgia Kirkpatrick. . . . Refreshments were served during the evening and favors were distributed among the guests while dancing.

Still, Nan was a working gal and these trips and events were adjuncts to her life.

The reason for Mrs. Lacy's recruitment of me that summer night was that a special research project was being
conducted with the Raleigh schools by Columbia University, and Miss English (the assistant superintendent) was
short one teacher. Columbia had a contract with the Raleigh Public Schools whereby the teaching for a period of
time would be done according to the John Dewey system.
It was an experiment with his ideas, and every month the
Columbia people would come down to monitor what was
happening. The progressive system Dewey used came into
disrepute later because teachers didn't know how to do it
right and it took a lot of work. I did it right. His theory
was that you learn by doing. He wasn't in favor of rote
learning. He wanted to arrange the learning around the
things that kids were interested in doing.

As a result of her inclusion in this experiment, Nan was
introduced to the Dewey theories at least two years before her move
to New York.

I was the youngest on the faculty and my salary was $100
a month. I was placed as the fifth-grade teacher at the
Centennial School, which was located at one end of Fay-
etteville Street, Raleigh's main street. The state capitol
was at the other end. The end the school inhabited was a
slum district and a lot of the kids in my class didn't know
who their fathers were. The principal (I thought she was
elderly—she was probably about 45) was a Miss Page. She
came into my class every morning about 9:30. There she
would park herself for most of the day. . . . It was my first
year teaching, and there she sat. I'll never forget it and I
never got used to it. One of the things my kids did was to
build a rocking chair, which they designed themselves. It
had a high back. They actually got the lumber from the
woods. It was very comfortable, and, once it was made,
that was where Miss Page would sit. At the end of the
year, she came up to me and told me I had my contract to

teach the next year. That was the extent of her comments on my performance.

A photo in one of Nan's memory books shows her standing on a parade float that says "Parent Teacher Association Uniting School and Home." A couple of school desks are in front of her with children seated at them, and another woman holds a placard that says "P.T.A. Stands For Our Schools First-Last-Always." The critical link between education, home life, and society, which Dewey talked about at length and which was to undergird many of Nan's later public arguments, began in such venues.

> I began that next year with Miss Page, but I didn't finish it. Miss English approached me a couple of months into the fall session and asked if I would like to transfer to Needham B. Broughton High School. What had happened was that one of the teachers there had started a school bank as one of the Dewey projects, but she was leaving. They needed a teacher who they thought was capable of carrying on this bank, and since I taught social science and mathematics, they felt that running the bank might be in my field. Of course, I told Miss English that I would do it, and my class and I kept the bank going. We were affiliated with one of the banks in downtown Raleigh. Every kid in school had an account in our bank. We studied stocks and bonds in the classroom, and we continued to run the bank even after the Depression hit. When that happened, the other students wanted to know what was going to happen to their money. I said to the kids that we had to do something about it. Being as creative as they were, they said, shucks, we'll get busy and raise the money and pay everyone off. They went home, baked cookies and cakes and had all sorts of sales going on. Paid off every cent.
>
> Saving money was part of my own personal custom. I would put $10 each month in savings and give $10 to the church. Then the Depression came along and I lost all the money I had in the bank. Also, I taught for six months

at that time without getting paid, and never did get paid for the work, although I did get a contract for the next year. For years after the Depression I never saved a penny because of the loss I sustained when the bank closed.

At this time, I was living at a dentist's home, a Dr. Bell, who had two kids. I roomed with Bet Piner, whom I met the first year I was in Raleigh. Miss English introduced us. We lived there two years. That wasn't too far from Broughton, and I could walk to the school. We didn't eat at the Bells'. We ate at a boarding house near NC State. We met a lot of people at that boarding house, and they were the crowd we ran around with.

At approximately the same time Nan was managing the student bank, the art teacher at Broughton had to leave and Nan was asked to take over that class.

I'd never taught art in my life and didn't know anything about it. At the end of the semester we had an art exhibition. It so happened that the woman who was the president of the state women's clubs came. She was impressed and asked the principal to introduce her to me. She asked me about my training and found out that I didn't have any. She then asked me if I would like to go to New York to study art. Of course, I said yes.

The Raleigh newspaper reported on this development:

Announcement was made yesterday by Mrs. R. L. Mc-Millan, chairman of the Picture Memory Contest for the North Carolina Federation of Women's Clubs, that Miss Nan Evans has been awarded a scholarship given under the auspices of the Federation. Miss Evans, who is a member of the Broughton High School faculty, will leave next week for New York City where she will study in the New York School of Fine and Applied Art during the summer session. She is a native of Greenville and a graduate of

East Carolina Teachers College. Miss Evans is working on
her master's degree, to which the work in the New York
school will be credited.

Nannie Elizabeth Evans, late 1920s

Arthur Raymond Young, a noted artist and illustrator, was her
teacher. Nan recalled:

> I had a wonderful time. The school helped me find a place
> to live and I lived in a room on the fifth floor of a building
> not far from the school. Never having been in art school,
> I didn't know what I was doing. I took two courses: life
> drawing and design. Life drawing was really and truly life
> drawing. I went into the classroom that first day and there
> was this nude, ugly as all get out, and here were all these
> students standing around drawing. My reaction was to be
> a little bit shocked. First time I'd ever seen a nude body
> posing in front of a group. They told me to take my place
> in the circle, so I did. I only took the one course. Later

I drew Lela Brown and did a nice job. Probably should have taken more courses in that. The other course was in design. I learned a lot in the course but didn't really enjoy it like the other. Another thing that has always been interesting to me in all the life drawing classes I've taken since, the models have always been women, and ugly ones, in positions you don't usually see people in. Later on, when I was doing work from models, we'd have people in and just do their feet.

Nan loved being in New York and was very excited by the two classes she was able to take:

Would that I had the creative mind to express in poetry, or to paint on canvas, the thrill, the excitement, the joy, the fear, of coming here, of being here . . . Ah, the city of brilliant lights, the crowd, the rush, the horns, and there and there they are, the news flashes of Times Square.

All she experienced was nourishment to the budding artist: the wind whipping through the buildings' canyons; the mixture of oil, gas, horse waste, and the crowd's aromas; the patchwork of elegant strollers and harried dock workers; the glitter of gaiety and the sadness of misery. She was a bit lonely at first, but soon her bubbly personality drew new friends. The rest of the summer passed with touring the city, going on dates, and working on her art. Her return to Raleigh was anticlimactic, and although she finished her master's degree at NC State that year (with its thesis being on an aspect of education at Broughton High School), New York had woven its spell.

After I got back to Raleigh, I decided that I wanted to go back to New York to study art. I asked Miss English what the chances were of getting a job at the Lincoln School, which was the model school at Columbia University. At that time Dr. Thomas Alexander, the professor of education at Teachers College at Columbia University, was

making trips down to Raleigh in connection with the
Dewey research project. In addition, he had recently been
made the dean of New College. Miss English told me that
she would ask Dr. Alexander the next time she saw him
if there were any chance that I could get a position at the
Lincoln School. When he came, she did; he called me,
and we went out to dinner. I told him what I wanted. Instead, he offered me a job at the New College, teaching
college.

His proposal included an offer that Nan could take eight credits
a year in art at Columbia. Her new job was to begin in the fall of
1933, so teaching in the Raleigh high schools came to an end and
her new life in New York City began.

THE YEARS AT COLUMBIA

"OF COURSE, THERE'S PLENTY OF ROOM FOR IMPROVEMENT

BUT THEN TO HAVE HAD HER SAY IT WAS GOOD WORK WAS

WORTH A GREAT DEAL TO ME." (1933)

Nan took a whole year of art training under Arthur Young.

> I worked hard, and he was a great teacher. At the end of
> the year I finally had something good, a scene of Morn-
> ingside Park near the school, and put it in the year-end
> exhibition. Someone stole it off the wall at the exhibition.

From her journals, indulging in her art always cheered her up
and was a source of her feeling good about herself.

> *Back to my room and painted a while then took my picture to art*
> *class. Someone chose it as the best picture on the wall today. First*
> *time anything like that has happened. . . .*
>   *Took my new watercolor to art class this morning. Say, I'm*
> *surely getting proud of myself. Almost get conceited at times. Art*
> *Young actually thought it was good. My first real landscape. I*

knew darn well I could, and I'll do something even better. Both of these snow scenes are good even if I do say so myself.

Unfortunately, her work duties made it impossible to submit an art paper at the end of the term and she got an "incomplete."

Nan's first year in New York City was one of acclimatization, and she went through many emotional swings. Her closest friends were in North Carolina, and taking the step of moving to New York was frightening at the same time that it was exhilarating. She had kept diaries before, sporadically, but starting on January 1, 1934, she kept a daily journal. It provides a closer look at her personal life during the three years she wrote regularly than at any other stage of her life. She records her feelings and emotions in depth and freely, but is vague (perhaps on purpose) on factual details. She had gotten accustomed to being in the city, and the journal records the ups and downs of a young woman in her twenties who was thrilled to be experiencing life independent of her family and community background yet had many lonely, homesick days.

> *How strangely things do turn out. One never knows what·a day will bring. What a peculiar make-up I must be. Have had the blues for a week. Here I sat last night down in the dumps so to speak—no dates, nothing particularly interesting to me. Everybody getting on my nerves. It seems to me I've spent the last two years just in such a manner. At times extremely interested in being alive, in one sense, extremely happy, and, on the other hand, terribly lonesome and blue. Always looking for something I haven't found. . . .*
>
> *No sooner had I gotten back to my room than Bill Glanz called. Went down and talked to him. Tried so hard to be sweet. Why don't I fall in love with him for instance? An excellent boy; good job, good family, a gentleman and yet . . .*
>
> *Why can't I fall in love as easily or even at all, the way others seem to. Oh, God! But I'm lonesome and in a sense tired of the life I live.*

She did seem to want to pack more encounters and adventures into any one day than others did. There is almost a sense that she feared she would miss out on something if she didn't participate.

She rarely went to bed before midnight. One entry relates that she sometimes felt that she was putting on a mask and needed to be the "pep" at any party or in every conversation. This also included her drinking, and at one point someone tattled to Dr. Alexander that she was "hitting the bottle." He fussed at her, and she records how furious she was that anyone would accuse her of this. She does, however, write about several instances of her having gotten "tight" and the results the morning after.

There were times when she had more than two dates with different admirers during a single day. The list of those with whom she had some sort of active relationship while living in New York City is long. There were around eight women with whom she spent significant amounts of time. About the same number of men were frequently on the scene, though none of these gentlemen stirred her heart. One of her more constant entries in her first year was her desire to find a companion who excited her.

Besides being lonesome and feeling she was missing something somehow, there were other parts of her life in New York that she definitely did not like. One was that she was always concerned about money:

> *Wonder what the best way to live on $1.86 is. How does one eat, get one's clothes from the cleaner and pay one's way about the city with such a large margin? I'm thankful that I had the ten-dollar deposit made on my room or I'm afraid I would have no place to lay my head tonight. . . .*
>
> *I don't particularly like this room nor the idea of staying at Seth Low Hall, but I suppose I shall have to make the best of it and get along the best I can. Where does my salary go? I don't spend any foolishly. I don't have any clothes. I don't spend a lot on food, scarcely enough, and yet I never have a cent. One thing surely is that I am gradually getting my debts in Raleigh paid. Still, I owe about $20 there besides my debt to Hugh and Bet. Oh God, will I ever get paid up?*

Nan's dislike of her living conditions plagued her throughout much of her time in New York.

> *Breakfast at Friedgurs with Sally was both appetizing and*
> *satisfying—the coffee was good and the toast hot, and I had fresh*
> *bread. How different from that at Whittier Hall. . . .*
>
> *Read until lunch, and when it was served it had to be lamb*
> *chops. How I loathe them. And broccoli. How I detest it. Gosh,*
> *what a terrible meal. Even the ice cream wasn't good since it was*
> *coated with raspberry sauce. . . .*
>
> *Bah. What a cold morning. Darn the service in this place. One*
> *minute you burn up and the next you freeze. Hell on getting up in a*
> *cold room, eating breakfast in a cold dining hall, and going down,*
> *still freezing. By noon they will run up out with heat.*

Yet she also recorded her excitement at being a part of the city
in her journal:

> *I like to go downtown. The people, the buzz, the rush, the stores,*
> *all are most exciting to me. Seems so real, so alive. Isn't just that*
> *the reason I am so rebellious here. Day after day in this environ-*
> *ment one gets so much of one side of life and misses so much that*
> *is so real.*

In addition, she took some ownership of the city whenever she
had out-of-town guests. As is common with most New Yorkers,
much of Nan's sightseeing took place when she had company. This
was particularly true when her mother came up for Easter in 1934.
It is a wonder both of them survived her visit, though Nannie Evans
was just sixty at the time and there didn't seem to be any need for
a slower pace.

> *(Saturday, March 31) Went over to Lisa's apartment and cooked*
> *our breakfast. Walked down in Harlem at 125th street and took*
> *a crosstown car to 2nd Ave. "L." Went down to Brasstown and*
> *walked around. . . . Took the "L" on down to South Ferry. Walked*
> *through Battery Park to the aquarium while it was pouring rain.*
> *Did we get wet? I'll say. Stayed in the aquarium about an hour.*
> *Still it rained. Took the 9th Ave "L" up to 66th Street and took a*
> *subway home. . . . Went to American Museum of Natural History,*

*the Metropolitan Museum of Art. Took bus down 5th Ave. to
42nd Street, walked over to New Amsterdam theater while it was
pouring rain; got tickets for the show. . . . Went to see "Roberta," a
good musical comedy. After the show we walked up to the doughnut
shop and bought a package of doughnuts; still it rained. Came
home nearly starving, made some coffee and had a midnight tea.
Finally got to bed about 1:30 worn to a frazzle.*

*(April 1) Up at 6:30 and went to Columbia sunrise service;
8:00 over to Lisa's apartment, back home and breakfast. Riverside
Church at eleven. Had to stand in line for about a half-hour, then
had to sit down in the basement and listen to the service on the
amplifier. . . . Took 5th Ave. bus downtown to see the Easter
Parade. . . . Took a couple of hours to get down to 60th Street . . .
visited the 5th Ave. churches. St. Thomas was beautifully decorated,
so was St. Patrick's and St. Nicholas. Walked down to Radio City
and went through the Spring Festival staged at the sunken gardens.
Walked crosstown to East River Water Front. Went in the New
Bldg. at the Museum of Science and Industry; the Grand Central
station, the hotel Commodore, the Empire State Bldg. . . . Walked
over to Penn Hotel and New Yorker. Had tea at New Yorker. Took
subway up to 50th and went to Radio City. . . . Home dead tired.*

*(April 2) Another full day of seeing New York City. . . . Didn't
get off on the start until eleven o'clock. . . . Took Mother to see
Morningside Residence Club roof garden; on down to the French
Catholic church and walked in on a wedding; then over to St. John
the Divine Church. Took the subway at 110th St. and went over to
Brooklyn to the Opera House. Came back to Wall St. and walked
the full length of it. Went out along the docks and got a good
view of East River, Brooklyn, and N.Y. buildings. Walked to the
Ferry house and took the ferry over to Staten Island. . . . Mother
got something in her eye. Worked trying to get it out nearly all the
way back to Manhattan. . . . Finally was able to go back on deck
in time for Mother to get a good view of the Skyline. Walked up
B-way. Went into the U.S. Custom House. Walked on up the street
to Schrafft's. Went in Trinity Church and the Equitable Bldg. Took
subway up to Grand Central. Walked up Park Ave. to Waldorf
Astoria. . . . Went in St. Bartholomew's Church. Went to Madison*

Sq. Garden . . . and down to Macy's where Mother bought Mattie a slip. . . . Came up to 116th and walked in Riverside Park. Went by Grant's Tomb and on to International House. Took a bus ride up Riverside and came back and ate supper at Childs and came home. Tired now; think I'll go to sleep early. Class tomorrow morning.

Nan also developed an interest in opera and bought tickets for the Metropolitan Opera when she could, though much of her opera-going was as the date of some young swain. At one point she went to the Brooklyn Opera and had the privilege of hearing and meeting Lily Pons, the coloratura soprano who had come from France in 1931 to take the operatic world by storm. Nan made her first trip to a zoo (the Bronx Zoo) and worshipped several Sundays at the Cathedral of St. John the Divine. She attended shows at Radio City Music Hall and other theaters, at one point seeing Duke Ellington on stage at the Capitol Theater, and she frequented both Schrafft's and Childs, iconic restaurants at the time.

Trips out of the city up to West Point, to Westchester County, and to New Jersey were also among her excursions. She went on dates that included golf, her first experience of ice-skating, and many long walks with beaus both in the city and the country.

One can never tell what a day in New York will offer. I have decided that though a person spent a lifetime here and went on an excursion in varied parts of the city each day, he would miss seeing some of the most interesting things within it. Quite possible to ride through the streets, in every section and get a general idea; but oh the places one has to walk to really see what may be in a dirty street, under the Brooklyn Bridge, through an archway and behind a door that you would have not opened unless you had someone who knew the place and its people to take you in. Who would have thought that such a place I saw today should manufacture lithographic plates? Such a tiny place, almost like a chamber in a dungeon that is finally reached after walking through the arches of a bridge on old cobblestones that have probably been laid for a century. Chinatown—what a compact place with people that look just as closed and mysterious as the stories of Pell Street imply. Wouldn't it be fun to enter those shops, provided you were with someone, or would that take some of the adventure away? Anyway, I don't think I'd care to enter otherwise.

She had the chance to meet and get to know some individuals whose contributions then and afterwards remain important in the development of modern educational theory, John Dewey among them. When he was introduced to her at a faculty reception, his comment was "My goodness, when did they start hiring children as teachers?" In addition, her duties in the social science department put her under the direction of Dr. William Withers, who went on to a distinguished career at Queens College; Dr. John Gambs, who became famous in the field of institutional economics; and Dr. Agnes Snyder, the author of *Dauntless Women in Childhood Education*. She also worked under the direction of Dr. Florence Stratemeyer, a founding figure in teacher education and curriculum. Dr. Stratemeyer was considered one of the most influential women of the twentieth century in the formation of principled teachers whose methods were based on reason. It was a formidable group, and exposure to these fine intellects must have been invigorating and probably honed Nan's ability to dissect and reassemble her thoughts and ideas in profitable ways.

Nan didn't know what she was supposed to do when she first arrived in New York, and these teachers didn't know either.

When I went to Dr. Alexander to ask if there were any other areas in which I would be working, he said: "I didn't bring you up here to tell you what to do. You figure out what to do. If you can't, you don't belong here."

On hearing about this, the professors told her to do supervisory work with the intern teachers (which required office hours) and to lead the seminars. She took on the roles she was assigned, although she became quite critical of her workspace ("How I hate that dirty, cold place") and felt disgusted with students who didn't show up for conferences.

She did struggle with some lack of certainty about her ability to handle all these new duties. Having the opportunity to follow her dream of studying art required that first she must spend most of her time studying the Dewey concepts and working with the under-graduates to incorporate these ideas into "units" to be used in their practice teaching. Helping compose these units was her primary job throughout the spring. By the end of the term, she finally felt she had progressed:

> *Things are moving along better in the seminar now. Guess we'll get some units written after all. What a job it is going to be to integrate all that material . . .*
>
> *A day set aside for work. How beautiful it has been outside. Warm sunshine! Spring! It is actually here. And I didn't put my foot out of doors. . . .*
>
> *Came to my room, locked my door so as to be alone, dressed in my pajamas and sat down to work. . . .*
>
> *Took me until lunchtime to get my thoughts organized. Sat down to work on a larger scale after lunch. Began to integrate the units handed in by the students in the Soc. Science seminar. What an impossible job it seems to be. I have dreaded it for over a week, and now I am down to it, trying to get something on paper. Dr. Snyder came in about seven-thirty. Saw my work and wanted to have it explained. Seemed to think it a lot of rot. . . . Huh! She doesn't like the generalization! Well, what of it. Finally got my idea stated to her in understandable language. Seemed that she began to see light. Even so much as admitted it was a good idea. Left by telling me it was a swell job but a difficult one. "Don't be discouraged."*
>
> *Went over to see Dr. Stratemeyer about the work. Went over most of it very carefully with her. Good news. Of course, there's plenty of room for improvement but then to have had her say it was good work was worth a great deal to me. . . .*
>
> *Went to Educational Seminar this afternoon. Very interesting. But gosh, it all seems so impossible and at times worthless. I wonder, are we getting anywhere?*

Nan ended up having other administrative duties as well. She later recalled:

> All the women undergraduate students were housed on the top floor of one of the dormitories when I arrived at Columbia. A few months after I arrived, the supervisor of these women, who was called the Dean of Freshmen Women, had to leave. Dr. Alexander asked me to take over the job, so I became a Dean of Women. I was about twenty-four or twenty-five at the time. . . . He gave me two other women to help me, though I was in charge.

One of these women, Sally Fair, had a father who was a friend of Dr. Alexander.

> Sally's connection with Dr. Tom made it very nice for all three of us. We were all under his wing and we all became great friends. Dr. Alexander considered us his kids and was always doing nice things for us, like giving us tickets to plays. We three women became very close friends and remained friends for many years.
>
> Each of us had "dorm duty" about three nights a week. By doing this job I got my room free, but I had to eat meals with the students, and I will never forget that. The students never started eating before I arrived. At my entrance, they all stood up and waited to sit down and begin until I was seated.

Nan did not enjoy this job, and by the second semester she had some negative comments on what it was like to be in charge of students not so much younger than she. She had been to an evening staff meeting and was frustrated when she returned to the dorm:

> *Got in about 12 and these crazy girls were making tea. Damn them, why won't they go to bed once in a while.*

And again:

> *Two girls have been in tonight to discuss problems. Surely had a*
> *taste of exercising "dean duties" lately.*

Yet she also tried to see the bright side:

> *One thing about this dorm business is that I am getting somewhat*
> *used to talking to a group of 50 with a little more ease than usual.*

Nan's New Year's resolution was to "make the best of everything and stop griping." Still, by the end of January her stress was resulting in physical symptoms: she was always tired, she had consistently low blood pressure, and she developed a bald spot on her head that drove her crazy. Her hands shook a little, an intermittent characteristic and not one resulting from any nervousness about a particular event.

> *Oh, God, how I wish my hands would not tremble. It has never failed*
> *to be embarrassing for me. I usually laugh it off when anyone notices*
> *it or says anything about it, but, in my heart, I am deeply hurt.*

She was always sensitive about it, but this tiny vulnerability remained throughout the rest of her life. Did it begin at this time? There was no previous mention of it, and there were later records of her disgust with it, so it is possible that there was some alteration in her physical system as a result of the stress she was feeling. The doctor said she would be all right, but her confidence fluctuated:

> *And all because of special nerves. What a terrible thing to have*
> *happen to me now. Ambition, what of it? What price glory. Is it*
> *all shot, or do I have a chance if I take care of myself? Rest, sleep,*
> *fresh air, exercise, and a diet filled with vitamins. How impossible*
> *all that seems here in the dormitory. But, by George, I shall have it*
> *all even if it is to say to hell with the work. . . .*
>
> *Damn my nerves and sensitivity. Wish to God I had the self-*
> *confidence some of these dumb kids around here have. I must*
> *develop it.*

Two days later she bounced back:

Believe the majority of the group are with me however. I did enjoy it, and golly, I wasn't ever afraid. Just sat there and defended my convictions. Geez, but I'm feeling proud of myself tonight. Hope I keep the self-confidence.

Then two months later she was full of angst again:

Knowing what you want to do. What a problem. Oh gosh I wish someone understood. What is this feeling of something hanging heavily just above us; why do I so want to escape and what is it I want to escape from with so much here that I like and have longed for. Oh, but freedom: Where is it? What is it? Ida! Bet! How I wish you were here. Could I talk to you? Would you understand or are you different also? No, I believe you would.

By May she had regained her optimism:

Had a most interesting seminar this afternoon. Miss Bain's group met with us. A good argument and nearly all of us took a part in it. Gee, but I'm getting brave. Feel terribly proud of myself. Well, I only hope I can keep it up. At least I am growing a little more self-confident. Maybe I'll reach the place someday where I'll have some nerve in public and won't be so darn bashful.

Some of Nan's anxiety had to have resulted from trying to create something entirely new in educational pedagogy. William James, back in 1890, had introduced the American intellectual class to the principles of psychology. By 1930, James's influence on Dewey had resulted in the idea of child-centered education. Yet this novel way of looking at child development and education was constantly bombarded by the world in which Dewey and his supporters, including Nan, sought to develop this approach. Nan and her associates were tasked with constructing the practical application of Dewey's pedagogy. Altering the methods by which education had been guided for decades and initiating a completely new approach like Dewey's placed additional pressure on the body politic.

In addition, Dewey thought that all true meaning in life and for life was found as the result of the prior experiences of the individual or society. For him, there was nothing outside of this way of understanding. Nan had a fundamental issue with that: she believed quite profoundly in a transcendent God, and Dewey's thesis seemed to reject that.

Nan had other doubts and criticisms as well; she was not totally convinced that the Dewey system would be effective. She was at the cutting edge of the progressive movement in education, but there were times when she questioned whether she belonged there:

> *What's it all about anyway? Have all of us gone crazy or are we really on the right track? How much retracing must be done to make the thing successful? How deeply am I interested? Social order! Sometimes I feel as though I should scream from merely hearing the phrase. . . . What is my social philosophy anyway? Opportunity, what am I going to do with it? Anything, nothing. How am I to know? Am I here temporarily or not? Yes, I do want to do my best now, for the time being, but I do not want to be dreaming. I want to live, to find real happiness, not sublimation. . . .*
>
> *Back to my room feeling disgusted. Had Soc. Sc. 15 at 1:30. Deeper and deeper into this thing called progressive education. Social philosophy. Yes! And what about it? One minute there's a joke and next we seriously discuss the most vital problems of life and what education is and should be. . . .*
>
> *Went to P.S. 43 with Mildred P. this morning and observed two geography lessons. I had a feeling of living in a modern world of conflicting ideas and order whose educational system is still in the medieval stages. Actually felt as though I had turned the pages of history back some forty years or more. Something must be done about such backwardness in such a city.*

Nan grew to like "Dr. Tom" a great deal, although her initial reactions in her journal that first year were that he was a difficult man to understand and know, and that he put too much pressure on her.

Dr. Tom was up there sitting with Ruth. Did he make me angry! What in the hell is he talking about anyway? Cheap living, bah! He knows nothing about it. Money. He knows darn well I don't have any or don't make any. And as to taking more courses and working on a doctor's, he's just simply nuts. I wonder, does he have a brain in his head? What does he think I came up here for anyway?

In truth, Dr. Tom wasn't interested in her wanting to be an artist. Permitting her to take the credits in that field was the means he had used to attract this talented individual to his program. Still, he did like her, and while he kept her in suspense regarding her future on several occasions, they had a good relationship, and opportunities eventuated that would have been implausible without his mentorship.

SEVEN

AN EMOTIONAL YEAR

"IT'S HELL IF YOU AREN'T IN LOVE

AND IT IS WORSE THAN THAT IF YOU ARE." (1934)

Good relationships make life sustainable and pleasant, and Nan made many friends, both male and female. Her art teacher, Arthur Young, was one of them. It was through him that her life became even more complicated. Art arranged a date for Nan on January 12, 1934, with a man named Dr. Arthur Lorch, apparently his best friend. Whether Arthur Lorch was affiliated with Columbia remains unclear from Nan's journal, but other documentation suggests he was an instructor in the chemistry department. It seems from Nan's account that he took his meals at the same restaurants her group frequented, attended many of the same functions, and was present at parties in the apartments of mutual friends. While all her admirers heretofore had interested but not intrigued Nan, Arthur was different. After her first date with him, she wrote in her journal:

> *Rather nice to have Arthur Lorch call this afternoon. . . . Enjoyed the evening so very much. He is most interesting. Strange feeling that I had while with him tonight.*

After that night, Nan was falling in love. Her journal from then on throughout the year records almost daily comments referring to Arthur. Their relationship was a mystery to her throughout the time she was seeing him. Her journal entries relate her turmoil, her bewilderment, and her anxiety, as well as her fervent desire for a permanent connection with him. A part of her angst quite possibly was her own fault, the result of her socializing with so many others that she did not send him clear messages. In addition, they seemed to have been at different stages of their lives and had come from entirely different backgrounds. He was Jewish and from New Jersey; he had finished his doctorate and was working in his profession. Nan, at 26, was more an ingénue.

> He surely is a hard person to make like you. I don't think I have ever been so sweet to anyone. . . .
>
> God, but I'd like to have him fall in love with me and need me . . . Oh God, was I ever in love before . . . I've never known such perfect happiness. How does he feel? I wish I knew. . . .
>
> Funny why I just don't give a damn about being with anyone else . . . Funny how one can be so lonesome with such a crowd around. . . .
>
> Darling, I love you. How can I show you, tell you, prove to you that I do with all of my heart? Don't you care, darling? After the dance now. How hurt I am. I'll never forget looking up into Arthur's face. To see him there that way dancing with someone else. A thousand and one reactions—just cold and then nervous. Every nerve and muscle in my body slowed. I couldn't help it. I wanted to leave but still I wanted to stay where I could see him every minute. . . .
>
> Darling, don't you love me? I love you. I've told you so. Don't you believe me? I've never told anyone else that. You loved me on the way home. You almost gave yourself away. Darling, why didn't you? The way you held me and kissed me and told me good night. . . .
>
> It's hell if you aren't in love and it is worse than that if you are. Wonder why he asked me to smile just before we walked out. Strange how he changed on the ride home. Well, I couldn't help but

feel the way I did and so act so cold. Who wouldn't, I'm still a
Southerner and I'm proud to the nth degree. Oh, if he doesn't call
me again and soon, I don't know how I'll stand it. . . .

Had fun with the whole gang and then had to come in and cry
myself to sleep because I love him so terribly much that I don't
seem to be able to stand it. . . .

To be in love is certainly terrible but then also it is the greatest
thing in the world. . . .

Surely we will find some way. A way that both of us will be
happy. You do care, I know you do. Yes, even with your very soul.
And, am I right in believing he feels the same way, yes? I must
keep my chin up. I love him and he loves me. We'll find our way.

There was almost a sense in her journals, however, that while she
pined, she was not going to stay home. Still, other men just couldn't
compare:

His type is so attractive to me and yet they aren't like Arthur. I
often wonder just why it is that Arthur makes me care so deeply for
him. I don't feel the same way about other men that I like.

Around this time, Nan received two job offers. The one from
a school in Pennsylvania was attractive but would necessitate her
moving out of the New York area. Her journal records many
questions and reflections. Yet Arthur seems to have been her
primary consideration in her decision-making, and she took the
chance that their relationship had a future and turned down the
opportunities.

A discussion Nan had with Dr. Tom about the Pennsylvania job
resulted in much anxiety. She apparently said something that he
thought indicated she did not appreciate all he had done for her.
She was unaware of this, but later in the year, he became angry and
fired her when she went to him about having a job at New College
the following year. "It was like a thunderbolt. I was told to get out."
Nan spent the next day anxiously waiting to see if he would relent,
but he left to go to Chicago for a conference and she had no choice
but to await his return. Finally, he granted her another interview:

I've seen T.A. We talked it over. What a fool I am. I should have known there are some things one can't say even though they be a truth. I can honestly say, however, that I am glad that I did not mean it the way he took it. I do realize how fortunate I am to be here in New College and that I have the best opportunity anyone could hope for. All I want is to know that I can have it again. Nothing would have ever been said had not those two jobs come up. All along there has been nothing that I have wanted other than to be here at N.C. again next year. It is what I have hoped for and worked for. I am terribly hurt that Dr. Tom took it the way he did. Goodness knows, I am thankful for all he has done for me. If he will only give me another chance. To play fair with me is all I ask. He has been fair in everything so far. If he could only understand and will forgive if it is true that I made such an implication as seems to have been taken.

Nan's personality was a bit impulsive, and she was undoubtedly headstrong. Having this rather frightening corrective must have been a jolt that taught her quite a bit about herself. There were very few times in the coming years when she allowed her emotions to override her thinking. In later years, while she did not distance herself emotionally from experiences, she learned to guard her tongue and trained herself to be sensitive to the motivations behind others' words and actions.

As a result of this contretemps with Dr. Alexander, May came with Nan not knowing if she would be returning to New York, not even knowing, until June 2, that Dr. Alexander was going to give her a job for the summer. At that point, he finally told her to go to the "Community," a communal living experiment in western North Carolina. This meant she would not have any encounters or dates with Arthur. She found that hard and referred to him almost daily in her journal the entire time she was at the Community.

The Community was located in Haywood County, North Carolina, deep in the Appalachian Mountains. It was an 1,800-acre farm about thirty-five miles southwest of Asheville in the Pigeon River Valley. Dr. Alexander's idea was to provide potential teachers with an experience of communal living in an environment where cooperation and collective effort were necessary for survival. Since the New College curriculum was based on educating teachers to be community leaders as well as teachers, the paradigm thus learned would benefit society, the ultimate goal of progressive education. The project involved not only communal living but also working with nature. It seems they were actually building some sort of small village because, according to Nan's journal, there was a lot of putting up of fences and construction of buildings both at the Community and at a "kids' camp."

Nan was a member of the faculty and yet was also a participant in the work. There were seminars just like at New College, but the staff at the Community also raised chickens and sheep and were involved in washing windows, peeling potatoes, polishing silver, washing pots and pans, picking turnips, scrubbing floors, moving lumber, and taking hikes with a professor and the group of undergraduate students. There was a work schedule for each day. At one point, Nan was assigned the job of chasing and catching eleven chickens, chopping their heads off and then plucking them. It irritated her that some of the group seemed to have such a hard time plucking the feathers off. With her farming background, it was just another job, and she knew how. By June 16 Nan was chairing the social committee and had to put on some kind of entertainment on Saturday nights. In compensation for performing these duties, she was back in North Carolina, in the mountains, and her artistic side was delighted. She loved the freedom of the outdoors and put scenes on paper whenever she had a moment to draw.

This opportunity did not last long. At the end of June, Dr. Alexander called her back to New York and set her to work cataloging the New College library. She enjoyed getting to know the system and knowing where everything was.

> *What a dirty job I had working in the office today rearranging all the books. I enjoyed it though! What a grand feeling it is to really do some work you can enjoy, that you can awaken in the morning and not live in dread of having to go to the job, but really want to go and really wish to get something accomplished.*

She worked there until August, when there was a break, and Dr.
Alexander had her ride to Raleigh with him. Just as the trip ended,
he announced that he expected to see her back at New College on
September 10.

Nan spent her break back in Greenville with her mother and
sister and devoted some time to rekindling her friendships. Mattie
told her sister that she had changed, although Nan disagreed. There
was also some kind of difficulty in her relationship with her mother.

> *When all were gone I wanted to just be near my mother. Why do*
> *we have such a strained feeling when my whole heart aches for it*
> *to be otherwise? Mother, just try to understand anyway. I can't tell*
> *you that I love you, but I do.*

Popping in and out of one's family life can be wonderful, but
when you have gotten used to your own way of doing things, coming
back into the family, however briefly, can also be uncomfortable.
On one occasion, when her mother and Mattie saw her off for New
York, Nan commented in her journal that she felt they were glad to
see her go. And she might have been happy to go as well. She had
found, even among old friends, that she seemed to have the same
problem she had in New York:

> *Why am I so miserably unhappy regardless of where I am? Even*
> *at White Oaks today among a group of my friends, old friends*
> *from Raleigh, I felt completely out of "cahoots," absolutely adrift.*
> *A feeling of loneliness that cannot be described. And what did I*
> *do? Play the game. It seems to me I always have to play that game*
> *and every instinctive emotion seems to cry no. But no is the last*
> *thing I ever am able to say. I have to laugh, sing, and play with*
> *the rest of them. The games they played were not of interest to me.*
> *And card tricks? How I hate them.*

She was also critical of the weather. She had acclimated to New
York and although it was just as hot in the summer there as it was in
North Carolina, it was not as muggy and sluggish, nor as filled with
mosquitos. She told her mother she would not live in Greenville

ever again. That statement would come true, though not for the reasons she thought then.

Back in New York on September 4, Nan was confronted with having to teach eighth graders in a Hackensack school. She was very unhappy with this assignment, but felt she had to take it since it had Dr. Alexander's approval. It was to be another attempt at putting Dewey's theories into practice, and she was to use the unit structure that she had helped develop the previous term.

In addition, she was to supervise student teachers from the New College undergraduate division. The first one, Peggy, she regarded as an "upstart" who apparently had the nerve to criticize Nan's methods. The second student was more amenable to suggestion, but still a bit unnerving:

> *Bobbie startled me by stating just out of a clear sky that I was the most puzzling person she had ever met. And then she proceeded to tell me why. Interesting, I must say, to have anyone tell you almost exactly your inmost feelings.*

The third student was Sid, who was, to her eyes, an abject failure as a teacher. In her opinion, he could neither teach nor control the classroom. Their differences were so acute that she sometimes took over the class.

> *Another day of misery. How I hate it. Oh, if I only had some job that began at nine and ended at five, with nothing more to worry about. An office job, something connected with education. How much I loved it this summer. Those squirming kids. How very much I detest it all. And I can't do anything about it but take it and work, work, work like the devil. Oh, God, what next? Have mercy on me and help me. Here it is almost twelve and I don't have the slightest idea what to do tomorrow. A unit; oh, for Pete's sake . . .*
>
> *I honestly wish I never had to teach school another day as long as I live. If things go right, I don't like it, and if things go wrong, I don't like it. I like education ok. I'm somewhat wrapped up in it, but I honestly detest classroom teaching. I believe I know how*

it is done and how it ought to be done but I surely don't like to do it. Why does it sap my energy so? Why am I tired? Why does it always worry me so much? I never have a minute to do anything that I really and truly want to do because I am interested. Today was a fairly good day and still I didn't like it.

With Dr. Alexander, there was always a carrot and a stick. He seems to have known that she would hate the Hackensack job, and that September he promised her a contract at New College for the next year and the possibility of a trip to Europe in the summer. She had noted in her journal that she was envious of the New College students' expeditions to Europe, so her desire was already there, and having that as a future prospect did help.

The bright spot in this new life was that she got a raise and could move into an apartment. She teamed up with a woman named Eileen and moved to West 122nd Street. She was thrilled to be in her own apartment and to be able to furnish it to her taste. She and Eileen made curtains, and somehow wove a rug that Nan thought looked very nice.

She was also thrilled to be able to entertain or to be alone. Her idea of being alone, as frequently as she says in her journal that she desires it, is not evidenced in the calendar she kept. She contracted even more engagements, inviting people to come for dinner and sometimes breakfast.

Something seems to promise a year of fun, a real friendship with a very interesting group. I truly hope so, for I have no pleasure to look towards in the work.

Arthur was still occupying a large part of her emotional attention, and whenever he asked for her, she made an effort to be available. Still, by the end of the year, when she was home again for a break, she was beginning to sense that her desire for a permanent relationship would not be fulfilled. Although she received a belated Christmas card from him, she didn't send him one herself.

During that tumultuous year, she also found solace from her constant worries about Arthur and life in general by attending Riverside Church. This interdenominational church had been open only a few years at that time. Although she skipped Sunday morning services quite frequently—late Saturday night festivities making her too tired to get up in time—going to church salved the soul wounds she couldn't seem to avoid. She frequently noted her attendance in her journal and commented on the peace she found by going. At one point she wrote:

> *Gosh, but would not all of us go nuts if we didn't have a god to worship. How sweet and beautiful the services were this morning.*

She was also reflective about religion itself:

> *Religion, I wonder what it is; just how much power it has or ought to have or what it really is. To me it seems to be all that is fine and beautiful in life. All that one can hope to have, to be. A love that lives on; that is the one high ideal that perpetuates ourselves; that governs every phase of our life. And yet those ideals so often have their very foundations knocked out from under us. Or so it seems. But something, somehow, away deep on the inside always comes back, and again one can usually see light, or a ray of it anyway.*

As a child, Nan had had the privilege of hearing her Uncle Offie debate visiting clergy:

> Maybe three times a year he [the preacher] would stay at Uncle Offie's. When they were discussing the Bible, either on Saturday nights, or on Sunday afternoon after church, I would sit in there at my uncle's knee. I don't know why I did; none of the others did. I once told my mother that Uncle Offie knew a lot more about the Bible than the preacher did.

She may have been critical because she felt, early on, that the circuit-riding preachers took advantage of their profession to live off other people. She questioned institutional religion all her life, particularly those organizations and people who did not examine their beliefs and who gave lip service to what she considered worn-out rituals. Her faith journey at all times included her own careful and extensive scrutiny of her beliefs and their decreed obligations.

Still, when she wrote her final thoughts for the year, she was positive:

> *1934 was the fullest year of my life so far. I have grown, have listened and watched things as they have happened, and have taken part in many exciting events. Experience has taught me a lot and I have a long way to go. Where I do not know, except that I trust the journey will be long, interesting, eventful, and fruitful. May my experiences be worthwhile, my choices wise, my decisions right and profitable. One never knows, and uncertainty is usually interesting and amusing. May there be happiness during this new year in all that I do and may any joys that I have be shared with others, bringing more joy and happiness to all with whom I come in contact. I'm still in love but I wonder, is it different and will it be happier that way.*

EIGHT

SUMMER IN GERMANY

"I CANNOT UNDERSTAND A POLITICAL MOVEMENT WHICH

AIMS AT EDUCATING THE WOMEN FOR THE HOME AND YET

DOES NOT TRAIN HER INTELLECTUALLY." (1935)

If Nan kept a journal for the first half of 1935, it has been lost. She kept a small two-by-three-inch diary, but it records only a few events and dates and there are no comments. What happened in her romance remains a mystery. Her journaling picks up again in the second half of the year, and while she continued to mention Arthur, her comments became less frequent. The experience of feeling love's emotional force, however, not only taught her to be cautious in listening to her heart above and despite all else, but it also encouraged her to continue looking for that fulfilling companionship she so desired.

She was stuck doing a job that she thoroughly detested, but she was in New York, and that meant some prospects that would not have been possible were she to have remained in North Carolina.

The second half of the year saw one of her hopes realized. One aspect of the Dewey plan for educators was that they have exposure to different cultures to broaden their approach to education. Nan was thrilled when Dr. Alexander informed her that she would be going to Germany that summer with the undergraduate students. The group was to travel through Germany examining its educational system. Although her expenses were covered, Nan had very little money to spend. Still, she had always longed to travel and was excited. Her passport described her as five feet five inches tall with brown hair and brown eyes. She sailed on June 29, 1935, on the new (1929) German ocean liner, the *Europa*. As she talked about the trip later:

> The group consisted of both undergraduate and graduate students. The person in charge of the graduate students was the head of the math department at Columbia, a Dr. Reeves. His wife and his son, Sidney, came with him. The person in charge of the undergraduate students was a Miss Buckley. I was her assistant. The night that we were to sail to Germany, we all partied beforehand because the ship sailed at midnight. I got sick and I thought it was too much champagne. When I got to the ship, they wouldn't let me on because my face was swollen. It turned out that I had the mumps. I had closed my apartment and everything. Either Dr. Reeves or Miss Buckley called Dr. Alexander, and he said that I could come stay with him. When I was well again, about two weeks later, he put me on another ship going to Germany. It was full of Germans and I didn't speak German. He told me to look at all the words and listen and it would be educational. He also told me there was a graduate student who was going who he would tell to contact me. About the third day at sea she called me on the phone and said that Dr. Alex told her that I would advise her on what to do. When she came, she was in her forties and was highly insulted that Dr. Alex had told her that I would advise her.

According to what Nan described in her journal, the journey felt strange and a bit unreal and, at the same time, natural. There was a contingent of Teachers College students on board, but she had not known them previously. Still, they spoke English, so she was not wholly adrift in a German-speaking world. It was her first time on an ocean liner, her first time surrounded by strangers whose language was unknown to her, her first time totally cut loose from all that was familiar, and thus she was truly alone. The gray expanse of sea and sky caused a jarring sense of there being no limits, perhaps heightened by the fragility left by her illness. But she realized, after her experience with the graduate student, that at least a part of her job in Germany would be to chaperone the undergraduate students on the trip. This intuition and understanding were probably only confirmed through a conversation she had with a young man shortly thereafter:

> *We spoke of the captain. What a responsibility he shoulders and how much confidence we have in our fellow beings. Just the mention of it made us wonder if our appreciation was as deep and sincere as it might be, for are we not almost totally dependent on our fellow man in everything we do, in everywhere we go?*

Her chief pleasure on board seems to have been singing in a musical group formed among the Teachers College travelers. Frequent comments from others about going from third class and tourist class into first class as the result of the singing group performances prompted a journal paragraph hinting at her ambivalence about the new progressive and socialist wave that seemed to be running rampant on the Columbia campus:

> *As I looked around the hall at the supposedly stiff necks sitting there, I did not feel that they were bored as so many people describe first class travelers. I have not found them so on this ship. Those with whom I have talked have been most interesting. At the concert they were interested in the music and were appreciative of it. . . . When tea was served, these people enjoyed it as much as anyone does and later, they went up on deck to play tennis, shuffleboard, etc. Certainly, they enjoy their dances; why shouldn't they.*

Her reaction to being among those who had wealth, not an experience she had had very often, seemed to have enlightened her.

The socialist attitude of equalizing assets rather than equalizing opportunity, and the communist desire to have a government in total control, rubbed against Nan's sense of responsibility and independence.

She also had time to think about the nature of male-female relationships. She penned comments about her own understanding of how a woman should look at the opposite gender as a result of a conversation she had:

> From what he said about the girls in the music group, I take it the men feel that all the old maids are out to get a man. I guess he is right. The illustrations he cited surely looked that way. Most girls do grow up with the one idea to find a man and marry him. I never felt that way. I wonder why? I usually look a group over and see if there are any interesting looking ones around to be good friends with, but somehow I never felt just what he expressed. I have always felt, and still do, that when I meet someone interesting to me that it will be a mutual thing, that both will know it, and both will just be natural about it all. . . .
>
> When Paul expressed his thoughts, I could hardly resist asking him why? For two reasons. First, I was curious and, second, I wondered if I were included in that group of girls. His answer made me think even more about it. He looked at me suddenly and said, "Not you. Your whole attitude and general appearance is that you aren't interested and don't give a damn." I asked if I were so cold looking or distant, or did I give the general appearance that I just wasn't interested in men and romance and fun. His answer showed me that he had sized me up rather well. I was puzzling; I worked and was interested in it, but the professional life was not my choice, but rather that of love and happiness. Said I'd never be a professional old maid schoolteacher. Well, I wonder.

When Nan landed in Bremerhaven in July 1935, she hoped to immerse herself in a foreign culture. The culture itself, however, was approaching the edge of a cataclysm, a civilization beginning its plummet towards chaos. Germany's president, von Hindenburg, had appointed Adolf Hitler as chancellor in January 1933. Hitler had immediately moved to strengthen his power, and by June of that year all his political rivals were either dead or imprisoned. In August of the following year, when von Hindenburg died, Hitler combined the office of the chancery and the presidency and became the *führer*.

The Nazi Party had come to power by pledging to cut unemployment in half within four years. The German people had experienced the same misery felt practically worldwide as a result of the 1929 stock market crash. They were also resentful of the reparations they were being made to pay under the Treaty of Versailles. Hitler not only exploited their misery and their fears but, through centralization of power, was able to bring about some amelioration of suffering for those he considered members of the "master race." He put in the Law for the Reduction of Unemployment in 1933 that encouraged women to stay at home, blocked Jews from civil service, and took those who couldn't get jobs and forced them to engage in "volunteer" labor "for the good of the state." He did in fact increase the production of goods by using (among other companies) Krupp and the Mauser rifle company to rearm the country surreptitiously. Through propaganda and the manipulation of statistics, Hitler could claim that he was making Germany strong. The forced labor of the unemployed was devoted to rebuilding infrastructure and cleaning up the cities, and this was regarded as "progress" as well as being appealing in its results.

By the time of Nan's visit, Hitler's propaganda machine and rearmament were fully organized and successfully progressing. He was very quick to identify the "problems" the Germans had—and singled out the Jewish race as one of the chief obstacles to a better future. This was possible because anti-Semitism in the 1930s was at a fairly high level not only in Germany but in America as well. Nan, while not anti-Semitic, comments in her journals on several occasions that so-and-so "is a Jew." Hitler's complete objectives, his plans to make Germany a "pure" Aryan nation, and his plan to dominate and take over Europe were not, at the time, apparent to the casual observer. The members of Nan's group were involved in looking at the government's educational theories, and their attention was not focused on the overall picture. By all appearances,

Germany had come through a painful period and was headed towards a more robust future.

Nan was aware of the Nazi movement but did not know its destructive intent. She later related the following:

> In the early days everyone, Jews too, backed Hitler. He was seen as doing a lot of wonderful things. Many of the small towns in Germany were walled towns. The people who lived in them lived in shacks, where they occupied the upstairs and the ground floor was where the chickens were kept. They were tiny places, very poor. When Hitler came along, he took all the kids out of these places and put them in schools and gave them the opportunity for travel and education. Hitler instilled pride and everyone liked him. One night we had dinner at the home of some exchange students who were Jewish and they were all backing Hitler.

Nan's group's tour of Germany consisted of visiting the major cities and being guided through at least one educational institution in every location. They were welcomed into each town by a ceremony the group called being *begrüßt* (welcomed): officials (mayors, college presidents, heads of the town's industries) welcomed them with gifts—cigarettes, cigars, bouquets of flowers, souvenirs—and a speech. While the entire group got tired of these occasions, this show of international friendliness was what the state, under Hitler, decreed.

Visiting classrooms and listening to lessons in a language she did not understand was tedious, and Nan alleviated her boredom by sitting in the back and sketching. At the end of the trip, she prepared a notebook of these sketches to thank Dr. and Mrs. Reeves for their hospitality. Later she wished she had kept it, or at least a copy, for herself. She also sketched during the long bus rides from city to city, particularly when she got tired of the group's prattle. Towards the end of the tour, when her money had run out, she spent evenings in her room drawing until the small hours. The need to create on paper was a continuing motif in her life.

Nan did not like the German classroom style:

Why do all the pupils yell when they speak? The teacher asks a question and pupils jump to their feet, and snap their fingers. It seemed to be a good method that had become a mechanical tool and one could not help but wonder where the reasoning training came in.

I glanced around the room to study the reaction of the students. Apparently, the majority of them were very interested in the work and I begin to wonder all over again about teaching, interest of the group, etc. Is that the way that they learn most and best? Is not the physical development taken care of in their gymnastics and sports programs? Is not the classroom the place for the formal work, academic learning . . . ?

The pupils and teacher seem to have a happy and friendly relationship and never have I seen pupils so well poised. I realize that in most cases the teacher and pupils are putting on a show for us. Today, it was different. We went to a school where no one was expecting us. I found the same poise, friendliness, that everywhere is obvious. Only once did I see anyone who was the least bit nervous and that was a Math teacher at one of the schools we visited yesterday.

Nan was impressed when the group went to see a children's camp.

The Wegscheide Children's Colony is attempting to put into practice the principles of education advocated by the great Pestalozzi and Fröbel. But why have not the Germans put these same principles of education into their school? . . . Such joy and happiness was radiated by all the students, and a true and sincere friendship apparently existed between the student and each member of the faculty . . . I felt that here was something like unto our New College community in North Carolina.

Nan was also intrigued by the youth hostels that were part of the Hitler Youth movement:

On leaving, we crossed over to the youth hostel. Why doesn't America do something of the sort for our youth? Here was an old soldiers' barracks turned into an inn for young people who travel over the country, usually on their bicycles. It was clean, convenient, attractive, and alive. The rate for overnight lodging is exceedingly reasonable. I understand that Americans too may tour the country and stop at these places. How I longed to travel with someone, maybe on a bicycle or a motorcycle, in just such a manner.

The group also visited a school for underprivileged students.

At another such village, we stopped to visit one of the Hitler Landjahrpein (a school where the poor girls from the city are permitted to come free of charge after they have completed the work at the Volksschule). They are girls who will not continue their education in the gymnasium and so are given the opportunity to live at such a school and learn the work and life of the peasants. While here, they spend several hours a day working with the peasants. When they go back to the city, they will probably work as maids, or maybe they will marry and become peasant wives. I understand that the peasant children have a similar opportunity to experience life and work in the city. There are many such schools throughout the country for both boys and girls. It is an effort on the part of the N.S. party to educate its children for work and to give them a job, thereby reducing the number of the unemployed.

Interestingly, the word *Landjahrpein* that Nan wrote in her journal does not appear to exist. The correct term for these camps was *Landjahr Lager,* which translates as "country year camp" or "country service camp." A German speaker speculated that the girls used *Landjahrpein,* meaning "country year pain" or "country service agony" as a sarcastic nickname. Would Nan have known that, or did she just pick up the word in listening to the girls?

When they reached Berlin, the tour included time at the Zentral-institut, controlled by the minister of education. The aim of this institution was to establish teacher training camps, edit and publish special magazines and pedagogical volumes, maintain a library and study room for teachers who wished to improve themselves, and become a repository for method books and magazines.

At the teachers' camp, the older teachers are gathered for a fortnight. At present they are invited to go at the sum of 2 M. [marks] a day. Young teachers just out of the universities do not have to go. At the camp, they rise at 6:00 o'clock, have flag exercises, then study German pre-histories, German folklore, study geopolitics, etc. In the afternoon, they have physical culture. They are given special instruction in National Socialism. We were given some material on the work of the institute and the youth movement. It is in German. I hope that I may be able to read it someday.

In her description of the re-education of the "older" teachers, Nan does not comment on the motives or consequences of this constraint to academic freedom. It was an unusual gloss for her, but perhaps a part of the general opinion by youth that they know more than their forebears (then and now).

Nan had been dating Sidney, the son of Dr. Reeves, off and on for over a year before the Germany trip, and she was invited to go with the couple and their son to some special events. These increased her knowledge of the Nazi movement: she socialized with Hitler's economic minister, a relative of the Reeveses, on several occasions, and she noted several other indications of the Nazi cultural ideology that in hindsight were portents:

We saw the raising of the Hitler flag, the salute and the chorus. The songs of the Germans are beautiful. Such wonderful organization, group spirit, cleanliness etc. . . . The gritting of feet stomping in rhythm was a new thing to me. I understand that it is a German custom. I liked it. When the group jumped to their feet and saluted "Heil Hitler," it was most impressive. They looked good in their uniforms. Men always do look good in uniforms though . . . One night we stayed in Berchtesgaden where we could look up at Hitler's place. Every once in a while, we would be on the streets when Hitler and his motorcade went by and we'd all raise our hands.

The flowers in Heidelberg particularly caught her attention:

> *The sight of the city office building just across the Platz from here was a picture. All around the building and one flight up was a row of geraniums in full bloom. . . . We do not see such at home. I do hope some of the many flags flying down the street were included in the picture. After asking the question as to why the flags were displayed all over the city, for about the tenth time, I finally learned it was to add color and atmosphere to the festivities of the season.*

As it turned out, the flower boxes were only in areas where foreigners were likely to go, and the decorations were part of Goebbels's propaganda ministry. The government strictly managed all group tours to ensure that the impression made on foreigners was favorable.

Nan also wondered how the Germans could erect so many new modern buildings when Americans were hearing so much about Germany having no money. She also was not convinced that the Germans could be in any way equal to Americans:

> *The trip to the courtyard and through the Zwinger Museum was to me one mark of culture of the old world. It probably sounds funny to say so, but it and Frankfurt and Heidelberg are about the only cities we have visited that I have seen any evidence of culture. The people we meet are not as cultured as people I know at home. They are nice, hospitable, etc., but not over polite.*

Hitler was finalizing his plans at that time for his conquest of more *Lebensraum* and planning for the integration of the peoples of the lands he conquered. Although Nan did not seem to realize the purpose behind the provision of training facilities in Germany, she did visit one:

> *Another one of these historical places turned into a school. German young men and women, citizens of other countries, come here for six months and are trained in trades and National Socialism and then sent out for another six months of apprenticeship. At the end of this time, it seems that they may return to their own country.*

*Just another part of the whole educational scheme. This work is
done free of charge for the student by the government.*

Nan's impressions of the people were generous, but she retained
some skepticism. She felt that most Germans gave the impression
that they were happy, but some, though they said nothing, exhibited
a sense of fear. In addition, she had negative thoughts about the
educational system's effect on the children's spiritual well-being.

*I'm still very questioning concerning the pupil's or child's place
in the home and his relationship to his parents. Only five weeks
during the summer, two weeks at Christmas, and 14 days at Easter
seem to be practically nothing for home life to me. Their idea
idealistically is to take a child from kindergarten age and develop
him intellectually and socially in keeping with the principles of
education of this school. I am fully in sympathy with the idea
but can't help but feel that home life and parent affection have
something to offer that no school or community can give to the
young and growing child.*

Her reaction to the relegation of women to the home was pointed:

*I cannot understand a political movement which aims at educating
the women for the home and yet does not train her intellectually
beyond junior college.*

She was also highly unimpressed by the Nazi attitude towards
the peasants. Riding through the countryside on a bus afforded
sightings of poverty that were, to her, indescribable.

*It is almost impossible to believe in this day of modern living. Why?
Germany, with all her culture, her intellect, her progressivism, etc.
It is hard to understand.*

The undergraduate student group to which Nan was attached
was booked into cheap accommodations; some stank, and one was
a brothel.

Our jolly mood came to an abrupt end when we walked into our hotel. The Kaiserhof was bad enough, or so the Math group thought, but, alas! The Deutscher Haus! What a place. On the outside it looked fairly decent but what a difference when we walked in. The manager took us through a narrow dark little passage out into a dirty small court where women were chopping meat and peeling vegetables. On the side was a dirty-looking kitchen. The odor was terrible. I had one whiff and thought, my goodness, do I have to eat food prepared in this place? We walked across the wet dirty cobblestones and went through a door that led us to a small winding stairway. Up to the attic we went. The bedroom was rather cheery looking, but three of us had to stay in this one room. We moaned and looked around to take it all in. The other room was a single one down on the next floor. Adjoining it was the so-called Johnny. What an awful place it was; long and narrow, no light, and an old outdoor Chick Sales type of stool. One of these supposedly chemical stools that smelled and looked terrible. One removed the lid and sat upon it. There was nothing else we could do for all of us were nearly pooped. The old kidneys must function at regular interval or else. We had the old washbowl to clean up in. There was not even a pitcher of water sitting beside the washstand. Once one used the water in the bowl, there was no chance of getting any more before the next day. My first reaction was, damn it all! I will not stay here. But, on second thought, I knew there was nothing I could do about it with my 2 pfg [pfennig] in my pocketbook. The reaction expressed by Elmira also warned me that I could not afford to say a word, but, on the contrary, had to do anything I could to keep the others from blowing off to Bucky and causing unpleasantness. We went down to supper. I simply could not eat it, especially after passing through that awful kitchen. Our bus drivers were there so we had a little fun with them and somehow managed to live through it.

Nan did not have enough money to buy souvenirs or visit some of the castles that charged admission. A continual complaint in her journal was how angry she was at herself for forgetting to bring her camera when she had no money to purchase another. She did some wandering about but, particularly towards the end of the trip, remained in her room occasionally to rest and spend her time drawing while the more affluent group members visited landmarks. Her impression of Germany was that it was mostly clean, but that the food was undesirable, and she often went hungry rather than eat boiled potatoes one more time.

> *Dressed just in time for lunch. And what a terrible lunch it was. I simply could not eat fish, nor the potatoes, nor the currants. I'm afraid I don't like German food. I finally did get stewed apricots for dessert, and that was about the extent of my luncheon. I was more than thankful for the Coca-Cola and waffle the men treated us to while we were visiting at the exposition just across the Rhine. . . . How delightful to be served a meal you can eat. I believe this was the first time I have really felt satisfied after a meal since I have been in Germany.*

There was one custom that particularly rankled: Germans, it seemed, would invite you to go with them for a meal or a drink, and expect you to pay your own way.

> *Had I known that, I might have stayed at home for I certainly have no extra pfennigs to spend.*

Even in the midst of all her traveling and new experiences, there were also periods when the depression that she had experienced in New York enveloped her:

> *Violet noticed my restlessness and asked what under the sun was wrong with me. The first time she ever saw me in one of my mood dispositions. Well, what of it?*

All in all, Germany left an impression of being alien. But being an artist requires paying attention and reflecting on one's daily experience, as well as integrating the events into one's understanding, and she did that. She was also fully aware that it was her job not only to assist Miss Buckley in ensuring a smooth tour but also to enlarge her understanding of progressive education's goals. Still, when Dr. Alexander sent a message offering her the option of staying on another month, she did not want to.

She sailed for home on August 10 on the *Columbus*. The crossing was dreary, with fog and rain almost the whole time, and Nan developed a nasty cold. She also had to face the anxiety of not knowing what the future might bring.

> *On Sunday we land in New York. I wonder what I shall find. I want to stay at New College. I want to be there in New York City at Columbia, but I don't want to teach. Gosh, there are a million and one things around that need to be done and I know I could fit in to many of them. Could do a good job of it too. Oh, if I only don't have to teach. When I think of last year, it is like a nightmare. I wonder when Arthur is coming back. The last of September he said. I wonder, shall I see him and what it will be like.*

She still had longings for Arthur but was beginning to withdraw a bit, feeling rebellious because the romance seemed so one-sided to her.

Nan felt a sense of homecoming at arriving in New York. It was no longer a strange place to her.

> *And so ends my first European trip. I am back again in the homeland, hopeful of what life might bring . . . . The trip has been wonderful and rich in varied experiences though not particularly happy. I was too tired out much of the time.*

NINE

LONDON AND OTHER TRAVELS

"NEXT, I GAVE WHAT I TRUST IS MY LAST LECTURE ON GROUP

AND INDIVIDUAL BEHAVIOR. FOR ONCE, I LAID DOWN THE

LAW AND TOLD THEM TO TAKE IT OR LEAVE IT." (1935)

Nan returned to New York from Germany on August 18. She left for England on the *Berengaria* on September 9, exactly three weeks later.

> When I got back from Germany, I planned on spending the rest of the summer in Greenville. While I was there, not more than a few weeks, I got a call from Dr. Alexander telling me to get myself back up to Columbia. The previous year I had been installed in an apartment in New York that belonged to the woman who was in charge of a group of students who were studying in England. She had to come home, and, when I arrived in New York, Dr. Alexander told me that he was sending me to take her place.

The voyage must have been calm and uneventful since this third ocean crossing did not cause Nan to record much. At the start of the journey she determined that she would use the time not just to observe but also to connect with people she did not know.

It is rather difficult to meet every stranger with a friendly smile so as to not freeze them. To just start talking with a stranger for the sake of conversation is not natural with me.

The following journal entries sum up her overall feelings in starting this new phase of her life:

How I do wish that some friend were traveling with me! Maybe traveling alone has its advantages but, somehow, I don't see it that way now. I get entirely too lonesome. Going to England to spend three months should be one of the greatest thrills of my life and in many aspects it is. But I do wish I had a friend along. . . .

It does make me feel good to know that, after having spent just one month in Germany this summer with the group, Dr. Alex and other members of our faculty feel confident in sending me over to carry through this job. I don't think it is the responsibility that I am anxious about, for even though I know it to be one of the hardest jobs connected with our division of the college, I take a certain amount of pride in being entrusted with it and shall do everything I can to make the work successful. . . .

Whatever adjustments I may have to make, how many hours of work I may have to put in, how many problems I may have to help solve, God grant that I may succeed in doing them well. May I be of help to the students and they to me. . . . God help me to grow along these lines during the next few months, that I may go onward towards being a better and less selfish person.

The confidence and humility expressed in this journal entry would be echoed in her speeches in the 1950s and 1960s.

Nan landed in England on September 26, 1935. The many military planes flying overhead made her wonder if war had been declared. The "Abyssinian Question," which eventually involved Mussolini's invasion of Ethiopia, was the political topic of the day and continued to be so throughout her sojourn. London had just celebrated the Silver Jubilee of King George V and there was a royal wedding between Prince Henry and Lady Alice Scott on November 6. Happily, Nan's four months there were mostly unaffected by

Nan's Certificate of Registration for England, 1935

turmoil in Europe—at that time, the British did not seem to believe any war would truly involve them.

The chaperone Nan was replacing greeted her at the train station and took her to Bedford Place in London, where she and the students in her charge were to live. The mural she envisioned in her journal, the composition during that fall of a creditable, worthwhile, engaging, and meaningful accomplishment, was about to be painted. Nan probably took a deep breath as she began her new assignment. She later explained:

> My duties were to be twofold: I had to hold a seminar with the students once a week concerning their progress, and I had to visit a lot of industrial companies which had some connection to companies in the United States and find intern jobs for all the students. Once, when I was at one of these companies, it was in the late afternoon and the manager offered me tea. He then asked me if I wanted "some of the cow." It was the first time I knew that people took milk in tea.

I also had to see to it that the students were enrolled in one of the London schools. Some were at the London School of Economics and some at the University of London. I thought that, since they were enrolled, I would take a course too. One teacher I had was Harold J. Laski, who became the Labour Party's leader several years later. His was one of the most fascinating courses I ever took. Everyone who took it loved it, and we sat on the edge of our seats to catch every word. . . . The other course was under Dr. Boaz, a world-famous anthropologist. I enjoyed it very much. I also took a course on English history.

Nan's records show that "Dr. Boaz" was the shortened name for Dr. Bronisław Malinowski. A pioneer in his field, his teaching would have been particularly interesting to Nan because he emphasized that any researcher must be actively involved in his work, not merely an observer—certainly a "progressive" idea. But, she wrote:

> *I hope he did not hear me just after class when I remarked that he was a "funny old duck," and looked up to see him nearby.*

There were approximately a dozen students in her care. They were staying at a house belonging to two sisters by the name of Staggel. These ladies turned out to have some definite views on how their boarders should behave. They didn't appreciate slammed doors, anyone being late for a meal, or noise of any kind after 10 p.m. They complained quite frequently that the group was bothering the other boarders and fussed with Nan about the expense of having any of the rooms heated or lit. Listening to the ladies' complaints and warning her students when they got out of line were aspects of the job that Nan found very unpleasant.

> *Personally, I think she has exaggerated the whole thing, but, even so, the kids are terribly inconsiderate and selfish about what they think are their own individual affairs. They think they are old enough to boss themselves. They never consider the other fellows in the house but seem to think of them as old fogies.*

There were several times when Nan had to intervene:

When I stepped out of my room I found that Fran, Kay and Everett had returned from a show. All were in the best of spirits but even so, I made up my mind to have my say concerning their evening out without word or message concerning their whereabouts. I called Kay and Fran into my room and had a little conference with them. It was a tough job on my part. It seemed so strange to even bother with saying anything for I knew they had only been to a show. Nevertheless, I minded my better judgment and took the matter up with them. This was the first with them and I trust there will be no second.

The first time was not the last. Nan was ultimately responsible for the social conduct of these students and she had to continue to chastise them, even into December.

Next, I gave what I trust is my last lecture on the group and individual behavior. For once, I laid down the law and told them to take it or leave it or they would suffer the consequences. That was that and so ended the meeting.

Being a disciplinarian was a new undertaking for Nan. Her only previous encounter with the necessity had been as the dean of students during her first year in New York, and at that time her commenting on the students' behavior was rare. But in London she felt it was her responsibility, and when she felt something was not right, she spoke up. This training bled over into her later public life, where she did not hesitate to call others to account when she felt they were on a path that was not productive.

Nan was in charge of the finances for the group as well. She was always very careful to keep both her and her group's accounts in order and was upset when any of her students tried to get more than they should. Besides parsing out the funds to pay for the group expenses, she put herself on an austere budget of one pound a week in order to have the money to see the sights and buy gifts for those at home. She did have to buy clothes, feeling she hadn't packed the correct gear, and while she was delighted to be wearing something new, it was money she thought she could ill afford.

At the beginning of her sojourn, she commented:

> *Conducting the group seminar all alone as leader was a new and, on my part, exciting experience. I admit I was a little afraid, yet I don't know just why. It went off well and I trust that I shall become accustomed to it, and I hope to become a more valuable member and leader of the group.*

By the end of December she was comfortable in the role, but she was much more critical of the students' work. As always, when under the aegis of New College's pedagogy, any advance in knowledge was up to the individual. Her students had been directed to take up some question regarding an era in the history of England—the division of eras had been made before Nan's arrival—and be prepared to teach the others during the seminars. Nan's training in group leadership, which had begun with the school children in Raleigh, was further refined through the intimacy of this three-month tenure as house mother, advisor, and supervisor. Learning which approaches were effective and which left issues unresolved was a valuable skill set in her later organizational activities.

One of Nan's chief complaints was about the weather in London, how cold she was in that house and how the chill of her room interfered with her ability to study.

> *I sat in my room and read until I was practically frozen and then went into the sitting room to hover closely around the grate fire that had just been built. After about an hour I began to get warm. . . .*
>
> *One could have spent a very profitable day reading had it been warm in the house. . . .*
>
> *Bought some woolies today and immediately put them on. Still I practically froze all day. It is bad enough to get outside and freeze but to come into a house or library or whatever it is and have to sit bundled up in your coat and still shiver with cold is to me inexcusable, especially when we are supposed to have central heating here. We surely do pay enough to have the heat on.*

The situation did not change in November or December, but Nan became busier with her duties and classes, with being a tourist and meeting Londoners, and so was in her room less.

She found the fog disconcerting, particularly the "black fog" saturated with soot and smoke from the burning of coal, and the climate was a significant drawback to her enjoyment. Unrestricted pollution sometimes made the air so dense and so unhealthy that being out in it was a serious cause of respiratory infections and, in some cases, death. While understanding this phenomenon had started to raise concerns in the government, it was another seventeen years before anything was done to improve the situation.

Nan had decided at the beginning of her stay that she would learn English history and generally improve her knowledge of the country. To that end, she planned not only a reading program but also visits to as many of the famous places in London and further afield as her time permitted.

> I determined to concentrate on the one field of history and to make all that I do as far as studying is concerned relate to the subject. . . . So often I feel that my interests and experiences are so divided that it is difficult to establish any firm knowledge on any one thing. But this morning, as is always the case after seeing a painting and sketches, etc., I immediately wanted to come home and sit down again to do some sketching on my own. I've always wanted to. I guess I always will. I want to do this and at the same time continue to concentrate on the field of history. Time cannot be divided and I wouldn't if I could. I shall study history, doing all the reading that I can and then possibly at some later date, I may practice my hobby of art—for I suppose that is what it is—and eventually realize one of my ambitions. . . .
>
> I'm a little worried about the amount of time I have for reading. I know that the only way to get it done is to sit at home and read, but then there are so many things one should see and do when in London that I can't see how I am going to get it all in.

Towards the end of November she was making some progress:

I spent practically the entire day in the library. Succeeded in finishing the reading of Adams's Constitutional History of England *and so can scratch that off the list of the books I have to read. They seem to be going off rather slowly but maybe, somehow, I will be able to get them all read. . . . Haven't done any reading at all for the Anthropology course, but once I have ploughed through Green and so gotten a general background for English history maybe I'll be able to devote more time to reading others.*

Nan managed to visit St. Paul's Cathedral, the British Museum (where, thanks to Hugh Lefler, her friend Bet's husband, she obtained a card enabling her to use the library), Westminster Abbey, Buckingham Palace, the National Gallery, and the Houses of Parliament. She poked into the Old Curiosity Shop, Selfridges, and Madame Tussauds; she rode down the Thames, and got out to York, Canterbury, and Greenwich. She was on the street when the royal bride and groom drove by in their wedding finery (and thought they looked like it might be a love match) and listened to the speakers in Hyde Park. Both the theater and the movies frequently saw her "queuing up." Once she had the privilege of hearing Yehudi Menuhin at the Royal Albert Hall. She and several of her charges went to meetings of the Fabian Society, an organization formed to promote democratic socialism through a program of reform. The society's ideas were very much in line with the ideas that had prompted the establishment of New College. Bertrand Russell was the featured speaker at one of these meetings.

What a charming old gentleman he is and what fun to listen to him speak, but he surely didn't say anything. It was all very light and spoken sarcastically from beginning to end. 'Twould be fun to know him personally. He looked and acted the very mental picture that I hold as representative of the English gentleman.

As many times as the weather permitted, Nan roamed the streets. As she had in New York, she loaded every day with as much as she could. Still, she was lonely and, as usual for her in her "down" moments, she wished she had a dear companion.

I wish it were true that I felt that bright and happy and hopeful all the time. But it seems that life isn't that way. Maybe if there were not the hardships, the worries, and the loneliness, one's life would not be so worthwhile, for one might not spend enough time in thought and surely one's appreciation of joy and beauty would not be so keen—and maybe one would be so familiar with the little things that bring joy to the heart that one would not feel a deep sense of appreciation.

Her on-and-off beau, Arthur Lorch, continued to be in her heart:

It's been a long time since I have seen him and still it will be several months more. Things will be different when I do see him, but I wonder how. I know that my attitude is quite changed even though I still care. What his attitude will be remains to be seen.

From then on, her comments reflect both pessimism and acceptance of the inauspicious prospects for her romance.

Besides the cold and the dreary weather, Nan was bothered most by what she thought were "queer customs." After going to the Tower of London, she commented:

Tradition seems to exercise the greatest power over the life of the English people. Their whole system of classes is based on it. They spend endless amounts of money keeping it going; many of their men are unemployed because their social rank does not permit employment of a laboring nature. Strong healthy men go through militaristic procedures during the changing of the guards just because of it. . . . I stood for quite a while gazing at the beautiful jewels of the state that were exhibited in the glass case and surrounded by an iron bar fence and wondered if there were not enough money lying idle to pay all the expenses of a government and its people for several years tied up in those jewels. True, they were the most beautiful I have ever seen. The one huge diamond in King George V's crown is supposed to be the largest one in the world. The banquet table at a state affair is set with golden dishes; the plates, the wine fountain, the salt cellars, the

> *spoons, the trays, etc. all are made of high carat gold. I wonder if the food is good.*

Her emotional tug of war between beauty and practicality was a fairly common occurrence in her ruminations, and being aware of and around beauty was an element of her artistic appetite. The temptation to clutter up life with busyness and things was always a part of Nan's struggle: Where should her abundant creative energy be expended?

Other "queer" customs jarred her as well:

> *Every now and then I am struck by something that is so different. When I was at the Davises' the other night, I almost gasped when I saw a supposedly well-cultured Jersey girl use her handkerchief and then pull up her skirt in the presence of a room with men and women about and place the handkerchief in the top of her stocking—which reached almost to her thigh. Too, I have tried to use my fork and knife the way Europeans do but I find it a very difficult way to handle my food; also, it looks terribly impolite to me, yes, even greedy. A young man leaves a girl on the street corner to walk home alone at night after a date. . . . A man in the upper class of society would not think of working for his living—he must have a white-collar job with the government or he does nothing at all. One must drink tea in the afternoon whether one wishes to or not. Ordinary people frequently dress formally just to go to a movie. One goes to the theater and has to queue unless he wishes to pay a high price. One is expected to give pennies to everyone who sings on the street. One has to eat in a restaurant without a napkin. One must always be nonchalant, speak very softly, hardly above a whisper, and never get excited over anything regardless of what may come or go. I go to an ordinary movie and sit in a reserved seat. We are presented with a print program listing all the characters and even giving a synopsis of the plot. After any public gathering everyone must stand and wait for the tune "God Save the King" to be played. The Duchess of Kent gives birth to a baby boy and the whole nation talks of it, lives it, thinks of it for ages afterwards. . . . One goes to the park and has to pay a shilling in order to go into the*

zoo and feed the wild animals peanuts. One has to hold a ticket in his hand when he rides on the bus or the underground. One uses "Could I, or Must I, or Should I," one never states, "I will, or I shall, or I am." One laughs over jokes that aren't the least bit funny. What a strange people the English are.

In addition to being puzzled and amused, she was also critical at times:

I'd like to give some of these lecturers a few points on how to lecture to a group. Why do they keep their heads down, eyes glued to a paper, or speak with their hands over the mouth or a glass of water to their lips? Wish they would sit up and assume a little more dignity in the classroom. The robe surely doesn't help them any for they look so sloppy in the careless manner in which they wear it.

Nan was also derogatory about the food and commented on the poor fare at the rooming house several times in her journal.

Wish the cook knew how to prepare a variety in the potato line. It's plain boiled potatoes every night. I feel like screaming every time I see them. It is a good thing I learned to eat carrots when I was living with Bet and Hugh for that is the only vegetable we get very often that I like . . . and I am always glad for I don't have to eat cauliflower. Lamb is supposed to be a good dish, but I thoroughly dislike it. We would have it about every other night. It's meat for breakfast and meat for dinner. But we do have excellent desserts. I do wish I could get a grapefruit for breakfast every morning. No diet is lacking if it has fruit and vegetables. Guess I'll have to continue buying apples and keep them in my room.

However, her critique of the English did not mean that she didn't want to know them. Her complaint about the first part of her visit was that she was not meeting English people who interested her:

There must be somewhere in London some charming and interesting young people. We have yet to meet them, but I hope we will be so fortunate. I do believe in being kind and friendly with all people, but there is such a thing as making friends with people with whom you have something in common. . . . I'd like to get acquainted with some really interesting English people. Surely there are some.

By the middle of November, however, Nan had begun to have a fuller social calendar and some of her loneliness was mitigated. A friend from New York had written several of her male friends and eventually three of these young men began squiring Nan around. From then on, whatever available time she had was filled. While they didn't cause extra heartbeats, these three young men were attentive.

The few charming friends I have made during the past month here, I wonder whether or not I shall ever see them again. Anyway, it has been great to know them. My idea of the English people has certainly changed a bit as a result of their friendship.

Then, sometime before November 24, she became acquainted with a Mr. Sopwith, a history teacher at the Latymer School in Cambridge. She felt comfortable with the young men she had been dating. With Douglas Sopwith, from the beginning, there was a sense of unease. He was assiduous in his attention from the first date. She enjoyed their outings yet was still hesitant about seeing him. Douglas's group of friends appealed to her intellectually, but they were also older and more confident in their knowledge and life path:

He then took me in for tea where I was introduced to about twelve men and sat down to tea with them. This short social interlude was most enjoyable. About three men were talking to me all at once. So much so that I hardly found time to drink my tea. They were charming and I was more than delighted to meet some Englishmen who were people I felt I had something in common with.

It seems that letters took precedence over phone calls in 1935, and Douglas Sopwith wrote her four times in the next month.

She records several dates with him but is always unsure about her feelings.

> *But when he told me goodnight, he suggested that I have tea with him on Saturday. I had accepted an invitation to a football game for that date and so made my excuses. Excuses just don't go in this country. He suggested Sunday and I had no alternative. Why on earth I should not wish to have tea with him I do not know. He is very good looking, extremely intelligent, just the right age, very charming, and certainly the best teacher I have seen in many years. I know I should be delighted to see him again, but for some strange reason I don't want to; least of all do I wish to have tea.*

Then, three days later:

> *This afternoon I have to have tea with Dr. Sopwith. I wonder what it will be like. O God! I hope I don't get one of those uncontrollable cases of the jitters between now and then.*

Still, the relationship did continue for the rest of her stay.

> *Ran over to the American University Union and left our forwarding address and later brushed up a bit for my tea date with Douglas Sopwith at four o'clock. I don't know why I have not looked forward to the few dates I have had with him, for each time I go out with him, I thoroughly enjoy it. This afternoon he took me by his brother's law office and we chatted with him for about half an hour. I found him very easy to talk with. . . .*
>
> *Later we walked up Charing Cross Road and Douglas insisted on buying me a diary as a going away gift. What a thoughtful person he is. In spite of my feeling of postponement of dates with him, I like him a lot. Before taking me home, he wished me to have a cocktail with him. We whiled away about 15 minutes in a nearby pub and then he took me home just a few minutes before seven. Had I not been giving the kids a party tonight, I would have had a date with him. I don't think I have met anyone quite so serious or concerned about life and what it should be. Neither have*

I met anyone who seemed so pleased, even grateful or happy, that one should accept his invitation to tea, etc. Can't make him out.

Nan's association with Douglas Sopwith continued after her return to America. They corresponded until at least June of 1937. The seventeen letters she kept demonstrate, on his part at least, a growing attachment. The last letter proclaims his undying love. Later in life, she mentioned him only once in talking about those months, acknowledging that he wanted her to marry him but that she adamantly refused to live in England and he somehow never made the trip to the United States. It is possible that the war interfered with his plans, but there is also a suggestion in the letters that he was in line for a promotion and hoped that that would eventuate. It would have to be assumed that Nan gave Douglas some reason for him to continue to pursue her. In the last of the kept letters, he wrote:

> The hope that you give me, that you might come to care for me, is all that I can wish for just now: but I want you to know, on my side, that I love you, that I want to marry you, and that I shall never want to marry anyone else. It may help you, dear, to think that I shall always feel myself bound to you and that, whether you come to choose me or reject me, it can make no difference to my love and my gratitude.

At this point, Nan had had three romances where some kind of romantic attachment on her part could be supposed: her high school beau, Chick; Arthur; and Douglas. Given the notes in her journals, it is safe to assume many other swains had fallen for her only to find their feelings unreturned. By the beginning of 1936, at twenty-seven years old, she was beginning to know just what characteristics she was seeking in a mate, but she still hadn't found anyone who met all her criteria while causing her heart to flutter.

....

Nan felt that the four months she spent in London were "among the most interesting and fascinating" of her life up to that point. Did she feel she had accomplished what she set out to do in creating the mural of creditable work that she had envisioned in her journal at the start of her time in London? Her last few weeks were filled with the practicalities of leaving London—signing out at the various government offices, organizing transportation and shipping, trying to finish reading those volumes on her personal to-do list, and attending to all the farewells. In addition, some of her charges were remaining in England to take additional positions and acquire more knowledge to round out their Dewey experience, and Nan was responsible for making those arrangements. She did not record any last thoughts regarding the group's performance. There was, however, a discussion at one of their December meetings about the group's reactions to the teaching style used at New College back in New York.

> *Everyone in this group is disgusted with the type of seminars we have had at the New College, and all are very anxious to have classes that are good lecture courses. All talked about how futile it is for young upstarts to get up in seminar and blow off about something they have no knowledge of.*

When Nan wrote of her reaction to New College students, it was even harsher.

> *Once again, I ask myself, is it not true that all our students talk very well, but actually are not so endowed with thorough knowledge about which they speak. When I listen to college students—at least many of them—give great discourses and make such broad and sweeping generalizations, I am always impressed and somehow feel myself very inferior. I have never been able to do such. I wish I could. At least they make a good impression, if that is what counts. But usually, I find with a little checking up and going a little deeper into a subject, they know not whereof they speak.*

Nan sailed for home on New Year's Eve on the *Washington*. While she may have felt the mural had not quite been completed, she was proud of her administration of the finances and hoped Dr. Alexander would be satisfied. She was happy to return to the United States if only to escape the cold and gloomy London weather.

....

Nan did get warm. Dr. Alexander almost immediately sent her on another trip. She spent the spring of 1936 touring the Southeast with a group of New College students and was in charge of the entire expedition. They spent six weeks going to different universities and visiting various industries; along the way they met the mayors of many towns and some state governors.

The students kept records of what they saw and their impressions, and Nan had to grade each of their journals. It is probable that doing this grading further honed her understanding of the need for experiential education and sharpened her analysis of the Dewey education system; getting direct feedback from students must have been enlightening—she had had the experience about which they wrote herself and could compare her observations to theirs as well as reflect on the students' perspectives in relation to their previous viewpoints and backgrounds.

For whatever reason, during this trip Nan stopped keeping a journal. Or, if she kept one, she afterwards disposed of it. Because she was willing to talk about her life later, and those conversations resulted in an extensive record, much information about her subsequent life is known, but the daily joy and sadness were no longer chronicled. No artistic impressions remain either. She did keep some of her earlier drawings, but her days may have been too filled with professional responsibilities to indulge in her desire to draw. Nan's artistic spirit had kept her aware of the need to absorb her surroundings and their aesthetics in the past, so it is reasonable to assume that she also paid attention to her environment on this trip.

Yet intellectual thoughts and artistic cravings were not her daily occupations. She was too practical for that, and she wanted to live, not just comment on life. The amusing and unusual incidents remained with her when she talked about that trip later.

One of the funny things I remember about that trip was that most of the tourist-cabin places and many of the restaurants of that time had slot machines. The students would all go to the slot machines while I took care of the details of getting us installed for the night. Then I would come in. Every time I would play the slot machines I would win. That was my spending money.

I also remember being in the mountains of North Carolina during that trip and a meal where we all ate a lot of beans. The roads from that eatery to where we were going to spend the night were pretty rough. When we finally arrived, one of the boys in our car leaped from the car and ran to the restroom. He said afterwards that he would never ever eat another bean.

Nan's eyes lit up when she talked about this trip. Was that because she did not have to teach in a classroom, because she loved to travel, or because she was "back home" in the South and comfortably knew her way around? Regardless, it was a break from the job she disliked.

The following fall Nan had to continue teaching, although it seems she was teaching at New College training teachers rather than in Hackensack dealing with children. In addition, Dr. Alexander made it a part of her responsibility to see how the junior and senior interns who had been trained in the Dewey methods were faring. This meant more travel since the interns were in schools throughout the states on the Eastern Seaboard. She enjoyed that. Unfortunately, after finishing those trips, Dr. Alexander informed her that another school in Hackensack thought they might use Dewey's methods, and Nan was to show them how to do it. She once again had to commute to New Jersey to a thankless job.

Nan's social life was active, although she did not mention Arthur's name when she later talked about her experiences. She remembered dating a teacher at Columbia named Duke whom she thought was a "Mama's boy," and there was a protégé of Dr. Alexander's named John with whom her mentor was anxious that she make a match—although Nan's heart did not agree. It is possible that Dr. Alexander was hoping that Nan would marry John because his own life was in transition, and she was, in a sense, a loose end that he wished to tie up.

....

New College fell on hard financial times in 1937, and before the end of the spring, a Dr. Tewksbury replaced Dr. Alexander. It was thought afterwards that Dean Russell of Teachers College had had his friend resign so that he would not be the head of a failed endeavor. Under Dr. Alexander's auspices, New College had analyzed and codified a series of theories that recognized seven discrete challenges they called "persistent problems of living":

- adjusting to and cooperating with other people,
- maintaining physical and mental health,
- achieving economic and political security,
- adjusting to and controlling the natural environment,
- interpreting and creating art and beauty,
- searching for guiding principles and ultimate values, and
- acquiring and transmitting social heritage.

This was the heritage that New College bequeathed to twentieth-century educational philosophy.

The announcement that the school would be closing caused an uproar. New College was one of the nation's most progressive school experiments, and the approximately three hundred students and staff at the college whose educational ideology had been formed by that movement fought this decision. While the deficit of the college in 1936–37 was $57,000 (a vast sum during this Depression era) and $37,000 a year would have had to be provided to subsidize the school, the students felt that, since the incoming class had been the largest in its history, it was the pedagogy of the school that was the true reason for its closure. The unrest was such that Dr. Harold Laski, one of Nan's professors in London the previous fall and a visiting professor at Teachers College, could not conduct his classes. At a dinner party in the mid-1950s, long afterwards, Will Russell confessed to Tom Alexander that he thought his decision to close New College was one of the worst of his life. Although some of the staff members who also taught at Teachers College would keep their jobs, Nan unfortunately was not among that number.

Dr. Alexander warned Nan about what would happen before he left and told her she had two choices. She had received her master's degree from North Carolina State University earlier, and he offered Nan the option of either staying at Columbia and working for her doctorate—and there was the implicit inference that he would find a way for her to finance this—or she could take a job teaching in East Orange, New Jersey, where a school was looking for someone who had been trained in Dewey's methods. For some reason, Nan believed that women with PhDs were destined to be old maids and immediately dismissed the idea of going for a PhD.

.

TEN

EARL WILLIAM ROLES

Nan accepted the job offer to teach at the Nassau School in East Orange but had to move there to do so. Essentially early twentieth-century American in its attitudes and ambiance, East Orange lacked the excitement and diversity of the city. Still, it was just west of Newark, so Nan was not wholly divorced from the currents of her former life. The family motto of "accept the inevitable; rise above it" must have become her mantra at that juncture. Frances Moseley, a woman whose family she had known in Greenville, offered to share her apartment—and the rent—and Nan, perforce, agreed.

Acceptance may not have been easy, but Nan did "rise above it":

> When I was at East Orange, whatever I was doing suited the principal. He came to me and said that a New Jersey education magazine was offering prizes for articles in education. He told me to submit. I did and I won.

Her article was titled "What Social Studies Shall We Teach?" and was published in 1939 in *NJ Classroom Teacher.*

The radical change of Nan's move to New Jersey was quickly followed by another, that of meeting Earl Roles.

> Earl and I met in October 1937. One night I was at a function at the Presbyterian Church. I ended up sitting next to Earl and he wanted to talk to me. He asked me a lot of questions; then he asked me out. I had a date the next night and said I couldn't. He then started calling me, but it was about two weeks before I had a night that I could go out with him. I remember before my first date with him thinking that something would be different by the end of the evening.

While Nan's closeness to Chick in high school might have been quite natural and comfortable, she had felt unsettled at the beginning of her relationships with Arthur and Douglas. So it was with Earl as well.

Nan did have requirements for a potential mate, and the only two men she had ever considered seriously had disappointed her. The criteria were never stated as such; to her, that would have been arrogant, a breach of good manners. What she wanted, however, was sprinkled throughout her journals in the comments she made about the men she knew, and these yardsticks narrowed the field considerably. First, the man must have an intellectual capacity that came close to her own. Second, he had to have ambition. She did not delineate how that was to be identified, but she loathed laziness and felt many of the "boys" she knew exhibited that characteristic. Third, he had to be kind in his dealings, particularly with family members. Fourth, she admired men who did things "properly"— men with "perfect manners are the type of gentlemen one naturally expects." She did not include honor and honesty in her comments, but they were character traits she took for granted since they were inherent in her own personality. She also never said anything about her potential mate being a "believer," but her faith was vital to her routine; were this quality not present in a potential mate, it would have been a significant negative. Enthusiasm and general enjoyment of life were important; Nan did enjoy her social life, and one of her concerns about Douglas was that he took life so seriously. Good looks were not a requirement, although she frequently commented about her male companions' appearances, so there had to have been some feeling that she wanted someone decently attractive. While not a dealbreaker, Nan loved music and dancing and a shared affinity would be appealing.

Earl Roles seemed to meet some of her criteria. He was good-looking, a physician (so his intellect could be assumed), and had already demonstrated his ambition to get what he wanted in his pursuit of her. He also loved to dance, and Nan had had some background with the violin and he with the piano, so that was another intersection of interests. She was open to finding out what he offered as a candidate for her affections.

> On our first date we went to a roadhouse and had dinner and did some dancing. Then, in the car on the way back, we went down a lane to a park and sat in the car and talked for a good long time. One of the things that Earl said was that he had always wanted to have a boat and that he would someday. He then said, "Would you like to be my first mate?" I thought it was a casual question and said sure, it sounded like fun.
>
> The next morning I woke up to find that he had sent me a dozen red roses, and the card said how happy he was that we had become engaged. I hadn't really thought that that was what had happened. I was dating a professor at Columbia when I met Earl, and the day after I had my first date with Earl, I had a date with this man. Earl asked me to break the date, but I wouldn't. However, it was the last date I had with anyone except Earl.

The conversation on that first date must have impressed Nan because she didn't come back with the "nothing doing" that was her lifelong catchphrase for refusing something.

Nan did want to fall in love, and she was perhaps more dedicated than most to finding a purpose in her existence. Life with Earl seemed to promise a partnership wherein she could leave behind her loneliness and become half of a whole—as her world understood feminine individuality at the time. Both the artist within her and the woman immersed in Dewey's holistic approach to life sought integration. The intuition that something is suitable, desirable, and fitting is an impulse that leads to creative consequences in most circumstances. Nan had written in her journal earlier that she believed it would "just feel natural" when she found her mate. While she recorded no conscious motive, no reasoning and weighing of pros and cons, her intuition seems to have propelled her acceptance of Earl's proposal.

Earl seemed to meet all of what Nan wanted in a mate and, one must conclude, did make her heart flutter. One facet of their later life together was their disagreement about a whole host of subjects, but most of these were intellectual and both seemed to revel in pitting their intellects against the other's. (Nan once made the off-hand comment that these disagreements were a part of their life together from the very beginning.) Earl was also a bit cocky and she liked his confidence in himself. For some reason, she did not object to some of the ways in which he proceeded to take over their lives.

> Earl, because he was used to his family—he being the only educated one—walked into my apartment the day after we got engaged and told Frances that we were going to get married. She said, "How wonderful." He then announced that the wedding was going to be in April, and said, "Do you want to be a bridesmaid?" My mouth dropped open. I didn't mind April, but my best friend was Bet Piner (Lefler), and I wanted to have her be my bridesmaid. But Frances was so excited, and Bet couldn't come anyway, so I guess it was all right.

He also told her early in their relationship that he preferred the name "Nancy" rather than "Nan." She was agreeable, perhaps because her mother's name was also Nannie, shortened to Nan by many, and there must have been frequent confusion. From the time they started dating, she answered to the name "Nancy" and did so for the rest of her life. Her heart's excitement must have been considerable.

Earl William Roles was living in East Orange when he and Nancy met. Professionally taken photos of him from around that time record him as very handsome. He was on the short side at five-foot-seven, although most men of that generation were shorter than those born later in the century. He had blue eyes and dark brown hair and was thirty-three years old.

That he was a doctor was an achievement for a boy who had grown up with parents who lived extremely frugal lives. His paternal grandfather was a plasterer who had come over from England in the late 1800s. He and his wife, Lousia, had eight children, with Earl's father, Will, being one of two boys. Will followed in his father's footsteps and was in some facet of the construction business all his life. Earl's mother, Eva, had a college education, and her family, who were also in the construction business, thought that Eva had married "beneath her" and disowned her. It was by the grace of Will's large family that the couple survived their first years. Eventually, Will built a group of two-story apartment buildings that Eva managed, and Earl and his older sisters, Ruth and Mae, grew up in that complex.

Earl was ambitious from early childhood. He was raised on the stories in Horatio Alger's rags-to-riches books and on the ideal of the handsome young hero in the Frank Merriwell dime novels. He had his first job at a bakery when he was about nine years old; this was followed by selling magazines from a cart, working in three different banks, and for a short period working as a draftsman (a skill he learned from his father). He later recounted, "I had as many jobs as I could figure out the time to do them." Part of this huge ambition came from his mother. She pushed him throughout his childhood to make something of himself, probably partially in response to her birth family's shunning her, but also because she found that her beloved husband was a bit too generous. He made their financial future so uncertain that they sometimes had to pawn items to pay their bills.

A part of Earl's program to better himself was his involvement in physical culture. He later recalled:

> One of the real interests I had outside of my education
> and my jobs was running. I was a member of the YMCA

in Camden for a long time and ran around their track a lot and enjoyed it. . . . I would run five to ten miles at night when I finished school or work.

Earl had graduated from high school by 1925 and had begun to think about what he wanted to do with his life. He was twenty, in great physical shape, and, while ambitious, did not yet have a direction. At that point a detour presented itself in the form of dancing. He had always loved Atlantic City, particularly its vaudeville shows, and dancing in front of an audience had allure. He also thought that perhaps being an actor was in his future. He found dance partners and for several seasons managed to work gigs from New York City to Atlantic City. However, this couldn't use all the time of a man accustomed to living at a fast pace, and another interest proved more advantageous than the stage. Quite by accident, he met a man who convinced him to go to chiropractic school, and another who assured him that he should add naturopathy to his skills.

Earl still didn't have a plan for his future, but his parents did. His father wanted him to go into the construction business with him. His mother disagreed, having a more ambitious program in mind. She announced one morning that she had gone to Hahnemann Medical College in Philadelphia and signed him up to get his degree. His having gone to both chiropractic and naturopathic schools probably gave his mother the idea that her son had an interest in the "healing arts." Students at Hahnemann who were going to be doctors spent two years working on an undergraduate degree, then combined the second two college years with the first two medical school years.

Eva, who held the purse strings in her family, had been able to secrete enough away to help him with a portion of the money required. Since Earl was used to holding down multiple jobs simultaneously, he earned the additional cash needed through professional dancing, teaching gymnastics to children, managing a band made up of some of his fellow students, and doing whatever short-term jobs he could find. He also applied to and received a gift from the local YMCA that came at a critical time—when the registrar at the college informed him that he couldn't go on unless he added to his account balance. That forceful an ambition and

Earl Roles, professional photo when he was
a dancer "on the boards," late 1920s

the ability to commit were commendable qualities, and Nancy's learning of the circumstances of Earl's education probably raised her esteem for her suitor.

Earl did his internship at Arnot Ogden Memorial Hospital in Elmira, New York. While there he demonstrated another attractive talent. He dated a widow whose brother-in-law was connected to *The Telegram* newspaper and that man invited Earl to write fictional stories about the lives of doctors. Earl had a flair for writing, and the stories, suitable for the Sunday Features editions, had just the right amount of interest and suspense to ensure a good readership.

Elmira was too far north for Earl, however, and when his internship was over, he decided to look closer to his home, Camden, New Jersey, and yet far enough from it to feel independent. He had had a junior internship at a homeopathic hospital in East Orange during 1931. The community and the people there were to his liking, so he chose East Orange as the place to begin practicing medicine. It helped that he had already met a good many people.

Any new practice takes time to become established, and there were probably not that many patients seeking appointments at first. His office hours were from 2 p.m. to 4 p.m. and 7 p.m. to 8 p.m., and Earl found that he had time on his hands. One of the doctors at the hospital invited Earl out to his country club and then invited him to join. For Earl, raised in a blue-collar neighborhood, this was extremely approbatory.

> I was young and single and flattered. To me the country club was an eye-opener because my parents didn't know anything about country clubs. It was the only golf club to which I ever belonged.

It was a compliment to his achievements and the image he projected to be made a member, but it was also expensive. Within a year, Earl discovered that keeping up with the other members represented a charge to his resources that was too high. He also learned a life lesson when he resigned: he was dropped from the invitation lists of those he had thought were friends. But for Nancy, his familiarity with "polite society," his social skills, and what had become a fairly wide breadth of experience were all appealing qualities.

....

Nancy and Earl had been engaged for about four weeks when they drove to Camden to meet Earl's parents. By then, the couple presumably had shared enough of their life histories to know how much they had in common and where their upbringing differed. Nancy had had extended family surrounding her throughout her young life; Earl had had much the same experience, with his father's large extended family living in the same neighborhood. They knew by that time that they were both highly intelligent and had tremendous energy and ambition. Earl's desire for success may have been more financially motivated, with Nancy having the traditional feminine hope for a life filled with a loving partner, a family, and a home; however, both felt that family came first, so they were probably quite in accord in their goals.

Nannie Elizabeth Evans,
engagement photo, 1938

Still, there was the clash of the city and the country, the North and the South, the day laborer and the farmer, the world traveler and the man whose adventures were usually confined to a three-hour car-ride radius. They were miles apart in their relative positions in their communities—Earl's father was a first-generation American blue-collar worker. In contrast, Nancy's family history in North Carolina began in the early 1700s and she came from one of the leading families of her town. Both families spent significant amounts of time together, but most of the Roleses were teetotalers and Nancy's relatives imbibed at nearly all holiday functions. Both families were matriarchal out of necessity, but Eva Roles, Earl's mother, was domineering and Nannie Evans was more genteel in her approach. Nancy recalled:

> We went down on a Sunday and had dinner. . . . I don't think I passed any judgments at the time, although I knew when I met his daddy that I would like him. One of the stories I remember about Earl's father was that he decided

to build cedar hope chests for his girls for Christmas. But he didn't want to leave Earl out, so he gave him one too. I still have that cedar chest.

At Christmas time I went home. Earl wanted me to go to his house, but I said nothing doing—if anything, he should come to my house. His response was that he couldn't on Christmas Day but would come later. He didn't go to Greenville except that one time before we were married. The only times he went after we were married were when we were living in Durham. But he adored Mama. Never could say enough good things about her.

The six-month interval during which Earl and Nancy were engaged was spent trying to connect their lives. From Nancy's point of view, it wasn't always a smooth transition, possibly because Earl had never before attempted to accommodate another individual in his thinking and planning. It is also important to remember that Earl had always been the pride and joy of his family. While his mother was often overbearing, her interference was always intended to build up her son and push him to succeed. As a result, Earl had a view of himself that meant he was at the center of his own life, a view that demanded he always be the one in control, always be the decision maker. Male dominance in relationships was also prevalent in the culture in the 1930s; it had been for a long time and frequently continues to be so. Nancy may have fallen in love, but she had also managed her own life for almost a decade; there had to have been some questions and some hesitancy. Still, while Nancy may have had occasional misgivings, it is more likely that she felt exhilarated that she had finally found someone who seemed to offer what she wanted. Having an expectation of future happiness and believing in the good will of the person you have decided to marry is a part of the romance of courtship.

Nan and Earl were married on April 14, 1938.

ELEVEN

SEARCHING FOR HOME

"BEFORE WE WERE MARRIED, WE WERE ALWAYS

ARGUING ABOUT WHERE WE WERE GOING

TO SPEND OUR HONEYMOON." (1989)

A newspaper notice of the wedding read:

> On Thursday afternoon, April 14, at five o'clock, Miss
> Nannie Elizabeth Evans was married in a private cere-
> mony to Doctor Earl William Roles in the chapel at the
> First Presbyterian Church, East Orange, New Jersey. The
> Reverend Charles A. Platt officiated. The chapel was
> beautifully decorated with palms and calla lilies. . . . The
> bride wore an ensemble of Eleanor blue crepe with navy
> blue accessories and a shoulder corsage of white orchids.

Nannie Evans, Eva and Will Roles, and Earl's sister Mae were able
to attend, and there was a reception in the church social hall afterwards for about forty. According to Nancy:

> Before we were married, we were constantly arguing about
> where we were going to spend our honeymoon. I wanted

to go to Canada; Earl wanted to go to Florida. When he turned right, going south, after we left our wedding reception, he said, "We're going to Florida because it's too cold in Canada and you don't have your fur coat out of storage." Earl was smoking at the time and he then proceeded to burn a hole in my wedding dress.

This was not an auspicious start and was further exacerbated by Earl's leaving the motel door open the following day when he went for the paper. Nancy came out of the bathroom just a little later completely nude—to the startled and leering eyes of a passing stranger who asked, "May I help you, madam?"

There were definitely compromises to be made, and Nancy was expected to make most of them. In Earl's defense, he was and continued to be utterly unaware of the effects of his actions on his new wife. He was very much in love, but he had claimed his prize and expected to go on with life as he understood it, with the single change being that he now had someone committed to him who would make life more pleasant and support his own plans. He did meet Nancy's criteria in all respects, but he also had attitudes and insecurities that caused Nancy much heartache during their years together.

Nevertheless, she had made her choice. Her life was perhaps different from her dreams, but it was also an existence in which she could anticipate companionship, security, and pleasure. Nancy's positive attitude carried her through some of the adjustments she faced. There were small quirks that needed to be accommodated:

> Earl never knew what to give me for anything. He once wanted to go out with me to get clothes and I took him that one time, but I never took him again. . . .
>
> For that first Christmas he gave me a cocktail set, with the ice bucket and glasses. He never drank much but I went with a group that did have drinks. I know that when I received it, it was kind of a shock because it wasn't exactly typical of him. . . .
>
> Earl knew I didn't care for candy, but somewhere along

the way he gave me a box of candy for Valentine's Day. I didn't eat it, but he did. Thereafter, every year for Christmas, he gave me a box of candy. It was really for him, and it became a joke between us.

And there were viewpoints on which she had to make a stand:

> One year he was very proud and told me that he had gotten me a wonderful present for Christmas. I had wanted a silver service and I thought that must be what it was. When I opened it, it was a set of pots and pans. I was so disappointed that I finally told him I didn't ever want something for the house, I wanted something personal. His heart fell; he thought he was doing such a wonderful thing.

The couple set up housekeeping in Earl's quarters at the site of his office. He had quit the country club by this time and was devoting his energy to growing his medical practice. Nancy continued to teach, but her dislike of it caused her to announce, after a little more than a year, that she had quit her job. Since an assumption of the marital relationships of that period was that the male was the breadwinner, Earl received this news with equanimity and didn't seem angry about her quitting. At one point later in life when Earl commented on it, he said that women were put into this world to raise babies and men were put into this world to take care of women. Perhaps he believed this in some ways even when he was thirty-three. Nancy certainly felt a husband's responsibility was to support his wife and family. Her primary male role model had been Offie Stancill, and he was a strong man who was very much the "head of the household." While Offie's wife, Mattie, was his partner in every way, she had her responsibilities and he had his. Nan always believed that when a woman took over the financial role, she emasculated her husband. She was never gainfully employed after that, although she was consistently proactive, energetic, and involved in life. She had chosen to be a wife and hoped to be a mother someday. To have Earl be the dominant partner and to have him control the finances and be responsible for the significant decisions regarding the direction of their lives seemed to her to be both logical and reasonable. However, she probably did not know at that point that Earl's need for control was so extreme.

While these domestic arrangements got straightened out during the first couple of years, there were still decisions to make about the direction of their lives. It may have been difficult, however, to think only of their personal affairs at that moment. Hitler's aggrandizement of power and Germany's annexation of eastern European countries promulgated intense talk in the United States about the possibility of war. Earl kept a diary for the months of April and May 1939 and his views reflected those of many. The term "conscientious objector" had not yet been coined but would be a true reflection of his thinking. Since Nancy had traveled in Germany and knew something about the people and the positives that Hitler had brought to the educational system, she was probably inclined to agree with Earl; her travel had resulted in her seeing the citizens of Germany as people rather than as "the enemy."

The German situation in 1939, moreover, was not the only news of the day. Mahatma Gandhi started his fast to end British rule in India in March; one pope died and another took his place; a Chilean earthquake killed over 30,000 people; and Lou Gehrig ended his string of 2,130 consecutive games played when he announced that he had ALS. Even in Europe, the news was not all about Hitler. Francisco Franco assumed power in Spain at the end of March; Italy, under Mussolini, invaded Albania at the start of April; and the League of Nations slowly fell apart as country after country resigned its membership.

....

Earl shortly began to feel that he needed to investigate other ways to increase his practice. Since he had taken a short course in plastic surgery earlier, he thought opening a plastic surgery clinic in East Orange might be possible. He went over to Presbyterian Hospital to investigate the idea, but a Dr. O'Crowley there told him he should take a five-year course at Bellevue. In his diary, he wrote:

It seems the old physicians want the younger ones to spend their time in school (while as a fact the older ones did not). At the present time I am perplexed. Should I spend 5 more years in preparation to bring me to 39 yrs. of age, just to pass the surgical board? We should have some home life with children on the way before it is too late. Should I go to some other town to practice? I would love a home with ground about it and some children pattering about. Nancy said today that nothing should stand in my way of taking the 5-yr. course. God bless her. She is always thinking of my future regardless of the cost to her happiness.

Another method Earl tried in his search for increased revenue was networking. He joined several business and physicians' groups, and those associations did help somewhat. Despite those endeavors, however, Earl remained unhappy with the size of his practice. With Nancy's full approval, he finally decided to specialize in orthopedics, even though doing so would require a year of training. When Earl shared his reasoning, he said:

> Why orthopedics? Just because I was interested. I wanted to be a surgeon rather than a family doctor and I chose orthopedics. I was always interested in developing not only my mind but also my body.

Nancy promoted Duke University:

> He applied and my friend, Hugh Lefler, put in a recommendation for him and also said that I had taught in Raleigh and was a North Carolinian. I think that helped, and Earl was admitted to the Duke program. We moved to Durham.

Nancy was ecstatic. She was back in her home state and among people about whom she cared. It didn't even matter to her that Earl had to spend his nights at the hospital while she roomed with "a lovely couple." Everything seemed to be coming together. She no longer had to teach, she was "home," and she had a loving partner.

Duke University, a private nonprofit research university, traces its roots to 1838, but when Earl and Nancy arrived during the late summer of 1940, the School of Medicine was only fifteen years old and orthopedics was a new specialty. Earl embraced the learning and the field. However, Earl had been comfortable in the metropolitan Philadelphia world of his youth. Its diversity and energy most probably had led him to feel that he had personal freedom and control of his life simply because of the anonymity he experienced there. East Orange, while small, was a suburb of New York City. Moving to a much smaller town with the consequent realization that he would be recognized and expected to interact with many of its citizens was a change. In addition, there was not the diversity of backgrounds he had known, with most of the population leading lives bound by relatively rigid and unfamiliar traditions. It was also a Southern tobacco town with a sleepy drawl and manner. This new environment must have been somewhat disquieting for him.

Before moving back to North Carolina, Nancy had become pregnant and had a miscarriage. Again in North Carolina, before Christmas 1940, Nancy miscarried. She soldiered on; it had to have helped that her closest friend, Bet Piner Lefler, lived in Chapel Hill and that she could make trips to Greenville to see her mother and be enclosed in the love of her extended family. Remembering that the tragedies of others were greater than her own—the instruction from the Brown motto—must have seemed significant at that time.

Earl received his certificate of "creditable completion" from Duke on June 30, 1941, and he wanted to leave immediately. Nancy was disappointed, but Earl wrote letters to suitable institutions that were advertising positions, and he accepted an offer from the Crippled Children's Hospital in Elizabethtown, Pennsylvania. Once there, they rented a second-floor corner apartment near the hospital in a building with a store on the first floor. Later, Earl remembered sitting in the front room of that apartment looking out to see complete darkness when the government instituted blackouts during the war. Nancy and Earl drew together as a team in the threat facing all Americans. This was a part of Nancy's dream—that she would have a companion on her life's journey, a hand to hold and a permanent escape from the loneliness that had so plagued her.

....

Earl was licensed to practice medicine and surgery by the state board of Pennsylvania on October 29, 1941. He was still a resident because it was customary at that time for anyone specializing in orthopedics to serve two years at a disabled children's hospital, write up at least 100 surgical cases, and pass an orthopedics examination before being allowed to become a fellow of the American College of Surgeons. This process he completed on December 13, 1942.

The United States passed the first Selective Service Act in September 1940. Earl had still been in school at Duke, so he received a deferment. When he left Duke, he soon took charge of all the statewide clinics in Pennsylvania for the disabled children's hospital and thus could avoid joining the service altogether. Neither he nor Nancy felt that this relief was unpatriotic. Nancy did not want her husband to leave her, nor did she think all Germans were evil, and Earl had voiced his opinion on many occasions that he was in the business of saving lives, not taking them. For Earl, war was an opportunity for arms manufacturers to get rich. As a child, he had been frightened by the propaganda used to elicit support for the First World War. He had seen posters of bayoneted babies and women forced to ride naked on horses, and his repugnance at this type of patriotism was probably at the root of his pacifist philosophy. He had the outlook of a globalist, believing that the world should and would eventually put the planet's interests above the interests of individual nations. He did agree, however, that challenges to the security of the United States had to be confronted at the present time. Earl was on one of his trips to the statewide clinics on December 7, 1941, when the Japanese bombed Pearl Harbor, and he was as appalled as all Americans at that destruction.

Earl was working hard to make business contacts and become as integrated into the community as time would allow during this period. Perhaps his flair for writing had come to someone's attention, since he was listed as a speaker at both a conference on

disabled children and a Chamber of Commerce meeting that year.
Earl started his comments in his conference speech by observing:

> In this day of wholesale slaughter of the youth of the
> world, it is encouraging to find so many people who have
> not forgotten the unfortunate cripple. We might philoso-
> phize a moment and say that there may be a great need
> for this type of non-war-minded person in the post-war
> reconstruction days to give the world mental balance
> against the war-conscious extremists.

Nan's attitude about the war was never written down or mentioned. However, the very lack of comments from her probably indicates her agreement with Earl's opinion. Her later writings and
art always promoted wholeness, community, and peace. She also
understood that, in the culture of that period, she was never to
stand against her husband's opinions publicly. Anything that might
threaten her husband was to be energetically resisted. Nevertheless,
she might have been ready to see enlightened development come
more quickly than Earl was, both in her country and across the
world. She had, after all, been trained in classic progressivism. But
maintaining a happy home life was probably her priority at the
time, and at that moment, Nancy was pregnant again.

It seems to have been a happy time for them, if not for the world.
In a photo from that period, Nancy's hair is in waves around her
shoulders, she is quite slim and is smiling lovingly as she pets a dog.
Photos of Earl show him at ease and extremely handsome. They
made an attractive couple, and certainly Earl was very much in
love. On April 14, 1942, when he was away attending one of the
state's clinics, he sent a telegram to Nancy that said, "Love and happiness to the dearest girl in the world on this our fourth anniversary.
I wish we were together to celebrate today."

Part of his happiness may have had to do with Nancy's pregnancy. She had learned that to carry a child to term she would have
to administer some kind of shot to herself every day during the
first trimester. She couldn't later identify what was in the syringes,
but the procedure was successful. After two miscarriages, Nancy

Nancy and Earl Roles with dog Duke, c. 1940-41

had to have been both very happy and very frightened. The couple welcomed their first child, Alan Wells Roles, on June 3, 1942. His advent brought the immediate family number to four since they also owned a dog.

They had found a puppy outside the house one day. Earl did not think they should keep him and took the animal with him to work. He shooed the small life out of the car and assumed it would wander away and become someone else's issue. When he returned to the car that night, it was still there, so he picked it up and brought it home. They named him Duke. Nancy recalled:

> I remember that once, when we went away for the week-end, Earl shut Duke up in the apartment bathroom. After we got back, it wasn't long before Duke made his displeasure known by ripping up every paper he could find and strewing the pieces all over the living room.

Duke was the first of many dogs the couple owned during their marriage; this was significant because Earl always maintained that he didn't want dogs and would only rarely let them in the house.

By the end of Earl's life, however, Duke, Apache, George, Tuck, Jeff, and finally Midnight had found their homes with the couple, even though they were always Nancy's responsibility. There was a tenderness in Earl that translated into an emotional reaction in favor of all who were helpless. Being an orthopedist, particularly one who attended disabled children, meant he had to either develop a hard shell or become a father figure. He chose the latter. That small puppy's helplessness tied Earl's heart to it and there was no alternative but to give it love—and since Nancy had always loved dogs, he had the benefit of pleasing her as well. This gentleness was a part of the reason for Nancy's love and loyalty and an aspect of both their personalities.

Alan was a healthy baby and Duke grew into a yapping terrier. In addition, Earl's love for music had not waned, and he had bought a baby grand piano. Nan also played the violin then, so the household became lively and noisy. But they were good sounds, and this was the life that Nancy had wanted. It was also a period during which she could think about art. She was at home for long periods and experimented with creating models in plaster of paris. She made a casting of Earl playing the piano that they both thought was quite good. Unfortunately, the piano could not go with them in their next move and the cast got broken.

They had been in Pennsylvania for almost two years when Earl decided it was time to look for a new position. He wanted to be in an orthopedic hospital, and Carrie Tingley Hospital in Hot Springs, New Mexico, offered him a job in orthopedic surgery. The salary was $6,000 for the year, a good income then, so Earl accepted. (Several years later, Ralph Edwards, the host of the radio show *Truth or Consequences*, promised to air the program on its tenth anniversary from the first town that renamed itself after the show, and Hot Springs won the honor.)

Earl went out early. He wrote Nancy daily about his new job and his impressions of the town and the people with whom he was working. In each of his letters, he encouraged Nancy to come as soon as possible, with a loving note always included. In July 1943, he wrote:

The worst feature is that I don't have you to talk to, Alan to play with, and lonely evenings. Hurry up and come down. I miss you. . . . Never are we going to be separated again. I know it will be another 2–3 weeks before we are together again and it makes me feel terribly unhappy.

As soon as their furniture was either shipped or sold, Nancy followed by car, with Alan and Duke, Earl's parents, and her mother. Earl had sent Nancy an itinerary with how far she was to go, where to stop, and what to do, but since Will was doing most of the driving, Nancy happily folded up the instructions and went along for the ride.

Hot Springs was close to the Rio Grande and was very rural. The nearest town of any size was El Paso, an hour and a half away. Nancy loved adventure and was happy to try out another type of living experience, but Earl immediately found the town too small, the people too different, and the opportunities too limited. Nancy might have liked living there for a while; the light in New Mexico was quite different from that on the East Coast. She likely absorbed its luminescent qualities and retained them until she could express them in landscape paintings many years later. One occasion, though, perhaps did sour her on New Mexico life: she came out of their adobe house one day to find Alan (not yet two) playing about four feet from a giant snake. Fortunately, the episode ended well.

Within the year Earl started looking for another job, and there seem to have been several opportunities. The couple left New Mexico without an entirely determined destination, although they headed east. Nancy had made it plain that she refused to live anywhere near Camden, and Earl agreed with her on this subject; being too near his mother's influence, and the demands both it and the larger family cluster would bring was apparently not what he wanted either. Nancy might have been influenced to go at least to Pennsylvania. Her sister, Mattie, had become engaged to John Greiner, an architect to whom Nancy had introduced her, and the couple was getting married in Lancaster within the next two months; Nancy would have liked to be in attendance, but she did not make it that far east.

It seems Earl had had some correspondence with a Dr. Bondurant in Cairo, Illinois, although Nancy was unaware of it at the time. They stopped there and Earl went in for an interview while Nancy waited in the car. When he came out, he had taken the job. In the agreement Earl signed, his salary began at $8,400 and would soon be raised to $9,600. Nancy later remembered the significance of their good fortune:

> It was a considerable raise and a wonderful opportunity to learn general surgery. He [Dr. Bondurant] got us to stay over, and he had a wonderful wife and a beautiful home. His wife fell in love with Alan and wanted him to stay with them overnight. The next day, Dr. Bondurant had a house for us. They also wanted Alan to stay with them a lot. Earl said OK, we'd stay there for a while.

Since Nancy was nearly nine months pregnant when they arrived in Cairo, Earl might have factored that into his decision to stay. Whatever had caused her previous miscarriages seemed to have been corrected through her successful pregnancy with Alan, but continued travel might have been considered a risk.

> Then one day it was time for me to deliver Barbara. That morning Earl got up and went to the hospital to perform an appendectomy. He told me to call if anything happened. He hadn't been gone an hour when my water broke and I began fast labor. I called Earl and a cab. Earl then called Mrs. Bondurant and told her I was ready to deliver. She said, "Tell Nancy I'll be at the hospital to pick up Alan and I'll keep him." After Mrs. Bondurant came, I went straight on into delivery. By that time Earl was operating. He came in when he finished. Mrs. Bondurant kept Alan a week; I had difficulty getting him back because she fell in love with him.

Cairo lay at the confluence of the Ohio and Mississippi Rivers. Its elevation was the lowest point in the state, and levees surrounding the town had been built to prevent constant flooding. Cairo had thrived during and after the Civil War, but the building of three bridges over the Mississippi in the early twentieth century had dried up its primary economic business of ferrying railroad cars and vehicular traffic. In addition, the town's record in race relations was one of the worst in the North. There had been many lynchings, and there was a high degree of ill will between the white and black residents. By the time Nancy and Earl arrived, the city was economically declining.

Again, within a year and with Nancy pregnant, Earl wanted to move on. He liked Dr. Bondurant but felt Cairo was a dead town. Searching again through the medical journals, he noticed an ad for an orthopedist in Cincinnati. When he got his final instructions for the interview, however, he learned the job was in Louisville, Kentucky.

In May 1942, the US government had designated the Curtiss-Wright Aircraft Company in Louisville as a wartime aircraft production plant. The factory produced the C-46 Commando cargo planes crucial to the war effort. It was a thriving business in a city that had some sophistication. Earl decided to talk with them. Nancy was happy in Cairo, but Earl's decisions were the ones that counted.

> We were going east anyway to see his parents, so we stopped in Louisville and had the interview. He liked it, so he took it. We finished our trip to Camden, and then came on back.

One of the advantages of this position was that the letter of agreement with Curtiss-Wright permitted Earl to open his own practice while working for the company. Nancy recalled:

> When he did this, he used the training he had done at Duke in orthopedics. He went to the large companies around here and offered to take care of their orthopedic work with accidents and such. He practiced industrial medicine from then until the time he retired.

The Curtiss-Wright salary was not as much as he had been making in Cairo, but the prospects were much better.

Earl's license to practice medicine in Kentucky was dated March 2, 1945, and the couple settled into the Louisville area for what would be the remainder of their lives.

TWELVE

SETTLING IN

"IT WAS A WONDERFUL NEIGHBORHOOD, AND CHILDREN

WERE LIVING ON BOTH SIDES OF US." (1989)

Louisville, Kentucky, was founded in 1778 by George Rogers Clark, making it one of the oldest cities west of the Appalachian Mountains. Named after King Louis XVI of France, it was sited beside the falls of the Ohio River. Those falls, the only major obstruction between the upper Ohio River and the mouth of the Mississippi, were central to the settlement's growth. Every boat coming down the river had to stop at the falls and portage around their plunging waters. The populace in Louisville provided all the services these voyagers needed.

The river also played an essential role in the growth of Louisville. In 1937, just seven years before Nancy and Earl moved to town, the Ohio rose thirty feet above flood stage and engulfed between 60 and 70 percent of the city. As a result, not only were many flood-prevention practices introduced, but significant suburban development was also undertaken on higher ground to the east of the city.

It was a friendly town with a churchgoing culture; Old Louisville provided a backdrop of taste and Southern traditions, and Louisville itself boasted a reputation for sophistication at an easy gait. At least so it seemed to the young couple. The city was the center of the bourbon industry, with a third of all bourbon coming from its distilleries. It was also the home of Brown & Williamson, at that time the third largest tobacco company in the US, and the all-time favorite Louisville Slugger baseball bat factory was there. In addition, the Kentucky Derby, the preeminent yearly horse race in America for three-year-olds, had been run at Churchill Downs since 1875, uninterrupted. The celebration held during Derby Week, perhaps the most festive of Louisville's society events, was becoming the city's largest annual event for charitable fundraising. Louisville also offered a university, a museum, an arts club, and a theater.

There was one additional advantage that Nancy and Earl found alluring: Louisville had four seasons. One could usually count on at least two months of fall and two months of spring. There was snow in the winter and temperatures over eighty degrees throughout the summer, but the long gray winter months of the North and the discomfort of extended blistering hot days of the South were absent. The only drawback to the climate was the sticky humidity associated with being next to the Ohio River.

For Nancy, not only was it a return to the South, but it also was a return to a place that was large enough to offer intellectual stimulus and the excitement of a city. Louisville provided the possibility of integrating into a community and eventually expanding from her roles as wife and mother to an identity that was all her own. Louisville also had an active artistic enclave, a significant attraction. For Earl, the city was large enough to offer him the chance to have a thriving independent medical practice. It was also close enough to the North to reassure him that his energy and ambition would not seem out of place, and it would offer the sense of anonymity that he missed in Durham.

All these positives about Louisville helped them look forward. Earl was enthusiastic about his career possibilities. For Nancy, the move offered fresh hope. Her rapport with Earl was sometimes precarious, and it was not always easy to follow her faith's dictates. He had a hot temper and would bang the door on his way out and then would stay out until he got back in control. At one point,

Nancy was so unhappy with their relationship that she turned to writing about it, presenting it as fiction, although it was a thinly disguised account of some of her experiences and a tongue-in-cheek chronicle of her feelings. When Earl read it later, he laughed, told her she had a good imagination, and asked her where her nerve pills were.

About twelve years ago my funny bone began slipping. Now it is lost and I am devoid of any sense of humor. It all began on our honeymoon when we were traveling in the Deep South. On our way to Miami, we stopped overnight in a little coastal town in which a friend of mine resided. While having dinner at our hotel, I related to my newly acquired husband some of my past pleasant experiences in that vicinity and inadvertently mentioned my friend's previous invitation to spend my honeymoon at her villa. My husband suggested that we call her. Shortly thereafter we were on our way to her island home where we spent the night. About a week later, we passed a very attractive gift shop. Remembering our delightful stay at my friend's villa, I suggested that we purchase a little gift for her. Like a flash, my husband's smile became a frown. Nevertheless, he pulled over to the curb and stopped. A bit puzzled by his countenance, I hesitated before stepping out. That was my mistake. He reached for my purse, counted my money, then became glued to the seat. I made my purchases and returned to a silent partner. After our honeymoon, while visiting with his family, he joyfully related many of our interesting experiences and enthusiastically inquired as to whether I had mailed the package to our friend. Noting my scowl, he decided to tease me and jovially related the incident of the purchases. Everyone laughed heartily and told me my first accomplishment as a wife would be to handle my husband.

A few weeks passed. We went shopping for furniture. I knew exactly what I wanted, and so did he, but it was not the same. We didn't argue, and we didn't buy. Days passed. One afternoon, returning from work, I was unable to enter our apartment. The key had been removed from my purse. I calmly relaxed and awaited my husband. In a few moments he darkened the entrance with a beaming face. Immediately, without so much as a casual hello, I was rushed into the elevator and a few seconds later, hurried down the hall. While fidgeting for his key, he bade me close my eyes, then, having swung me off my feet, carried me across the threshold into a completely furnished apartment. Never since have I attempted to buy anything for the house without him. Even when just contemplating making a purchase, I solicit his advice.

Before meeting my beloved, I was a strong-willed, independent individual. Subsequently, during our five-month engagement, he tamed me completely. The word "obey" was not included in the ceremony. It would have been superfluous. When I said, "I do," I became a slave to my lord and master. He does not have to wear a crown to be my King. Even when we are walking down the street, he is several steps ahead. I worshipfully trail him at a respectful distance. Once, my attention was diverted. I stared at an approaching couple. The man was walking attentively beside his feminine companion. My old self-esteem was aroused. For one brief moment I imagined myself his queen, enjoying his obvious homage. My husband, pausing at an intersection, chanced to look backwards. A little surprised with the dreamy look in my eyes, he purchased my thoughts with a penny. To him it was humorous but not pathetic. I was admonished and advised to keep pace.

Sometimes, by sheer stubbornness, I win, or think I do, but not without inviting his anger because of my failure to respect his wisdom or judgment. Once, I sincerely desired a large *Webster's New International Dictionary*, and secretly hoped I might receive one at Christmas. We had little wealth then and did not shower each other with expensive gifts. However, when he asked what I wanted I eagerly made known my wish. With many words and much advice, he flatly refused. Twenty dollars would be spent on me, but not so foolishly. My little dictionary was entirely adequate. We spent the holidays in Philadelphia and, as was our custom, went shopping together on Christmas Eve. I refused to find any clothing under twenty dollars that I liked. Finally, in desperation, he pushed me into a second-hand bookshop. My sarcastic tongue touched off his ignition, and his anger blazed. Fortunately, they did not have the dictionary. We went home in a huff. At midnight when the family gathered around the large tree, most everyone was jovial, but we were not speaking. When Santa had presented his last gift, he returned to the tree for a final inspection before saying goodnight. There was a letter near the top for me. It was a lovely card from my beloved enfolding a twenty-dollar bill. Late the next afternoon we departed. On the way back to our abode, we stopped in Washington for my husband to keep a professional appointment. While he was thus engaged, I found a bookstore. A week later when we were again pursuing our studies at the university, some friends dropped in to welcome us back. There was much talk about our holiday experiences and how each one had been remembered. I could not believe my eyes or my ears. My husband proudly exhibited my dictionary and actually beamed when his friend commented on it being such a thoughtful and appropriate gift.

My beloved is wonderful around the house. If he changes a light bulb, it breaks. With a crowbar he is perfect. However, I never object to his fixing anything for I am confident in having a perfect job. In the end, we are forced to hire an expert craftsman. Once my spouse attempted to reach out the upstairs hall window to hang a screen. In so doing, he twisted his back and injured a rib. The screen was left dangling and he retired. The next morning, he could not move. Ordinarily, if his big toe hurts, I humor him, but this time I could not. When he called for help, a brilliantly lighted though invisible placard loomed in front of me: "It is all in the mind." Recalling that I had never been permitted to have a pain. I decided to apply some of his own psychology. As I entered the bedroom, he groaned, but summoning forth my courage, I urged him to get up. It was necessary that he go to the office. That was the wrong medicine. He passed out completely and I was a little frightened. Gathering his clothing and denying my emotional concern, I proceeded to pull on his socks. This brought him to, but my suggestion that he slide to the side of the bed so that I might continue aroused his anger, and he ordered me out of the room, declaring me a most unsympathetic wife.

Somehow, he slid downstairs and drug himself to the breakfast table. Since it was late and I had to drive our child to school, we left him there. Taking his car, for I intended driving him to the city, I returned to meet him steering mine out of the driveway. He passed but gave no sign of recognition. Sensing his terrific mood and a possible sadistic reaction, I was warily concerned and turned immediately to overtake him. Strangely enough, he was completely out of sight. The early hours of our evening together were strangely quiet. Eventually, temptation won; he broke his vigil determined to arouse my sympathy. He related in detail his agonizing drive to the hospital, the warm and sympathetic solicitations of the nurses, and the kindness and patience of the doctor. I could hardly suppress my anxiety but did succeed in remaining silent. His bewilderment was complete. As he stared at me his countenance slowly registered an alarming concern. What on earth had happened to me? At length I was persuaded to partially explain. He listened with obvious disapproval. Finally, his eyes almost smiled; but he retaliated with a loud "Huh, you never had a pain" as he left the room.

Counted among our friends is at least one couple we both consider exceptionally well adjusted and happy. The husband is a golf enthusiast and his wife never complains.

I doubt that he has ever asked her permission to do anything, or even given it a thought. He grants her the same
independence. Nevertheless, one Sunday afternoon when
he was recapitulating a few of his plays before a number
of guests, he stated that he had played so much golf in
the past week that appeasing his wife had become trying.
In all seriousness he turned to the masculine element
and remarked that earlier in the day he had actually had
to plead his cause. They all laughed with that knowing
smile, "I know what you mean, brother." His wife opened
her mouth to protest but did not. She turned to me and
exclaimed softly, "The old storyteller." A week later the
phone rang. My husband was not in. On inquiring if I
could take the message, the voice at the other end of the
line laughed. I learned that on Saturday this friend had
invited my husband to play golf and been told that my
permission was necessary. Shortly thereafter, the head of
our house returned. I gave him the message and asked
why the little white lie. He laughed and went on out to the
golf course.

Last weekend we invited a number of friends to a card
party. Just before they arrived my husband went out on an
emergency call. While he was detained our guests chatted
socially in the living room. Several were enthusiastic fisher-
men, and a few tall stories were told. Eventually, one of
the men began a tale about his culinary accomplishments.
He described in detail how he had fried enough doughnuts last Monday to supply his family a week. Before finishing the tale, his wife, overhearing the last statement,
interrupted and spoiled the story. "Of all things; there was
never a doughnut cooked in our house." I laughed and am
still laughing over the expression on two faces. Maybe my
sense of humor is going to return.

Most of these fictionalized incidents actually happened, and they
were all highly frustrating. Some Nancy could dismiss as the result
of Earl's need for control, while others were harder to understand.

The incident with the dictionary happened during their second year, and Earl continued to reverse himself whenever he decided to do so. Nancy got angry frequently, although protesting Earl's actions or decisions did not do any good, and she learned to keep quiet most of the time. It was only later in life that she began to understand that his reversals resulted from his learning to look at something from a different angle.

She also found out early on that Earl could not, in his mind, afford to have her ill or hurt. That may have been caused by his fear of losing her. It was also an affront to his need for control. As a result, while he was highly sympathetic to the plights of others, for her there was little compassion. At the beginning of their marriage, when they were moving into their apartment, Earl was in another room. Nancy was up on a stepladder and fell. Earl poked his head around the corner and said, "Oh you're all right, aren't you?" and walked out. Nancy learned never to complain about physical issues. There was one occasion much later when she fell and broke several ribs but didn't even mention it for over a week.

Nancy also told her best friend once that Earl would make comments asking her how she could know anything, that she was just a woman. Nancy remarked in relating this that she made up her mind that she *would* know. In referring to that story, her friend noted that maybe it was a good thing because it spurred Nancy on to learn more, to know more. On the other hand, when he was much older, Earl reflected that Nancy had the patience of a saint. Perhaps he did come to realize how unaware he was at times.

Finances were a bone of contention. The Depression had hurt both their pocketbooks and Earl kept as tight a hold on the money he made as he could. This was an attitude that remained throughout his life. He never had credit cards, and it became evident that making and keeping money was in itself a pleasure for him. A poor childhood can make an adult generous, but it can also result in parsimony. Earl fell into the latter category. The tone of their monetary discussions was set in these early years of their life together: Nancy was to ask Earl for whatever money she needed each time she needed it, and she was to detail and justify every expense. An itemized budget in Nancy's handwriting from December 1, 1949, to December 1, 1950, gives a report on every penny spent. Even the sum of twenty cents for shoe polish was listed. At one point she wrote on this spreadsheet that she had given $16.55 to the church. "This total should have been $39.00—that is 52 Sundays @ .75 a Sun. = $39.00 but I didn't have it." Her total expenditures for the year were $4,059.05.

Earl's penny-pinching resulted in Nancy's having to ask her mother for money at one point to buy underwear for her children. And, even though she hated to sew (perhaps because her mother had had to make her living as a seamstress), Nancy made shorts and halter sets for the girls from curtains she had replaced. Whether individuals are rich or poor, budget minded or free spending, money is always something about which they are aware; for the Roles family, both because Earl worked hard and because of his attitude, it was a backdrop to their lives.

....

The neighborhood of Riedlonn, where Nancy and Earl found their perfect house at 609 Emery Road, was built at the crest of the hills overlooking the Ohio River, a fifteen-minute bus ride east of downtown. It was initially developed around 1920 on land that was part of an old 1837 estate. Woods formed the backdrop to the rear yards of the houses on three sides of the small neighborhood and vehicle ingress was limited, thus making it a safe place for children. Given that the couple had two children and were expecting a third, this was an important consideration. They bought the house immediately upon viewing it and were in their new home within two weeks of arriving in town. Nancy recalled:

> Emery Road was delightful in every way. We would pick blackberries from the woods every summer and make blackberry jam. It was a wonderful neighborhood, and there were children living on both sides of us. The Kiesels had two boys. The Daltons had two older boys, and Lisle was the same age as Barbara. They were delightful neighbors and we got to know them right away. Dorothy Dalton

came in to meet me with an offering of food almost immediately; she was so lovely.

The house was a red-brick center-hall colonial of approximately
2,500 square feet. As you entered the house, the living room was on
the right and the dining room on the left. Behind the living room
was a small, enclosed porch that opened onto the backyard. Behind
the dining room were the kitchen and breakfast nook. A kitchen
door led out the left side of the house and had a small porch over
which honeysuckle grew; it was there that the milkman made his
deliveries.

The stairs in the front hall led up to the second story, where
a master bedroom, two small bedrooms, and a bathroom were
located. One could open the door to steps to the attic from the
upstairs hallway. This area was, at different times, a guest room,
Alan's bedroom when the senior Roleses visited, a playroom, and
an art room. One side of the attic had a gas heater that was lit with
a match for an actual fire, apparently not illegal at that time.

The steps to the basement were located off the breakfast nook and
under the stairs to the second floor. The basement had a coal-fired
furnace, a small bath with a shower, and a laundry room. At some
point, a large chest freezer was installed, in which large quantities
of food and pint cartons of ice cream were stocked. Nancy, the girl
from the farm, was fully prepared to buy in bulk and either freeze
or can fruits and vegetables, and the basement was the repository
for both.

The garage was located just off the main basement space and
presented some difficulties: reversing the car up the gradient during
icy conditions was almost impossible. Earl eventually enclosed the
area and, since there was a full bath on that level, made it into an
additional bedroom. According to Nancy:

> There was a girl, I don't know how we learned about her,
> who lived in a rural area and wanted to go to high school
> in Louisville. So, she came and lived with us for about a
> year and stayed in that room.

Behind the house, there was a fence surrounding the backyard with a gate at the rear property line near the woods, and the garden between the house and the woods was terraced. The Second World War was still being fought and food was scarce when the Roles family moved in; everyone who could had a Victory Garden, and Nancy grew flowers, fruits, and vegetables in hers. When the children grew a bit older, the yard was their playground. Nancy drew many sketches of Alan in his Daniel Boone coonskin cap playing in this safe, enclosed space. The drawings sometimes depicted Alan alone and sometimes included the neighborhood boys in scenes of their fantasies. According to Alan, "She took our backyard and made it a wilderness of many levels in those sketches. A stone could be a palisade."

The house at 609 Emery Road was neither small nor large. It was an appropriate home for a young couple and was gracious enough to provide them a residence in which they could entertain with pride. There was even a button on the dining room floor, hidden by a rug, that could be used to call a maid in from the kitchen—although Nancy used it on very rare occasions. The thirty-six-year-old wife and mother worked hard to decorate her home with her own good taste and to keep it looking nice. She only once had to accede to Earl's decorating ideas—when he had a set of dining room furniture delivered, presumably a payment by a patient; it was heavy English mahogany and much too large for the room. She did not like it but was stuck with it for the rest of her life.

Earl's success at Curtiss-Wright included a $1,000 raise after just one month, and his independent practice grew rapidly. The couple was delighted with their decision to settle in Louisville, and Earl's raise enabled Nancy to hire the domestic help she needed in the last months of her third pregnancy.

It was not long after we moved there that I hired Jessie Mae to clean for us. She worked for the Daltons, and I got her through them. I think she worked for me two or three days a week at that time. She was a jewel. She cleaned well, she washed, ironed, and she took care of my kids

whenever I wanted to go anywhere. She was very bright,
but she hadn't finished high school. I got after her and
told her I'd get her enrolled. We did that, and I think she
finally got her high school diploma. She worked for us until after we moved out to Woodhill Valley; that was a little
too far for her to come.

Jessie Mae cost $5 a day in the 1940s, and having "help" was simply
a part of life, not a status symbol. Nancy's view would have been
that she wanted both the help and the backup Jessie Mae provided,
and Jessie Mae wanted the job. Jessie Mae was a part of the family
and was given complete respect. All the children knew that they
were to obey her without question and always treat her with the
same courtesy they were to accord other adults.

The couple had been fortunate in their choice of a home in
Louisville; the neighborhood was not only friendly, but it was
also social. Gatherings in each other's homes as well as organized
community events brightened their lives. Nancy recalled:

> Fortunately, most everybody in Riedlonn was about the
> same age, and had children about the same age as ours.
> After a bit, we knew just about everyone in the neighbor-
> hood. The whole group used to get together at the end of
> the road once a year for a barbecue.

There was a plot of open land there, perhaps designed to be a
small park. At this event each summer, the men in the community
would dig a pit and roast a pig in it all day. A small stage was set
up and framed with shelves that held prizes donated by the nearby
storeowners for the bingo games that would follow dinner. Lights
strung across the area on poles contributed to the festive ambiance.

The only other community event was held during the Christmas
season at that same undeveloped lot. The community would gather
to sing carols, and one of the older men would dress up as Santa
Claus and appear at the close of the singing with candy for the
kids. These group events must have been reminiscent for Nancy of
the gatherings at her Uncle Offie's farm for holiday occasions—

everyone knowing everyone else, a spirit of gratitude and thanks-giving prevailing. They were also events that strengthened the bonds of friendship that Nancy was forming. Two of her closest friends for the rest of her life were Riedlonnites.

This lively community also attracted stray dogs, some of whom found a home with the Roles family. While Earl would not permit these dogs to live in the house, it was hard for his soft heart to fight Nancy's and the children's eagerness to adopt. Earl's history with dogs ran from the puppy Duke, through all the strays that Nancy befriended, to quite late in life when he was happy to have a large dog in the house with him for security.

There was one incident while the family lived on Emery Road that illustrated his reluctance to have dogs and was a cause of friction between him and the rest of the family. There was always activity on Emery Road, with children and cars using the pavement. Most of the dogs in the neighborhood would chase the tires of any car for a few feet. One of the dogs Nancy adopted did so one day and then in his excitement nipped a child playing nearby. This made Earl furious. He put the animal in his car, drove across Louisville and let the dog out, assuming that was the end of it. Within a short period, the dog showed up again. Earl then put the dog back into the car and drove it across the bridge into Jeffersonville, Indiana. The children were so desolate that they talked him into driving them across the river to search for the animal. They were unsuccessful, but it was not long before another dog decided 609 Emery was its home base.

THIRTEEN

EMBRACING MOTHERHOOD

"THE IDEAL AMERICAN FAMILY IS FOUNDED ON LOVE." (1950s)

This move to Louisville felt different to Nancy. She sensed she could establish satisfying friendships, and the community seemed to offer a range of opportunities for creating the "creditable work product" she had envisioned in her London journal reverie. The couple also thought that Louisville was a good place to raise children. Nancy was pregnant when they arrived in Louisville and their daughter, Carolyn Jean Roles, was born on May 18, 1945, exactly fourteen months after her older sister's birth. The following two years were spent being a mother, forming friendships, and putting down roots.

In addition, Earl seemed to be content with the city as a place to build his practice. He had become a physician almost by chance and an orthopedic surgeon quite possibly because of his wife's encouragement. He then fell in love with his profession and with treating the people who came to see him. His heart especially went out to the children who suffered. Throughout his practice he would come home and share his concern for a particular child with Nancy, and she frequently thought that he might bring one of them home

to live with their family. At one point, he wrote a poem after having
treated a little girl.

AS I STOOD WATCHING

As I stood watching
With her temperature so high
And a pulse that was missing
I asked myself why
A child should be suffering
A condition untreatable
With knowledge galore
An illness non-remediable
When the angels shall take her
And escort her to Heaven
I am sure there will be
A chariot of roses, for one almost seven
Now when God sees his charge
With her beauty surrounding
A place will be made
With the bugles all sounding.

There is no date on this poem, but its composition may have
been bubbling in his subconscious because of the dramatic turn of
events in his family's life. Nancy had become pregnant again, and
their fourth child, Earl William Roles Jr., was born on April 8, 1947.
Nancy recalled:

At Billy's birth, he was recorded as being healthy and normal in every way. I was overjoyed because my water had
broken a week beforehand, yet the doctor had told me to
stay at home. But, after a normal birth, Billy didn't urinate
for three days. Then he did, but he immediately went into
a coma and some of the personnel there thought he was
dead. They gave him some sort of a shot; for some reason,
this brought him out of shock. Afterward, X-rays showed
that a large section of his brain had been destroyed. They

kept him in the hospital for five weeks. I had trouble feeding him; I had to press his cheeks together to get his muscles to pull on the nipple of the bottle. I remember staying up hours at night trying to get him to take what was in the bottle. . . .

Billy grew normally at first, but several months later, when he was about eight months old, a bump on the top of his head appeared. The doctor told me to watch it and come in if it didn't go down. It went down, but after that Billy began deteriorating physically.

Eventually, Billy was diagnosed with cerebral palsy. Nancy took him to the Medical College of Virginia in 1948, tried and failed to get him admitted at Johns Hopkins, and, finally, sought a consultation at the Cleveland Clinic, where they said that Billy's brain scan showed minimal function and there was no hope of his growing normally. Nancy kept a journal for a while, recording Billy's medical condition and the oscillations of his life. It contains nothing surprising. She noted seizures, constipation, vomiting, head jerking, difficulty breathing, and days of dullness. She recorded anything hopeful as well: the days when he seemed attentive to his surroundings, appeared to have energy and was playful, and seemed to enjoy a changed position or attention from his siblings or music. Perhaps the most painful and poignant entry was the following:

> *My child has had a look of agony and distress in his eyes at least 3/4 of his waking hours since the first swelling of the fontanelle. The light in his eyes has gradually become dimmer and practically faded away.*

Nancy and Earl spent a little under six years dealing with a child who never grew out of being an infant. They treated Billy as a regular family member, and he was cared for with the same attention as Alan, Barbara, and Carolyn. They fitted him into their customary routines, and Billy was taken along when they traveled to visit family. Nancy treated her son with anything that might help, but mostly with massage, continually encouraging the growth of neural pathways that simply did not exist. There was never a time when the couple gave up hope for a miracle.

On the morning of February 20, 1952, Barbara and Carolyn, then eight and seven years old, told their mother that they didn't feel well, and she let them stay home from school. Perhaps because of this complication, Nancy let Billy sleep while she dealt with breakfast and Alan's and Earl's departures. By the time Nancy got upstairs to bathe and dress Billy, Barbara and Carolyn were in their parents' bedroom at their mother's dresser pulling out their baby books and beginning to look through them. Billy's crib was on the other side of the room. Nancy had heard Billy scream a little while before, which usually indicated a seizure, but since his episodes usually didn't last long and frequently were over by the time she got to the crib, she hadn't rushed up. When she did get there, Billy was not breathing. She picked him up, put him on the bed, and worked frantically to revive him. After a few minutes, she sighed, went to

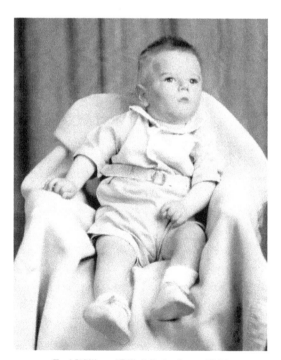

Earl William "Billy" Roles Jr., c. 1947

the phone, and called Earl to tell him that Billy had died. She later recalled:

> Billy was cremated and there was a funeral. . . . It was a short one; most of the people in the neighborhood were there. He was better off; everybody was. But he was a beautiful baby, and I still think he was a blessing to the whole family. We all learned so much from him. I had never seen anybody have a seizure before Billy. I had no idea what it was like or what it was like to tend to someone like that. We took him everywhere with us, which I think was the right thing to do. I remember very well how many people asked me why I didn't put him into an institution. What was I there for? One of my purposes in life I guess; I'm awfully glad I could do it.

This remembrance was related about thirty-five years after Billy's death. The heartache had long since diminished, and life had gone on. Despite that, a part of the heart is damaged when one's child is ill, particularly when one's child is lost. Nancy was Billy's caregiver and had total responsibility for him. The fact that Earl was a physician provided no benefit. For both, the overwhelming helplessness must have been dreadful. Yet sometimes the heart grows stronger in its recovery, and one becomes more aware and sensitive to the pain in others. For Earl, the result was to make him a more sympathetic doctor. For Nancy, the desire to lead a valuable and creditable life was reinforced. Evidence from her later activities makes it plain that her experience caring for a special-needs child fueled her work towards helping increase the potential of all women and children. When things quieted down, Nancy gave her children Dale Evans's book *Angel Unaware*, which describes the actress's journey through a similar situation. All three children read and remembered it. Nancy's family motto must have been particularly poignant in these circumstances. Not only did she have to "accept the inevitable and rise above it," but she also had to continue to "look out" at the world and avoid staying submerged "looking in" at her loss. It must have been challenging to remember to count her blessings.

....

In addition to her concern for and devotion to her youngest, Nancy had the management of a home and the daily life of three active children. During this time, the late 1940s and 1950s, Nancy's core desire to create wholeness was tested. She sought to use the concepts of progressive education in raising her children, a radical departure from the accepted approaches of the time. These attempts probably would not have been possible were it not for her faith and her mother's example of what it meant to be a parent. Since Nancy did have that bedrock background, she was able to permit her children the freedom to develop their own interests, viewpoints, and individuality. She later articulated in one of her speeches the principles on which she and Earl agreed:

> The ideal American family is founded on love. It is disciplined, enlightened, and cohesive. It is a core of democracy, a stage for freedom, a school for social consciousness, and a court of justice. It fashions the social order and fosters national greatness. Members shoulder responsibilities and share privileges and pleasures; they respect and encourage individual differences but exhibit unity and harmony. . . .
>
> The individual does not choose his family relations and he cannot completely sever his ties. His attitudes and actions mold, enrich, or destroy the patterns and quality of his family portrait. Heirs of an honorable family inherit privileges, powers, duties, and responsibilities that must be preserved and enhanced; their position demands leadership, vision, courage, cooperation, and action.

While Earl left most of the daily arrangements to Nancy, he was always an essential presence in the children's lives. Although he wanted her to be the disciplinarian so he wouldn't have to be (and supported her use of forsythia switches to correct objectionable behavior), he also encouraged their children. Dinner table conversations often involved lively discussions during which the children were urged to voice their thoughts. They learned from their parents

Barbara, Carolyn, and Alan Roles, 1945

that one's opinions should be backed up with information, knowledge, and irrefutable facts.

Commenting on the rhythm of those times, Nancy said that it was the custom to hold dinner until Earl got home. His office hours ended at five, although it was usually at least an hour or so before he saw his last patients and did his rounds at the hospital. The children would watch for him to drive up and run to the door to greet him. He would pick each of them up and hug them and swing them around. When one of the three was not there, he would be disappointed and want to know why.

Dinner was a family meal, eaten in the dining room on the heavy mahogany table Earl had brought into their lives, and they always said grace using Earl's childhood prayer. The meals were well balanced and included dessert, probably because Earl had such a sweet tooth. There were never any restrictions on food, although portions were smaller than they would grow to be decades later. Breakfast was more hurried, but the family gathered around the Formica table in the breakfast nook every morning for a substantial meal, one most assuredly influenced by Nancy's farming background.

Nancy doled out chores to the three children—setting tables, washing dishes, cleaning rooms, taking out the garbage, straightening shelves, and shucking corn for a penny an ear so she could do the canning and freezing. She taught her daughters to bake cakes from scratch and to use the Ironrite in the basement. The girls pressed Earl's shirts, the small napkins he had them sew for him for medical procedures in his office, and even the towels and the underwear—which might seem excessive but was probably a legacy from Nancy's country background that required tidiness in all areas. It was as well possibly a reflection of her artistic desire to have everything in neat semblance.

She listened to their nightly prayers and helped them memorize Bible verses; she caressed Barbara's head when her breathing was difficult because of her hay fever and she couldn't sleep; she rubbed Carolyn's back when her ear ached; she never missed meetings and events that had to do with her children; and she always stood up for them. Once, when a fifth-grade teacher was particularly critical of Barbara because of her sniffling in class and Barbara cried about going to school, Nancy went straight to the principal. The teacher was reprimanded and never shamed Barbara again. As Nancy stated later in one of her speeches:

> We may teach a child, train him in all the social, cultural, and ethical knowledge and morals, provide every opportunity for his growth and advancement, and he may in the end fail you. But give a child intelligent love and discipline along with truth, and he will never fail you.

She raised three children who went on to be successes in their own lives.

Nancy also got to apply her artistic talent by leading activities for the children's Scout troops. These projects often took place on the dining room table and included such childhood classics as block-printed Christmas cards, driftwood sculptures, foil decorations, and papier-mâché flowers. One of Nancy's legacies was her desire to promote creativity in others; later in life she would make that effort a community-wide endeavor.

In the evenings, the family would often listen to the radio after dinner; *Fibber McGee and Molly* was a big hit. Then in the early 1950s, Earl bought one of the first televisions in the neighborhood, and everyone came over to watch the national political conventions in 1951. Once the TV replaced the radio, favorites included *I Remember Mama*, *What's My Line?*, *The Ed Sullivan Show*, and *Perry Mason*.

These were the years of Nancy's keeping watch while the children raked leaves and burned them in the street, played hide-and-seek at twilight, and chased lightning bugs to put in glass jars. These were the years of broken arms and cut knees, hay fever, and frequent trips to the doctor. These were the years of shuttling children to school and music lessons, tangled hair and home perms, parakeets and gerbils, and monopoly and canasta games on the back porch.

....

These were the bright years of family trips. Nancy drove the children to Greenville every summer for a two-week visit with her mother. Earl was never along, and Nancy got to make all the decisions. As they wound through the Smoky Mountains, she taught the children "She'll Be Coming Round the Mountain When She Comes," "Carolina Moon," and other songs she remembered from earlier trips with friends. Then they would stop in honky-tonk Gatlinburg to eat hush puppies and go on the rides.

On one of these trips, around 1950 or 1951, Nancy decided to take her children and mother to Atlantic Beach, North Carolina, for the weekend. Visiting the ocean and walking the beach gave Nancy great pleasure, and perhaps harkened back to the time she had spent at the ocean while living in Raleigh. On this occasion, Nancy's Aunt Martha had told her that the old family Bible was being kept in a bank vault in Wilmington, and Nancy promised she would retrieve it. However, they were in an automobile collision a few miles outside of Wilmington. Nancy later recalled:

> My mother landed in the hospital, two of my children were hurt, and our baggage was broken and scattered along the highway. The name of the bank, and of its offi-

cial, was lost. I spent the next three weeks with my mother in the hospital and did not get to the bank. Shortly thereafter, Aunt Martha was killed when she was hit by a car as she was crossing the road to go visit her daughter.

Nancy tried many times over the years to find the bank and the Bible, but never succeeded.

Nancy also visited her sister, Mattie, at least once a year on the annual family visit to Earl's family in Camden. Mattie and her husband, John, lived in Lancaster, Pennsylvania, which was on the route. Sometimes Nancy got to stay with them while Earl and the kids went on, but more often her visit with Mattie was all too short. Earl didn't take many vacations at this stage since he felt he had to be in Louisville to build his practice, but he did want the children to know his background—he also wanted to show them off—and he got the royal treatment on these visits.

The couple used the once-a-year car trips to Camden to encourage the gathering of knowledge—learning geography as the family traveled east on the Pennsylvania Turnpike, memorizing the parts of a car, being tutored about the various organs and processes of the human body (they could long afterwards describe in detail the movement of food from its introduction to the body through to its evacuation). This was all done with good spirit and no objections.

Both Earl and Nancy were fascinated with words, so another custom on these trips east was the requirement that each child choose ten new words from the dictionary (which was brought along) and use them frequently during the ride until they were cemented in their vocabulary. Earl's impetus was his desire to have a large vocabulary. He'd studied Latin in medical school, and perhaps his lifelong interest in language began there. He was a committed reader of the *Reader's Digest* vocabulary quizzes, and he became a supporter of the 1960s push for an international language called Esperanto. Nancy's fascination with language was the result of her desire to express her thoughts in writing as accurately as possible.

....

These were also the years during which the family grew closer through spending significant time in close quarters. A year or two before Billy died, Earl joined the Richmond Boat Club, located on the Ohio River about five miles east of the city. Both he and Nancy remembered Earl's marriage proposal when he asked her if she would be his first mate, and he felt it was time to get a boat. He bought a twenty-eight-foot Steelcraft and rented a slip. Nancy wholeheartedly endorsed this development. The club had a private pool and a swim team the children could join, and river excursions with the family held enormous appeal. Nancy recalled:

> It was a marvelous thing to have done. Our first boat was a cabin cruiser. We began going out every weekend and taking the kids with us. When we went on Sundays, we would take guests as well. I always fixed up a big fried chicken dinner, and we would have dinner on the boat. We would go up to Twelve Mile Island, which at that time had a beach at the north end. The kids would swim, and they learned to surfboard behind the boat and then to ski. The next eighteen years we spent on the river, and we had two or three different boats, all named the *Nancy ABC*.

The family had many happy times aboard the boat. In addition to weekend day trips up to Twelve Mile Island, the family took at least one overnight trip a year up the Ohio, the longest being to Cincinnati. Sometimes they would go from the Ohio River to up above the first set of locks on the Kentucky River.

The boat had a cabin with the steering wheel on the left and a booth-style table on the right. The table could be lowered to the level of the seats and thus provide a sleeping area big enough for the girls. Forward of this, one stepped down into a galley area. It had two bunks that Nancy and Earl used and a small kitchen with a stovetop and a refrigerator. Alan slept on the bench at the stern of the boat, and the head was in the bow. The *Nancy ABC* was not a particularly pretty boat, but it was made of steel and Earl felt it was safe.

One of Alan's enduring memories showed that Nancy and Earl remained in a loving relationship:

> Once we were out at night when the majority of the guests were teenagers. The young people were in the back of the boat and on the top of the cabin, while Mom and Dad were steering; the chair for the steering wheel was big enough for two small people to squeeze into it. Next thing you know, we were in the middle of the river with a barge searchlight on us. We were heading right for it. We had a good time kidding Dad and Mom about what they had been doing in the cabin rather than steering the boat.

And sometimes we block out those memories that are not as good. Carolyn once laughed and said that Alan did not remember all the times the boat was not working, when the engine wouldn't start or the bilge pump failed. Earl was notoriously bad at any handyman job (and left all house repairs to Nancy) and he was always more upset than was warranted when his rosy plans for a river cruise did not pan out.

Earl considered the hours he spent on the *Nancy ABC* to be his leisure time, and, besides the annual trip east, he was not at all interested in other vacations during those years. The couple had gone on one trip to Europe with the Jefferson County Medical Association in the late 1940s, but the only other trip they made while the children still lived at home was to Bermuda. In late May 1954, Earl phoned Nancy from his office and said that one of his patients was going to Bermuda on the maiden voyage of the Swedish American Line ship the *Kungsholm*. Did she want to go? With Nancy's wanderlust, there was no question. For dinners on board the vessel, Earl and Nancy were seated at table 72, and one evening Nancy rose to make a toast to Earl:

> This honeymoon is better than the first one—in a way.
> Just as filled with sunshine and surprises every day.
> Just as rough and smooth as the waves on which we ride.
> Darling, may my captain keep his first mate by his side.

FOURTEEN

COMMUNITY INVOLVEMENT

"CAN WE AFFORD TO COMPLAIN ABOUT MEDIOCRITY AND

CONFORMITY—AND TALK ABOUT EXCELLENCE—UNLESS WE

EXHIBIT AND DEMONSTRATE THIS EXCELLENCE?" (1953)

Earl's ambition during these years was to make a place for himself, and that included, as always, joining organizations. He became a member of the American Medical Association, the Kentucky Medical Association, and, as soon as he moved to Louisville, the Jefferson County Medical Society. He was soon admitted as a Fellow of the Southeastern Surgical Congress. He became a charter member of the Louisville Chamber of Commerce in 1950 (and eventually was named an Ambassador of Good Will of the City of Louisville). He also joined Kiwanis and the Masonic order. These were promising pathways to success, and he enjoyed his memberships.

Nancy's social and organizational activity began before Billy died, only to increase exponentially later. Because she never seemed to require much sleep, generally wanting no more than five hours, her roles as mother and wife left her with time to become involved. She had already moved quickly to find a church when she arrived in Louisville. She later recalled:

When we moved to Louisville, our next-door neighbor
Dorothy Dalton went to the First Christian Church, and
we went down there with her several Sundays. But Earl
didn't go to church, and it was a long way to take the kids.
I wanted to go to one nearer, so I started going to the
Crescent Hill Christian Church.

The fact that Earl didn't attend church was not a comment on
his faith. He knelt beside the bed to say his prayers every night of
his life, even on their honeymoon. If asked about attending church,
he would say that seeing his hospital patients was more important.
He did eventually join Crescent Hill Christian, but it was about
fifteen years after Nancy did. Nancy was a faithful attendee, perhaps
partially because she wanted to set an example for her children, but
also because her faith was important to her. Her involvement with
that church grew steadily, and it turned out to be her first step into
the community. Part of the Dewey mandate was the necessity for
community leadership, and Nancy began to build her influence in
her world at Crescent Hill.

The second group Nancy joined was the American Association
of University Women (AAUW). This organization had been
founded in 1881, and its purpose was to advocate for equity for
women, primarily in education and research, although it also
worked to assist women in finding careers. These goals appealed
strongly to Nancy, and she worked hard to attain them—directing
her attention towards enhancing educational opportunities not
only for women but also for children from poor backgrounds. Her
first job in Raleigh had been an eye-opening introduction to the
environment in which children from low-income urban families
had to struggle.

Next came the Crescent Hill Woman's Club (CHWC):

Everyone on our street was friendly and I quickly had
friends. Several of the women were members of the Crescent Hill Woman's Club. A member of the church, a Mrs.
Mamie Lamb, invited me to join. At that time, I had just
joined the American Association of University Women,

and I hadn't thought about joining another club, but I did. Shortly after that, this same Mamie Lamb asked me to join her literature group in the club, which was the most prestigious group there. I've always liked literature, and poetry is something I've liked to play with. At one point someone at CHWC asked me to turn in some of my poems for a statewide contest. Several of them were published.

Back when Nancy was spending her fall in London as the chaperone for the New College group, she had commented in her journal that she was turning her attention more and more to literature:

> *I wonder why I did not become literarily conscious when I was in college. And I don't wonder at all. I know why. I went through high school hating the subject because of one teacher I had, and so was determined to have no more than was necessary of the subject when in college. What a mistake it was and how much I have regretted it since graduation. These several years I have been conscientiously trying to make up for it and I seem to be making very slow progress.*

Nancy did make up for it, and not only through the literature groups. She and Earl became members of a Great Books group through the AAUW and continued their membership in that program for the rest of their lives. Nancy frequently reviewed the books being studied. She also became a writer and poet herself.

It was in the literature groups that Nancy made many of her closest friends, with Evelyn Wolford perhaps being her dearest. It is often said that one can count one's true friends throughout life on the fingers of one hand. Nancy had many true friends, many more than her fingers—and toes—could count. She had a grace that drew others to her, and her wit, intelligence, and loyalty enfolded them and made them want to be in her circle. But Lela Brown from her childhood, Bet Piner Lefler from her young adulthood, and Evelyn Wolford from the early 1950s on were those she held closest to her heart. It was Evelyn to whom she turned in her low moments; Evelyn who knew how upset she sometimes became with

Earl; Evelyn who stayed by her side in many of the organizational efforts in which she became involved; and Evelyn who held her hand when misfortune threatened. Nancy wrote a poem later that most probably was about her gratitude for Evelyn's friendship.

THANKS FOR A FRIEND

There is an ear that hears my voice
Though no word is spoken.
There is an eye that sees my heart
Though it be bright or broken.
There is a hand that feels my touch
Though I be far away.
There is a mind that understands
Though I have naught to say.

And God with love
Grants me this friend
In trust, that I may know
The joys and tears, the kindred fears
Of mankind, friend or stranger.
That I might seek and understand
His wonders in this mighty land—
And lend my heart,
My mind and strength
To righteous thoughts and wholesome deeds
To still the conflicts and the pleas
Of lonely souls—
That they might find, a friend like mine—
Whose ear and eye
And heart and hand
Reflects God's love for every man.

Nancy's artist's eye saw the world through a spiritual lens, and that perspective was the motivation for her commitment and dedication in all her public activities.

Nineteen fifty-two began a twenty-year period during which

Nancy dedicated much of her time to improving the lives of others. The core idea of her endeavors at New College was social progress, and it was to social progress that she turned her attention. Another of the primary groups through which she did this work was the Women's Auxiliary to the Jefferson County Medical Society. Her activities with that group became her first significant commitment towards creating a "creditable work product." While today the proportion of female physicians in the United States has risen to 36 percent, in 1950 just 6 percent were female. The wives of the male doctors had created their association in 1922, but their efforts were more in support of their fellow members than in contributing to society. Nancy soon sought to change that emphasis.

> Several of my friends who were doctors' wives had no use for the medical auxiliary in Louisville, but others were very enthusiastic. Mary Ulferts and Elizabeth Bowen were members, and they had become friends of mine. I think Elizabeth Bowen was the first one who asked me to do anything in the Auxiliary. I think she was the president at the time. The first committee assignment I had was So-cial. It wasn't long before I was asked to do all sorts of things. I met a lot of people, made a lot of friends, played bridge with a group of them. Some of my closest friends were from that beginning.
>
> Then, out of a clear blue sky, one day in 1953, the nom-inating committee of the Auxiliary called and asked me to run for president-elect. I practically fell over. Martha Bernhard was president when I became president-elect. We became very good friends, a lifelong friendship, and I had a good year and made a lot more friends. That year also was the first time I balked about something the medi-cal auxiliary was doing. Martha said "good for you" about what I'd said, and I replied that I didn't want any part of it and that I would resign if they didn't like my opposition.

Although the issue that caused Nancy's opposition was long forgotten when she relayed this memory, the remembrance of her friend's support remained strong. Membership in the Women's Auxiliary helped the couple establish themselves socially and Earl was to say later:

> My life outside of my medical practice—that is, my social life—has mostly revolved around Nancy. She has been active in many local, state, and national organizations and has a large coterie of friends. I have joined in the activities that occurred because of her life.

....

Volunteerism is frequently a direct service—from one individual either to another individual or for a charity. Nancy aimed higher, preferring to attack societal problems through focusing entire organizations on the issues. In 1954, her inaugural speech to the Auxiliary was predicated on her efforts to encourage the membership not only to acknowledge the relevance for themselves of the issues facing their world, or, as Dr. Alexander would have put it, the "persistent problems of living," but also to seek the knowledge and the skills needed to resolve them. The first four of the problems outlined at New College (adjusting to and cooperating with other people, maintaining physical and mental health, achieving economic and political security, and adjusting to and controlling the natural environment) figured in the direction she wanted to see the Auxiliary go during her tenure. In addition, the political nature and inspirational tone of many of her future speeches were forecast:

> Sometimes we face events or situations of a tragic, of a fortunate, or of an honorable nature without knowing why. If tragedy is our lot, we are fortunate indeed if we are able to analyze the situation, accept it, and rise above it. If good fortune is our lot, we enjoy our good fortune only to the extent that we share it with others. If honor is bestowed upon us, we merit that honor, as St. Paul so beautifully stated it, only to the degree that we prefer it in others. I am deeply grateful for the honor you have just bestowed upon

me, for the faith you have manifested in me, and I humbly and earnestly pray that I may be worthy of your trust.

As we begin our new year of auxiliary work and fellowship, I should like to see us broadening our vision, serving with knowledge and inspiration, and seeking to achieve our goals through educating ourselves on subjects relative to the medical profession and then disseminating this message of medical service to our community through positive action.

The natural course of events and trends of the times influence the thinking and action of individuals and groups. Those who possess or develop a keen insight evaluate the trends and capitalize on available opportunities. Those who do not drift along, accepting or rejecting what comes their way.

Nancy went on to set forth the challenges she saw for society in general and the Auxiliary in particular at that time:

First and perhaps most imminent is the fact that locally and nationally there is an accelerated increase in juvenile delinquency and adult mental illness. Both are basically health as well as sociological in nature. Second, there is the constant and growing demand on the part of the public for an expansion and extension of medical care and health facilities to our indigent populace. Third, there is a definite trend or demand for the acceleration of preventive medicine and that such measures or preventives may be made available for all people. Fourth, there is the ever-present threat of disaster that may result from natural causes such as tornadoes, floods, accidents, etc. as well as man-made threats from atomic or hydrogen explosions. Fifth, there are always present in every civilization many independent and related groups who are striving for mutual humanitarian achievements, but who suffer a certain amount of friction and discord. Such conditions create emotional conflicts that hamper the greatest possible achievement. Sixth, there is evident a desire on the part of every American to realize for every American the democracy outlined in our National Constitution. There is the cry that Civil Rights be extended to all people, that Americans overcome their prejudices and work cooperatively for mutual blessings and achievements.

Her conclusion referred back to the humility with which she sought to approach her term of office:

The above-listed natural causes, or trends or factors, have their medical or health implications and so have become some of the problems that challenge our thinking—our capacities for a broadened vision today. As we proceed through the year, let us be ever mindful, ready, and willing to assist and to cooperate with our parent organization. Let this continue to be primary with us. Also, let us approach each problem, each challenge that presents itself to us, with insight, with vision, with inspiration, and with an understanding heart. Individually and as a group we are democratic—we respect the right of every man or woman to seek to associate himself or herself with others who are seeking to promote the common good. If the tendering of such rights of association are requested of this group this year, I humbly pray that we may possess the vision, the intelligence, the courage, and the stamina to face such possible requests justly and righteously. May we listen sympathetically to the voiced expression of any or all of our entire membership, make our decisions wisely and democratically, and abide by such decisions with loyalty and good faith. And now as we adjourn this meeting, may we keep a vision before us, begin studying to show ourselves worthy of inspiration, and resolve to go forward cooperatively, harmoniously, cautiously, and with love and understanding in our hearts.

This is my Prayer.

Her speech was an ambitious motivational address. It was the first time in Louisville that she had gone on the record with her fundamental outlook. Until this point, Nancy had largely been a member of groups, but with this speech she set herself apart as a leader. Since she was speaking to the medical auxiliary, her points were tied to that perspective, but she would issue challenges with similar intent from many different platforms. She followed her presidency of the local medical auxiliary with presidency of the local chapter of the American Association of University Women. She then went on to be president of the state medical auxiliary and the state AAUW organization and then served on the national boards of each.

Because Nancy knew that what she was advocating was a fairly progressive viewpoint, she had to couch what she said in language that sounded conventional and in terms that would appeal to basic understandings of societal good. Furthermore, the idea that women could make a real difference was radical in mid-century *Father Knows Best* America. Urging women to think independently and, further, to do something in the public arena about the results of their thinking, was a gamble. In addition, Nancy had to be careful that she promoted rather than damaged her husband's career. In truth, she had no desire to cause controversy. Her social understandings were traditional: she believed in individual responsibility and, if assets were accumulated through proper conduct, she thought enjoyment of the resulting resources was appropriate.

What was more avant-garde in her philosophy was her genuine desire to enable all people to have the opportunity to make of themselves what they could without exigent circumstances holding them hostage. She was later to become somewhat more strident when she got tired of the lack of proactive behavior of her fellow members in the AAUW. At a regional AAUW meeting, the inclusion of black women in membership was discussed, but no action was taken. When she reported this to her local group, she said:

> When those who would lead take no stand, or present no
> original ideas, nor offer no new avenues of approach—

but repeat the usual shopworn patterns—yet talk about excellence, how can we rise above the mediocrity and conformity we vociferously decry? Can we afford to complain about mediocrity and conformity—and talk about excellence—unless we exhibit and demonstrate this excellence?

Nancy also joined the League of Women Voters, the Art Center Association, and The Arts Club of Louisville. When most people join an organization, they become members and perhaps eventually officers. Nancy fast-tracked. Within her first year in AAUW, she had assumed chairmanship of at least three committees. At Crescent Hill Christian Church, she was soon teaching the adult school, participating in Women's Day worship services, and periodically giving sermons; by 1955 she would also be on the board of directors. She was also heading up programs at The Arts Club. She had lived in Louisville for less than ten years, but she had become well enough known that she was being invited to give talks at various churches and meetings around town. There is a letter in her files from an assistant to Dr. Leland Miles of Hanover College in Indiana that indicates that Nancy had agreed to participate in a TV show called *Casing the Classics*, for which Dr. Miles was the moderator. It was on the local television station, WHAS, every week. There are directions for her participation, saying that the book to be discussed was *Babbitt* and that she and the others invited would be talking about the book. The show was recorded on November 25, 1953.

Before that year was out, Nancy was asked to be the Woman's Club president. She was not elected by one vote—her own—but she was relieved because she had already been asked to do something on the national stage of the Women's Auxiliary.

When you get to be president of leading organizations, your name gets to be known. Because I was president of the AAUW, I was asked to be on the board of the Louisville chapter of the American Cancer Society. I served on that board, then, on Elizabeth Bowen's recommendations, on the board of Norton Hospital for several years. It was while serving on Norton's board that I learned a lot about how these organizations get money. While I was serving, Children's Hospital and Norton's merged to become Norton's Children's Hospital, and we built a new facility. The people who ran things there expected me to give money, but, even more, they wrote and told me how much I was supposed to give. I was expected to give several thousand, and I ended up giving them about two thousand. I know this—you don't stay on those boards very long unless you give money.

In 1955, Nancy got involved in a project that was very surprising to her and turned out to be quite educational.

I was briefly involved in politics. I was president of either the local or state medical auxiliary or AAUW, and I guess I had a certain rating in the community. I got a call from Henry Heyburn, who was very prominent in Kentucky politics. He asked me if I would run on the Republican ticket for the state House of Representatives. I said thank you, that I was very flattered, but that I knew nothing about politics. He said that didn't make a difference. I told him I would consider it and call him back. We all talked about it, and decided it was a good experience, so I decided to do it.

I did all sorts of things that candidates do. I don't think we ever thought that I would win. I made speeches and

Nancy's business card while running for political office, 1955

traveled all over the state. The newspapers did cover us, even though I was certainly the "underdog." Once, we went out to Lakeland, the mental hospital; I saw all these young kids mixed up with the older ones and I had quite a reaction to the place. When we came back, all the newspaper people were there, and they wanted to know what I thought of my visit to Lakeland. I told them.

After the newspaper people left, someone on the committee came to me and said I shouldn't have expressed my opinion. I asked why and said that it seemed to me that was what I was supposed to be doing, letting the public know what I thought. He said the object was to get elected; then you could do what you wanted to do. I understood later that I missed being elected by only 100 votes. That was the year that Happy Chandler ran for governor and swept the state. It was remarkable that I came so close, but I'm glad I didn't get into politics.

Nancy and the children (Alan, Barbara, and Carolyn)
posing for a newspaper article about the 1956 election

Nancy also became president of the PTA at her children's junior high school during the 1957–58 school year.

> About the time I was getting involved in both the medical auxiliary and the AAUW, my three children were in junior high school. I seldom went to PTA meetings. I don't know why I ever got sucked into being president of the PTA at Barrett Junior High School, but I did serve. One of the programs that I helped start was a program to train the girls for babysitting in the daylight time. Gave the girls a chance to make spending money. The principal didn't want it, but the PTA put it over anyway. I thought making sure the school was up to date was the purpose of the PTA. We did put two or three other programs through that year. One was to get a kiln for the art department. Every one of the problem kids who were placed in the art class turned out better because of it.

Nancy's name and/or picture appeared in the newspaper on twenty-three occasions in the 1950s alone. These depicted her as the president, chair, leader, delegate, speaker, or hostess at various functions. Some had her pictured with prominent dignitaries; some mentioned notable public luminaries. Those items do not record the whole of Nancy's attendance at and involvement in events. Many events were either not deemed newsworthy, or the reporters simply didn't know about them. One such event was the Kentucky Governor's Conference on Education to which she was a delegate in 1956.

It was one of Nancy's gifts to form abiding friendships, and that resulted in her having colleagues in her efforts to address those issues that she felt needed reform. Nancy used every opportunity presented to promote the possibilities she could see on the horizon. She had written in her journal as far back as 1935:

> *Determination and faith and conscientious work have a lot to do with shaping our lives; how we handle or take advantage of fortunate experiences and succeed or don't succeed in shouldering*

*the responsibilities has a lot to do with life during the present and
also the future.*

She went from being a young woman who asked herself what road
to take, whose hands sometimes shook and who was embarrassed
to be in front of a group, to being a woman sure of her path and
quite adamant about methods for achieving success. She had found
her voice.

Yet even with her priorities of following her faith, raising
children, and volunteering with organizations, she still needed
more. While her schedule allowed limited time for pursuing her
art, she didn't give it up entirely. She became friends with several
women who liked to paint, and she would take the children with her
and accompany these ladies to the Louisville parks to capture the
scenery in charcoal and oil. She used half of the attic as her studio
and made several attempts to paint her children's portraits. She was
never satisfied, but her final effort depicts the three in their grade-
school years. Nancy also painted a portrait of a friend's children:
there is a letter from Bet Piner Lefler, in which Bet refers to the
amount of trouble Nancy is going to and offers to pay "for the
pictures if you will let me." Nancy also contributed her talent to
events in her organizations, and many of the displays and props for
programs demonstrated her distinctive artistry.

Still, Nancy found she had the energy to add yet another intellectual investigation. She took classes at the law school from 1959
to 1961.

> Several projects I worked on during those years resulted
> in my becoming interested in jurisprudence. I decided to
> go out to the University of Louisville and take a course in
> their law school. I got an A, and I thoroughly enjoyed it,
> so I took some more courses. However, at that time I was
> president at the state level of either the medical auxiliary
> or AAUW, and that involved a lot of traveling. It turned
> out that I missed a lot of my classes, so I decided to wait
> until after I stopped doing that kind of thing before I went
> back. But I never went back.

While Nancy was engaged with all these activities, Earl continued to pursue his medical practice, which grew quite large. Energy and ambition had always been common denominators for the couple, and he too found another outlet for his vitality. Ways of making money always attracted him, and he found a profitable side business when a patient came to him with the proposition that they become partners in real estate investing. A need for capital was probably behind the offer, but Earl knew that his patient was successful in the game and accepted the proposal. He later said:

> Most of the time we were purchasing second mortgages and, once in a while, third mortgages. Over time I bought about $20,000 worth of mortgages from him and found myself in that business.

Fortunately, this enterprise did accrue a profit, and Earl got a lot of pleasure from being involved. Nancy was not at all interested in real estate or this side business her husband enjoyed. She was, however, pleased that he was doing what he wanted to do. His involvement in the enterprise took a considerable amount of Earl's time, and Nancy needed time herself. The parallel efforts worked out for them both.

FIFTEEN

TEACHING SUNDAY SCHOOL

"IF WE DIE TO SELF-LOVE, CHARITY COMES ALIVE:

IF WE DIE TO PRIDE, WE RENDER SERVICE TO OTHERS:

IF WE DIE TO ANGER, LOVE COMES IN ITS STEAD." (LATE 1950s)

One of the seven "persistent problems of living" that Nancy had helped articulate at New College—searching for guiding principles and ultimate values, and acquiring and transmitting social heritage—occupied her time both in organization work and in another role she took on, that of teacher of an adult Sunday school class. While Nancy had never enjoyed being a classroom teacher for children, she enjoyed teaching adults. She found delving into exegetical work stimulating. She had been accustomed to preparing in depth for the units she helped construct in the Dewey system. Perhaps because of the nature of that experience, she was open to examining the possible meanings of the weekly Bible lessons. Her keen mind and artistic soul would notice more than what a simple look at a Bible commentary might reveal. She recalled:

> At one point a new class was being started, and Rev. Hutchings came to me and said that someone had strongly recommended me as a teacher. I took the class and taught

it for years. It was a small class for women, perhaps eight or ten of them. Later on, there was a couples class that a man there was teaching. One Sunday he couldn't teach—I don't remember why since he was there—and the classes were combined. After that morning, he wouldn't teach anymore. Years later, he and I were talking and he asked me if I wanted to know why he had quit. I looked at him, and he continued, "I was so plain jealous. You were so good I didn't want to teach anymore." It never dawned on me that anyone would be jealous of anything I did.

Nancy's children became accustomed to seeing her studying and writing at the dining room table. She spent hours poring over her Bible, concordance, dictionary, and other volumes that enhanced her study. In a talk at the Bethany Christian Church in 1963, she said:

> Each man's spiritual growth, his value, is measured according to the way he responds with what he has to the needs of his fellow man. Through men God's voice is spoken and heard. One does not need to be a Paul, or a Rhodes Scholar, or a genius to hear and interpret God's voice. One does need to sit at the feet of Jesus and listen to his voice of love.

While she didn't refer in any way to herself in a lesson she presented to her class in June 1955, the following excerpt does represent her understanding of a fulfilling life:

> When we review the lives of those we refer to as living most abundantly, in the sense that Christians generally interpret the meaning of the phrase, we find men and women who have sought or are seeking a definite goal. Many of these individuals apparently have determined the nature of their goal early in life, and so have spent most of their efforts in pursuit thereof. Even in their preparation we find such people living full rich lives and then, as they

have realized their goals, they have enriched the lives of others. We do know that many who do determine a definite goal and pursue it to fulfillment are persons known to live in close communion with their God.

One must first determine the nature of his goal before he can adequately prepare himself for pursuing it . . . and proper preparation is the keynote to all success. He who is well prepared has the eyes to see, the ears to hear, and is possessed with an understanding heart. How little we as individuals and perhaps likewise as a nation prepare ourselves for our greatest goal. Whatever our profession or station in life, our greatest goal is to love and serve God and our fellow man. All history teaches us that this can be accomplished best when man is in tune with God. While in communion with God, one is led, inspired, and empowered. Man does not get in tune with God without preparing himself for this harmony.

Fourteen of the Sunday school lessons she wrote for her adult classes have survived. She began each with an outline of the subject she would tackle, described what she thought the biblical passage said, and then discussed her conclusions. They are deeply considered ideas derived from the Scriptures. Some of her insights were original, some thought-provoking, and some surprising, but all were the product of profound reflection.

When she talked about Simon of Cyrene, who was the individual pulled from the sidelines to help Jesus carry his cross, she stated:

> The significant facts are: (1) That he could have been anyone, and (2) that he was just passing by. Just accidentally there. He was not seeking a chore. (3) That he was called or compelled to carry the cross. It is an interesting incident because it is so universal. Universal in that it just happened. Universal in that it was thrust upon him. Universal in the fact that real burdens are always thrust upon us; and, finally, universal in that once an individual accepts his burden and seeks to shoulder it, it becomes a joy.

On prayer, Nancy wrote:

> Honest praying is not our postscript at the close of day,
> nor the phrases we voice at the beginning of a meal, nor
> the recitations of saints cloistered behind garden walls,
> nor the cries of the sinner before an altar. It is the ex-
> pression of the secret yearning of the heart whenever and
> wherever one acutely feels or desires the presence of God.

When Nancy wrote about Paul's letters to the Corinthians and
his chapter on the unity of the followers of Jesus as one "body"
with all their gifts necessary for the maintenance of the whole, she
suggested that this extends to the whole human race:

> Man, collectively, is a body, baptized with one spirit. Jews,
> gentiles, blacks, whites, all are members of one body, one
> whole. Each group is a member. Each has its own func-
> tion. No one is more important than the other. The body,
> "mankind," could not function if it were all the same. Nei-
> ther can any one group cast aside, enslave, or coerce the
> other. The more feeble members of society may be the
> most necessary. The most uncomely may produce the most
> comely. In the body of mankind, there can be no schisms,
> for if one member (group) of society suffers, all suffer; if
> one member (group) is honored, all are honored. No one
> of these member groups of society should do the work of
> the other, whether these groups be races, professional, sci-
> entific groups, cultural, or what not. Neither should one
> group be jealous of another. Each member group must de-
> velop and use its gifts to the best advantage because of the
> joy in doing that for which it was created, that the whole
> body (society) may function joyfully and well.

When talking of Nicodemus's questions to Jesus, Nancy theorized:

> To be born again, one must already have been born once.
> Born again means to repeat the process. All life is a con-

tinual, repeating process. The same thing happens over and over again. But each time it reoccurs, it happens in a different way, and in a different environment, and the results of its happening vary. In our span of life, we experience love over and over again. Each time it is different. As children we love our parents—here the kingdom of our loving is of a certain type, in a certain environment, and because of it and its setting, we enjoy wonderful experiences. Then we grow into adolescence. Here we love all over again. A new world opens up. We are born anew. We see and experience and enter into a new kingdom. It is founded on the past, but entirely different. Then as we grow older, we find a mate, fall in love. Here again, we are born anew into a new kingdom. It is totally different from the old. Then again, if we don't love our mate anymore, we sometimes find another, but that is a new love also. Love born again. Different in environment, in how it happened, and in what it offers. Perhaps even later we know another love, the love of parenthood. And so, we are born again.

Until we are "born" into each of these kingdoms, we are unable to appreciate the joys of these kingdoms. As we are continually reborn in love, so it is with other phases of our living. We experience travel, over and over again, but each time it is different; even if we return to the same place on our vacation, something about it is different.

In another lesson she developed this thought:

Actually, on earth, in all instances of nature, and in all human experiences, when something dies, or we die to something, something new comes to life. If we die to self-love, charity comes alive; if we die to pride, we render service to others; if we die to anger, love comes in its stead. Death in nature is a beginning, a new birth. In character, the death of one type of personality is the beginning of another. We cannot separate life and death.

She went on in another lesson to comment on the "born again" nature of successful marriages during her discussion of the tensions between Paul, John Mark, and Barnabas.

Each of us fails. We accept obligations then find the obligations cost us more than we are willing to give. This is often true in marriages. Unlike Barnabas, self-interest enters in. We are so set, so strong in our convictions, so righteous in our own actions that we are ignorant and blind to the good qualities of others. . . . Our families suffer when we fail to sympathetically understand and appreciate a spouse. When we argue with one another, or separate, or isolate ourselves. When, because of our temperament, our differences in background, or our frustrated youthful dreams, we cease to communicate with one another. These failures affect others, particularly our children, in many ways. Sometimes our self-righteousness rejects all efforts of others to realize harmony and understanding. Sometimes it makes those around us, particularly youth, skeptical and unhappy. And we ourselves go into a shell, become frustrated, irritable, and even more prejudiced against someone we formerly loved.

Then again, sometimes a failure, when it is openly recognized, becomes a disciplinary medium. Then we, like Paul, need and seek help from friends. We learn to compromise on little things, to encourage each other to develop their own personalities and innate abilities, and to discourage our own tendencies to dominate. Failure, when properly viewed, may be the occasion for our greatest growth and achievement. When we face truthfully and objectively our own failures and recognize that we are not wholly righteous—that others have a worthy point of view—we ourselves mature. We find new awareness, new interests. Respect and sympathy for others broadens our own horizons—and we find a way to compromise. Then communication is re-established and the more significant objectives are more clearly viewed and sought.

Nancy taught the combined adult class at Crescent Hill Christian Church for over ten years. Towards the end of those years, she and the family moved and not only was she living farther away but most of her friends had moved on, and Nancy began to feel that going there did not make sense any longer. She joined Christ Methodist, which was much closer to her new home and seemed to be a better fit. The pastor there, a Dr. William Slider, could fill the pews with close to 200 people even on a hot, humid summer Sunday. His sermons were long—some even to the length of forty-five minutes—but they were so good that the radio station in Louisville eventually started broadcasting them. Nancy must have been delighted to have the opportunity of listening to an intelligent voice. She remained a member of Christ Methodist until after her daughters were married and her son had moved back to Louisville; Alan wanted his parents to join him and his family where they worshipped, so they did.

But by then Nancy had found that she was no longer interested in being involved in any church, and she continued to attend more because of Alan's wishes and Earl's willingness to go than for any enlightenment. She had arrived at a point where she believed that the ritualistic proscriptions and dictums of all the churches were detrimental to man's progress towards communion with God:

> We should not let the church as such rule but rather let the
> free spirit within the church rule.

She had embraced a spirituality that was an amalgam of her strict Protestant heritage, her continuous intellectual study, and her love of nature.

SIXTEEN

ROOM TO BREATHE

"SATISFACTION CARRIES WITH IT THE LONGING TO

PERPETUATE OUR PAST AND THE LONGING TO PROGRESS

TOWARD UTOPIAN SOCIAL, ECONOMIC, CULTURAL, AND

MORAL EQUALITY." (1960s)

The influence of surroundings on one's ability to be creative is demonstrated throughout literature and in our daily lives. While that is a fact, individual reaction to each distinctive environment varies across the spectrum. For Nancy, while living on Emery Road did not preclude imagination, inspiration, and the ability to be an effective advocate, being able to live in a more rural setting had always held appeal.

As their children became teenagers, Nancy and Earl often talked about finding a new home, one with more space. Emery Road had been ideal when the children were small but eventually felt cramped. The couple began to spend many weekends looking at property. Nancy wanted to live in the country; the city boy resisted that idea. Then, in mid-1958, Earl saw an ad in the paper for a house on Woodhill Valley Road. In less than two weeks, he signed the contract. Nancy related:

It sort of answered all our desires. We paid $50,000 for
it. Earl had the mortgage paid off in two years. I liked the
house, and the woods and the land were what I loved. I
was tickled to death. Of course, we all loved Riedlonn, but
the Daltons had already moved, and it was time. Moving
didn't bother me a bit. I was getting my wish of being in
the country.

Woodhill Valley Road was a new development of (eventually)
eleven homes just off Route 42, the main thoroughfare from Louisville to Cincinnati at the time. It was situated in Prospect, Kentucky,
about six miles east of Riedlonn. The house was at the end of the
road and was surrounded not only by the five-and-a-half acres
they bought but also by a twelve-acre park associated with the
development and by a huge estate that went all the way to the Ohio
River. Nancy recalled:

> That made it possible for us to have a horse. At one point
> we had two. The one we had the longest was Pal. I fell off
> Pal twice. The first time was when I was riding him and he
> went between two trees that were too close. I fell under the
> horse, but Pal kept still until I could get my wind back and
> get up. The other time was near Route 42 when the strap
> on the stirrup broke. I fell off and blacked out; I came to
> with men from cars that had stopped standing over me.
> But I wasn't hurt.

The house was situated halfway down a hill with a circular
driveway before the front door. On the left, a steep side hill dropped
off from a side patio. A lawn in the back of the house gently sloped
down to where an old barn sat. The property then sloped a bit
more before leveling out into a field. Little Goose Creek ran from
the estate on the right, along the back of the property line and to
one side of the park. Thus, the house was encircled on three sides
by the creek, but the water was far enough away and low enough
that there was no threat of flooding. The structure was mid-century
modern and appeared to be a small, single-story brick building

from the front, but from the back was clearly a good-sized two-story house, totaling about 3,800 square feet.

The front door opened to a generous hall that on the left led to one's choice of the dining room or living room. The living room had a large picture window looking out over the valley. Nancy spent many hours reading there, where she could glance up and be sustained by the beauty before her. The small dining room and kitchen were in the front, and this main living area also included a spacious enclosed sunroom off to the left. From the front hall to the right were two bedrooms, each with a bath.

The downstairs contained a large terrazzo-floored family room used for entertaining and later as Nancy's art studio. There were, in addition, two more bedrooms, a small bath, and the laundry and utility room. The garage was built into the right side of the home on the lower level. As with the garage on Emery Road, Earl eventually enclosed the space, this time making it into a poolroom.

The living room at Woodhill Valley was the perfect place for Earl's baby grand piano. Nancy's comments were in keeping with her typical logical approach:

Earl and Nancy in the kitchen at Woodhill Valley, 1961

I took music all through high school and could pick out any tune by ear, but I never learned the left hand. All three children took music. The way I looked at it was that it was right that they be exposed to it, learn to read music, know about it. But it was Earl who loved music. I don't think he missed a day playing the piano and then later the organ.

Gaining an appropriate place where he could indulge this avocation may have been an incentive for Earl in his purchase of the property. In addition, having Earl engaged in something he loved after dinner was helpful when Nancy wanted to delve into the subjects that interested her or when she became engrossed in writing.

Woodhill Valley also afforded Nancy a landscape that urged her to put pen to paper and brush to canvas. Her creative impulses were becoming more insistent. Finally, she once again had room to be outside and feed her spirit with God's natural world. The skies above Woodhill Valley bestowed frequent sightings of common crows and ravens; bright cardinals and finches flitted by; and the mockingbird's song imitated many of the native species. Hawks, owls, and bald eagles announced their breath-catching presence. There Nancy was surrounded by summer's muted roar of cicadas, the comforting ribbit of frogs at the creek, the certainty of sweat bees and hornets. Present were the earthy colors of the prickly sedge, the glow of the cheerful daisies against the dark foliage, and the ubiquitous goldenrod and ragweed.

Nancy loved to roam "her" valley, drawing sustenance from its pulsating life, and many days occasioned solitary meditative walks. She was as renewed by nature as she had been as a child. She had always enjoyed getting her hands in the soil and, with Earl not being very handy, took care of all the landscaping. She had a Gravely tractor that she rode to mow the acreage, and she once planted a sizable garden in the lower field (a venture she didn't repeat because of the extensive toil required).

A poem she wrote in 1960 takes its inspiration from this milieu:

ALL ARE ONE

I see twigs of tree tops
Swaying quietly—
Slowly, swiftly, stiffly
To the will of the winter wind.

I hear whispers murmur—
Whistle a weird, minor note
That lifts, and drifts my soul
In outer space.

I feel the warmth of a kindred spirit,
The caress of a pair of eyes.
They see through mine, a vague outline
Dividing and meshing earth and sky
Beyond the glass of our enclosure.

I sense a throb—
The drumming rhythm
Of universal life,
Where strife creates
Heat, motion, power.

I am one.
I am all that breathes
And leaves, in time
Slowly, swiftly, quietly—One signal accent
Tis the Will of the Master Mind.

....

When the family moved to Woodhill Valley, Nancy did not decrease
and may in fact have increased her community involvement since
the children were now teens and did not need her constant attention.
Nor did the move dampen her desire to effect positive change.

Nancy was still a woman who sought to invigorate her audiences towards new ways of looking at the world, both at her church and in her speeches for wider groups. Because she had accepted the presidencies of the state medical auxiliary and AAUW and had served on regional and national boards, she had the platforms she needed. This required a good deal of travel. Although Earl did not go with her, he was supportive of her commitments, even when they meant she had to be away. Records survive that indicate that in 1961 alone she traveled on organization business to Berea and Frankfort (Kentucky), New York City and Rochester (New York), Chicago, and Washington, DC. As vice president of the southern region for the national medical auxiliary in the early 1960s, she flew to Alabama, Georgia, Florida, Louisiana, Illinois, and California.

Nancy chaired so many meetings, ran so many groups, and gave so many speeches during the years of her committed public service that it was a good thing she had taught Barbara and Carolyn how to cook. Earl always expected his dinner on the table within a half hour of his arrival at home, even though he did not keep to a consistent schedule. Frequently, during the girls' high school years, Nancy would phone home and give them directions for starting dinner because she was held up at some event.

The following quote from one of her speeches provides an example of the earnestness and fervor she brought to her talks:

> Innately, man desires to progress. This desire is linked with our love and respect for our past. Because of this desire, which is linked with the past, we speculate and venture into the future . . . the unknown . . . looking not only for adventure, excitement, thrills, new horizons, but looking for satisfactions. Satisfaction carries with it the longing to perpetuate our past and the longing to progress toward utopian social, economic, cultural, and moral equality. One does not know satisfaction, except as his new ventures are applied to and absorbed into his past, emotionally, intellectually, culturally, or morally. One's present pleasures and attainments . . . those already realized or yet to be achieved . . . are without meaning unless they are known

and appreciated by, measured by, in terms of the past. One may attain fame in a new environment, but in his own mind, in his own egotistical world, he measures or evaluates his personal achievements by his past. One wants his family, his race, and his native land to share and approve his gains or recognitions. One has the desire to pass on to his closest kin the benefits of his achievements and to perpetuate among them his future, his memory, and his personality.

John Dewey and Tom Alexander would have listened to this speech with smiles and nods of agreement; searching for guiding principles and ultimate values and acquiring and transmitting social heritage were two of the principal challenges they had articulated.

Nancy did not restrict herself to philosophical thoughts. Her teaching, public speeches, and activities continually promoted her agendas. She fought for adequate public education for children, despising private education and its elitism. Her early training ensured she would focus much of her attention on this. In one of the speeches she gave, she said:

> All education should become moral and religious—the home, the school, the church, and the community must cooperate in promoting one great enterprise—the Kingdom of God. This kind of education, with free and equal opportunities for all, is an ideal very close to my heart. I do not wish to spend so much time on it here, but I am concerned with the present trends on the horizon—I refer to the present revival of denominational schools, the release-time programs—the reverting back to more private schools—all of which I am bitterly opposed to.

She was bitterly opposed to segregation as well and was a proponent of the civil rights movement, just gaining momentum in the late fifties. In another speech:

> I'm sure all of you are now following with a great deal of interest and possibly concern, the Supreme Court trials

concerning segregation in our schools. There is no moral ground for the policy of segregation in education. Segregation in our schools will eventually be ended. It will be the primary step toward eradication of segregation in all its forms, and a great step forward in realizing the brotherhood of man—not to mention the tremendous extension of human rights that will be a natural result.

As a child in the South, she had grown up observing the burden the Jim Crow laws had placed on the backs of black people and thoroughly detested all forms of bigotry and prejudice. In addition, she supported all activity that led to better services for the Native American population, she was in favor of the goals of unions (while appreciating management's perspective as well), and she was fierce in her fight to change what she saw as a dysfunctional justice system in its treatment of youth.

Before a statewide audience at an AAUW leadership conference during the 1960s, Nancy emphasized the concerns she thought should be the priorities for the organization's leaders. Her speech reflected the same aims she had developed during her years at New College:

> Dr. Millicent McIntosh, on the occasion of the ground-breaking ceremony for our AAUW Education Center said, "An educated woman thinks not of herself and what she deserves, but what she can give, what she has inherited, and how she may enlarge, improve, and expand that inheritance for younger generations."
>
> What are our special responsibilities, our obligations? We have inherited the knowledge and culture of the ages—we are obligated to preserve the best that we have inherited, to share this inheritance with all, and especially with those who are not so fortunate. We are responsible for using every talent we possess to further truth and righteousness. We are likewise obligated to seek to destroy the continuing evils that infest the society of which we are a part.

We owe our community, our state, and our county our service as our community is called to direct the peace and harmony of all mankind. We owe our neighbors and colleagues the liberty and freedom, the cooperation and sympathetic understanding that we enjoy—the helping hand that lifts the burdens of sorrow, misfortune, ignorance, and intolerance. We owe our neighbors and friends our faith and confidence in their ability to realize their own potentialities.

Because, as educated women, we have inherited these responsibilities, these obligations, we are concerned—concerned with social and economic problems; with the status of our cultural and educational institutions; with foreign affairs and international relations.

Nancy then listed specific current concerns and concluded by challenging the conferees:

Are you sufficiently concerned about any one? Will you become informed about your community needs? Will you accept your special responsibilities, take the initiative, seek the cooperation of others—to correct, to inspire, to promote and expand your inheritance? Are you prepared, as you undertake such action, to fulfill your obligations to your family, to continue to be a woman, a wife, a mother? Will you budget your time, lead a balanced life, preserve your feminine charms, and remain a sympathetic, understanding human being? If so, you will grow, and you will discharge your special responsibilities to society.

Nancy's reputation as one concerned about how matters were handled grew as the years passed and resulted in her being seen as an authority. She was, in fact, something of an authority on many subjects, but specifically she became one on rules. As a Registered Parliamentarian, she carried her small brown copy of *Robert's Rules of Order* with her, and she was often invited to meetings throughout the South simply to play that role.

Later on, when she was no longer as active, her reputation had the national AAUW board coming to her for help with their problems:

> One of my very good friends was president of the local AAUW chapter here a few years ago. She published something in the *Courier-Journal* that had something to do with the national AAUW's position that was not to the liking of the national board. They called on me to see what I could do. I went to my friend and told her that I'd been asked to straighten the issue out. She said that she thought I was the right person to deal with it. There ended up being a lawsuit between her and the national board. She lost. The national AAUW bylaws were changed because of the issue involved.

Other more nationally significant changes were emerging in the early 1960s. Setting aside the civil rights debate that was raging and about which Nancy had spoken publicly, something of a crisis had also begun developing in the health field. New medical discoveries and better nutrition had advanced individual life span, and many of the older population were poor. A movement to set up a health insurance program for those over sixty-five, eventually known as Medicare, was gaining traction. It began with what was considered a reasonable step: government health insurance for those with disabilities. The proposed congressional action to enable this met with opposition from physicians because it mandated that doctors decide who was eligible. They were afraid it would result in governmental interference in their private medical practices. Nancy related:

> Because of the times, the national AMA decided that it had to have a political arm and formed the American Medical Political Action Committee. Mrs. English, who was the national president of the AMA auxiliary, recommended me for membership on its first board, and I was the only woman. When I was asked, I made it very clear to Mrs.

English that I wasn't in favor of certain aspects of what was proposed. But I was told by the board that my part was to work on the education side—informing the public about issues that concerned the medical profession—not the political side. At that time the medical association was getting criticized heavily, and they wanted the auxiliary to get involved and promote the good things that the medical association was doing.

When I came on board with AMPAC, the AMA board asked me to give a speech, maybe because I was the sole woman. I wrote the speech and sent it to the AMPAC board. They sent it back without any changes. When I was making the speech in front of the national AMA board, everyone applauded. After the speech, one of the members of that board went up to the AMPAC board secretary and thanked him for writing the speech that I had just given. The secretary replied, "What do you mean? I approved the speech, but Mrs. Roles wrote every word of it."

Nancy continued to disapprove of PACs for the remainder of her life, and she was appalled at the money candidates accepted from interest groups. Her resignation was accepted at a meeting that the chairman had not been able to attend. He told her later that he would not have accepted her resignation had he been there because her input was so valuable. He was well aware of her opinion about political contributions but still wanted her participation. He made sure that she was honored for her contributions with not only a resolution in the minutes but also the presentation of a plaque.

Thirty years later, when Nancy was no longer an active participant in any of the medical organizations' work, she contributed once more to the national health debate. She had always told her children that there were areas in life where they could make a difference and areas where they could not; they should focus their work on what they *could* affect. Because of her background, Nancy felt that perhaps she could influence one issue before the nation. In May of 1993, Hillary Clinton was pursuing a mandate for nationalized health care, and Nancy agreed with it. However, she had her own plan for how to proceed and wrote Mrs. Clinton to tell her how it should be done:

> We are willing to pay for a full coverage program for every citizen so long as every citizen shares and shares alike respecting the services; provided that they are attainable to all and the cost is born by every citizen. This can be accomplished by levying a one-cent national sales tax on every dollar spent per day (one cent on one dollar, two cents on two dollars, etc.—no fractional tax).
>
> The one cent per dollar spent per day allows for no exemptions on anything. A dollar spent is a penny made for health. . . . The more a citizen spends per day, the more he/she pays for health. At such a low rate, no one suffers and no individual or group is discriminated against.

Nancy estimated a yield of one hundred sixty-eight odd billion dollars per year. Hillary did not reply to Nancy's letter, and the issue of a national health system versus private institutional health support continues to plague society. The problem with Nancy's solution was that the government would not likely leave that amount of money in a special fund for health care any more than they had left the social security system funds alone in the past. However, Nancy was forever optimistic and forever seeking ways to better society's outlook; she continued to be a classic progressive her entire life.

....

While Nancy was considered an enjoyable and lively person with whom to associate, she had long since given up being reticent if she disagreed with what was happening. Her strongly voiced opinions about the tactics of the AMA were not the only incidents when she followed what she believed to be right even when there was opposition. On several occasions there were those who became angry. Her friend Evelyn considered Nancy to be a feisty woman, although not difficult, and once said:

Nancy would sound off at the conventions of these organizations, whether she was in favor of or against the resolution being discussed, and she always had good reasons for what she said. But you don't make yourself popular by giving good reasons for or against things when others are on the other side.

Nancy remembered the reaction to one of her speeches vividly:

> At one of the meetings of the national AMA group, I made a speech. It was usually my custom to send a copy of my speeches to headquarters and sometimes they would write back with comments. In regard to this particular speech, they wrote back and said they were delighted. No changes offered. I made the speech. But the response was peculiar. No one came up to me and said anything about it.
>
> After the meeting, I went on and caught my plane. A woman from another state who had been at the meeting was sitting with me. She said something about the speech and wanted to know how I felt about the reaction. I said that I felt they apparently didn't like it. She said that was why she asked. She wanted to tell me why the reaction had been so peculiar. "The reason is we were all so jealous we couldn't see straight. We just knew that what you said was true and we couldn't say it."
>
> Two or three weeks later I got a letter from a member of one of the local auxiliaries in that state. The woman who wrote said that I probably noticed that no one came up to talk to me. She said she wanted me to know that they weren't interested in what I had to say, didn't want to hear it, and that if I wanted to get very far in the Auxiliary, I had better change my tune. Of course, I remembered what the woman on the plane had said.

Another incident taught Nancy how the workings of organizations could sometimes be skewed inappropriately:

There was a lady from Ohio who had been asked to run for president of the national auxiliary and had accepted the nomination. I was on the national board at the time, and I found out that there were several on the national board who disliked her. These women came to me to ask me to run against her, but I wouldn't do it. Somewhere along there, all of us were at a meeting and when the minutes were read, they weren't correct. The particular paragraph had to do with candidates for national office. I got up and said that wasn't the way I remembered it. No one supported me. Then they passed the uncorrected minutes. After the meeting, one of the board members came and apologized to me. She said she knew the minutes weren't correct, but they made it harder for the woman from Ohio to be elected, and the group of them simply couldn't sit by and see her elected president. She won it anyway and I was delighted. I hate to see things like that happen.

At other points, Nancy had to confront officers of the AAUW.

I did serve as president of the state AAUW, but I couldn't get along with the AAUW regional vice president. I figured that I was president of the state and I ran it, but she tried to run the state and I wouldn't put up with it. Our concepts of what the regional vice president did were very different.

The regional convention was held here in Louisville and I had a lot to do with it. When the time came to collect the money, she wouldn't give the state what it had spent. We had it out. In the meantime, a lot of trouble was going on in the national AAUW. I didn't like it at all. I wrote to the president and told her what was going on at the state and regional levels and that I thought the bylaws needed to be changed. I never heard from her.

The next year we were having a meeting at Ashland—I was still president—and, as usual, a figure from the national board came. I invited her to stay with me over the weekend and I took her to the meeting. Evelyn Wolford and Carolyn Rosenkrans were with us in the car, and I was driving. The two in the back seat got into a discussion on what was happening at national. The national representative said that they needed someone on the grassroots level to get concerned. I told her that that didn't do any good. She asked why, and I told her I had written the national organization about everything that was happening that I felt needed changing and had never heard back. She said, "Little do you know." Apparently, every member of the national board had received a copy of that letter and had spent hours discussing it.

After her visit, she went back to the national and repeated what I'd said about it not doing any good to write to national. Then they wrote me and asked my thoughts. They ended up restructuring the whole organization. At the next national convention, the restructuring—a lot like I suggested—did get passed.

Nancy was asked to be the chairwoman of the "restructuring" committee, and she said much later that having rewritten the national bylaws of the AAUW was one of the community service accomplishments with which she was the most satisfied.

She was also very proud of one of the local AAUW projects she chaired:

> At one of the AAUW conventions the question came up about how few women went on to get their PhDs in comparison to the number of men in doctoral programs. The gist of the comment seemed to be that there wasn't money for women candidates. I remarked that it seemed to me that every time something came up like this, all the group did was ask for money, but that, in my opinion, not too many women applied. The more I thought about it, the more I decided to find out if women did apply and didn't get accepted because they were women, which I didn't believe. So I decided I was going to send a letter to every

outstanding university or highly recognized college and ask
them—percentages, et cetera. My question was: Do you
discriminate against women? The answer came back: They
don't apply; we'd be happy to give more women scholar-
ships if they applied, so naturally it does all go to men.

As a result, I wrote up the survey and gave my opinion
and, of course, the local AAUW accepted it. I then presented it to a state meeting. When I got through, the state
wanted to approve the entire thing. We went ahead on our
own and sent copies to a lot of people. The thing was sent
to the national board to see what they thought about it.
They wrote back and gave me $1,000 to have it reprinted
and sent to every state university.

The written conclusions criticized the lack of opportunities awaiting
women after graduation in contrast to those of men. It also set forth
the obstacles that she and her committee had found women faced
throughout their schooling.

Perhaps because of that report, Nancy was nominated for appointment to the Commonwealth of Kentucky Board of Education. That nomination was also quite possibly because she had been
included in *Personalities of the South*, one of the "list" books that give
the vitae of famous people. It was not a vanity publication, as many
are, but had a good reputation as a Southern "Who's Who."

Fortunately, Nancy's intelligence and personal charisma were
equal to the challenges she faced. In 1961, the local AAUW
named their contribution to the national scholarship fund in her
honor—the first time that the fund contribution had been named
for anyone. Part of that choice may also have been because the
fund had been set up to encourage interest in college among
Southern women, and Nancy was a Southerner. The nomination
included the comments that "Nancy combines a really staggering
schedule of outside activities with a full complement of duties for
husband, three children and home. And she does it all with the
charm and aplomb of the true Southerner. . . . Nancy Roles has
been enthusiastically accomplishing things ever since her youth in
North Carolina."

At that time, Nancy was on the boards of directors of The Arts Club (and chairing the Beaux Arts Committee), the Kentucky Cancer Society, and the Crescent Hill Woman's Club; was still teaching at the church; and was attending law school. In November 1960, she and Earl also allowed their house to be shown on the CHWC "Merry Christmas Tour," and it was featured in the newspaper with a descriptive write-up. They had been in the house for just two years, but Earl had permitted Nancy to have the living room decorated professionally and he was very proud.

Nancy clearly was not idle, but she seemingly had the time to become involved in politics again. As a candidate, she had gotten to know Thruston Morton, who served three terms in the US House of Representatives, was Assistant Secretary of State for Congressional Relations in the Eisenhower administration, and then was elected to be one of Kentucky's US Senators in 1956. When he ran for re-election in 1962, she co-chaired a group called Kentuckians for Morton.

Nancy seemed to have enough going on in her life that it truly was chock-full. Late one night, she penned the following:

PULSE

Time—we measure and set
   But the darkness of the elements
   And the whims of humankind
Regulate the rhythms
   Of our movements and our minds.
Speed—we seek and value
   But the clocking of the pace
   And the visions of the goals
Temper the advances
   That shape our earthly mold.
Love—we feel and ponder
   Her enigmatic charms alert the soul
   All wisdom and beauty vibrating
Man's destiny eternal—
   God's timeless creating.

Was Nancy feeling the press of her activities? She was impatient to see her agendas making progress, and she wanted to paint. Indeed, time seemed to be as fast-tracked as she had always been. She was comfortable being that busy, however. Her friend Evelyn once said that she thought Nancy was happiest when she was running her meetings. As busy as she was, she never had time for gossip (and detested it) and she was never personally critical. She was consistently positive in her approach, a person who could be trusted to hear what you said with a sympathetic heart. Her children saw her as a cheerful person who enjoyed her life and did not hover over them. Earl practically idolized his wife, although he was careful not to let her think she had any upper hand. Her friends enjoyed her pluck and vim. When Nancy was asked, she said she was just "having a lot of fun."

SEVENTEEN

FAMILY FIRST AND FOREMOST

"WE ARE RESPONSIBLE FOR USING EVERY TALENT WE POSSESS

TO FURTHER TRUTH AND RIGHTEOUSNESS." (1960s)

By the summer of 1962 Alan was back in Louisville after his sophomore year at Florida State University, Barbara was off for two months touring Europe before starting her first year at Randolph-Macon Woman's College, and Carolyn was a rising high school senior. The children were growing up. Their attitudes were being formed and they were voicing their opinions more strongly. The Roles family dinner discussions became wide ranging and animated. When Barbara returned from France and invited a young Frenchman she had dated to the house for dinner, he was surprised at how lively the conversation became. He was even more astounded at how civil the environment remained and how even delicate subjects were permitted and addressed. Nancy and Earl had both learned how to guide the dialogue so that arguments did not escalate into attacks. Nancy, in particular, had mastered the art of asking pertinent questions that would return the debate to the subject's essentials. She had also learned how to avoid voicing judgments so that her children would not feel she was criticizing them. They might learn her opinion later, but always in a different context, when their own ideas were not a part of the conversation.

Nancy missed her son and elder daughter, although they wrote letters regularly so she could keep up with some of what they were doing. In 1963, she saw the last of her children off to college at Miami of Ohio. She and Earl then began a period of visiting their kids for different parents' weekends at the respective institutions. Alan graduated from Florida State in 1964 and started law school at the University of Kentucky. Carolyn joined him at U of K the following year.

Further, Nancy and Earl began noticing that their daughters were making connections with partners of the opposite sex who might become important in their own lives. Barbara had, by this time, met her future husband, Wink McKinnon, and Nancy and Earl entertained him at Thanksgiving that year and for the Derby the following year. At Christmas 1965, Barbara came home with a ring on her finger. Since Barbara had one more semester before her college graduation and it was the custom of the era that the bride's mother handled wedding arrangements, Nancy had plenty to do and drew back from activity in her plethora of organizations. Barbara's wedding was a sizable affair, with almost three hundred guests and five pre-wedding showers. The size of Barbara's wedding was exceeded the following year when Carolyn married Kent Thomas, a Louisvillian she'd met at the U of K. Those of Nancy's friends who had not been able to throw showers or parties during the previous celebration rushed to get Nancy's permission to be involved. According to Nancy:

> I know this: I fully expected all my children to go through college and then get married. I know that we said that if any of them got married before college, we would not pay for college. I did expect all of them to meet the person they would marry while they were there. Barbara and Carolyn both did. Barbara was married a few weeks after she graduated, and Carolyn did the same. I know that Earl didn't mind putting out the money for the weddings. He was awfully proud. Alan married the following sum-

mer. I know that I wasn't like other mothers, crying and such when my children left home for college and then to begin their married lives. I was happy for them. My point was, that is what they *should* do.

In addition to Nancy's public life and her involvement with family, she and Earl maintained a fairly heavy social schedule. Entertaining had always been a part of their life in Louisville. According to Carolyn:

> I can't remember the names of any famous people they knew, but there were times at Riedlonn, with some frequency, that there seemed to be someone who would come to dinner who was from out of town—maybe new patients of Dad's, maybe through Mom's work. I remember our having black people from Africa and a woman in a sari with the red dot.

After the move to Woodhill Valley Nancy continued to entertain both local friends and out-of-town visitors. Cocktail parties were in vogue and the couple would throw at least one a year. Smaller dinner parties were held more often; card tables for these fêtes were brought out from the closets and covered with the appropriate linens. Earl was always happy to host these functions, and they served the purpose of repaying the hospitality of others as well as cementing friendships.

....

From 1962 until after 1968 Nancy had additional domestic involvements that required her close attention. Earl suddenly "came down with" hay fever. Never before and only twice thereafter was he affected, but he was miserable and sat in his chair in the bedroom much of the time because that was the only room that was air-conditioned. Doctors have a reputation for being the very worst patients, borne out in this instance, and catering to Earl was a time-consuming job.

She was also managing arrangements for her aging mother:

> By the 1960s, Mama was dividing her time between her
> house in Greenville and coming for visits to me and to
> Mattie. She stayed longer at Mattie's, but I think that was
> because she was more of a help to Mattie. Mama wouldn't
> stay at anyone's house without paying. I wouldn't let her
> pay per month, but she did pay for things for me. Half
> the time she'd put her social security check in my account.

By the fall of 1965, Nancy's mother was living at Woodhill Valley
almost full time, so she had to be home more or take her mother
with her wherever she went.

Nannie Evans's health got worse during the year after Carolyn's
wedding. One morning in November 1967, she accidentally set
fire to her breakfast. Nancy recalled the following day as a turning
point:

> Earl and I were fixing breakfast and I heard her scream.
> I ran in and she was standing next to the desk and she
> was screaming, "Call the fire department, the house is on
> fire." I had a hard time convincing her it wasn't. When I
> finally got her out of the room, she shuffled. I took her to
> the sunporch to have breakfast with us. When she ate, she
> saw only half of her breakfast and she cleaned only half
> of the plate. Earl said that she had had a stroke. I walked
> her around and around and around. She could still talk
> but the stroke had affected her mind. That went on for
> almost a year, but it went from bad to worse.
>
> The first thing the doctors did was to give her tranquil-
> izers. They made her holler and tear at her clothes. It was
> the most pitiful thing I've ever seen in my life. Lord knows,
> if I have a stroke, let me go. In Mama's case, it wasn't that
> way. She just gradually went. Good thing she didn't know;
> she didn't want to be dependent on any of her children.
> I'm awfully glad it happened in my house. When Mama
> got sick, I resigned from the national groups and dropped

most everything. I stayed at home and helped Mama, and I'm glad I did.

Of all the influences in her life, none exceeded the high opinion and respect Nancy had for her mother. In reflecting on the situation, Nancy wrote perhaps her most cherished and praised poem. It was titled "Ninety-One." The poem was read before a large audience at The Arts Club and apparently a third of those present ended up in tears. It was later included in The Arts Club's published volume, *Spots of Time*. To be chosen, the poem had to be selected by a committee of three university professors from three different schools in three other states.

NINETY-ONE

The aged speak—
WORDS—parrot-like
through day's darkness
and night's blazing hell.

They sing—
hymns and nursery rhymes.
With strained throats
    they shout
    poems of youth's delight
    Then whispers command a reverent mood:
    scripture is reviewed,
And reason, lately slipped away,
peeps in—a latent game to play,
'Til darkness wins.

They die—a thousand times—
to live again
soul's earthly span.
They curse, scorn their fate.
Damnation preached to childhood's ears
Summons new its devils.

They pray—Our Father Who Art . . .
loudly, softly, beseechingly.
In despair they calmly say
Now I lay me
Then scream.

SOMEBODY LOVE ME.

Two other poems by Nancy were probably written about this time on the same theme: "Moments" and "Wandering."

MOMENTS

The wheels of a clock are many
Small, large, medium—and flat.
They all turn.
Some whirl, some are lazy, some scarcely move.
They make the hands go round.
Seconds tick, minutes pass, hours change.
It is a day.

The days of the past are myriad
Dull, bright, hazy—and long.
They are gone.
Some flew, some flew by, others lingered.
They formed the present mood.
Fears shout, spirits sleep, thoughts explode.
What is tomorrow?

WANDERING

As a child
I walked alone—
Many long walks
The snow was wet
But not so cold
As fear that reigns
When thought and reason
Freeze the heart and hand of men.

The lonely strolls
Were silent nights—
Many stars twinkled.
The paths were long
But never straight
As rules that bind
When mind and soul explore
The love and joy of freedom.

In timeless space
I roamed the fields—
Many worlds faded.
The sun was bright
But seldom warm
As sparks that light
When pride and greed confuse
The end and dream of being.

One other of Nancy's poems that was written around this time showed a more positive emotion. "Amid the Beauty" won second prize for poetry in The Arts Club competition and then, revised, was later included in *Spots of Time*.

AMID THE BEAUTY

When grey green earth reflects
In dawning light
Exotic glows—not seen but known—
My soul leaps out
And in the silent atmosphere
Is warmed and stirred.
No language speaks
No brush portrays my mood;
A dream, vibrant and unbounded.
Soft morning vapors
Gently kiss blushing leaves
Sparkling on crested waves
Lately blown from icy climes
To cradle autumn's glory.
In space, encompassed,
The rhythmic swirl
Transforms identity.
Against the azure sky
Sentinel branches form a web
And I conceive a pattern
Newly born.
No conflict here!
Each falling leaf quietly lays its treasure.
Earth waits
'Til mind exploits.
Posterity inherits the merits
Of man's divine reunion—
And seeks anew
The glory of His kingdom.

....

While Nancy was taking care of Nannie, Alan graduated from the University of Kentucky Law School and became a US Marine. He took the bar exam in the summer of 1967 and passed it on the first attempt, which enabled him to be a part of the Judge Advocate General's Corps (JAG Corps) as a second lieutenant. He met his future wife, Pat Blair, while stationed near Washington, DC, and they married in August 1968.

Barely two months after Alan's wedding Nancy's first grandchild, Barbara and Wink's son, James, was born. The new grandmother spent time at Barbara's assisting the new mother but then started campaigning for the young family to come visit in Louisville. Nancy wanted her own mother, who was still conscious although not terribly alert, to see and bless her great-grandchild. Barbara managed this at Christmas, and Nannie Evans died three weeks later.

Nannie's children initially kept her home in Greenville since it was rented out and income-producing. Nancy's brother, Bill, lived in Greensboro at that time, so he managed it. When he no longer wanted the responsibility, the home was sold. It eventually became the property of the college, now called East Carolina University, and is used for student housing. The farm continued to be leased to local farmers until 1995 when Alan handled its sale.

Whether it was the result of having to care for her mother physically, or her working in the yard on her beloved Gravely tractor, or her travels to the northeast, or her usual pace, Nancy had to have hernia repair surgery in February 1969. She was 61. She had already dealt with a broken arm the previous year and this subsequent surgery did not keep her down long. In late March, Nancy and Earl went to Barbara's for their grandson's christening and returned to Louisville after a stop at Alan's home. They were soon back East because Earl's mother, Eva Roles, after complaining of shortness of breath for only one day, died of congestive heart failure on May 23.

The household at Woodhill Valley was active in the 1970s and 1980s through visits at least once a year from Mattie and the frequent comings and goings of Barbara and Carolyn and their families. Barbara had three children, James, Sarah, and Robert. Carolyn, who had divorced and remarried, was soon to have two, Sam and Allison. With Alan's two, Rob and Elizabeth, Nancy and Earl had seven grandchildren. Nancy made herself available to babysit whenever she could; there were several times when she took the young ones to meetings with her because she would never say she was unavailable when asked. Nancy and Earl might have been "empty nesters," but they were seldom alone. When Barbara and her husband took their yearly fishing vacation in Canada, Nancy kept their children. Since Alan's kids lived nearby, they came out to Woodhill Valley almost daily during those visits. One summer Barbara's son Robert stayed for a full six weeks.

These summers were a pure pleasure for Nancy. The kids called their summer visits at Woodhill Valley "Grandmother's Camp," and they loved their vacations with her. While "camp" was in session, Nancy had as many young people as her friends could provide come out to Woodhill Valley, and she entertained them all. She took them for rides in the cart behind the tractor; supervised projects in the garden; roamed the woods with them (and the dogs); painted them playing in the creek; took them on horseback rides; did arts and crafts activities; and took them to the pool. When she had just Robert McKinnon for the day, she would teach him about art:

> If I took Robert out to the museum in Louisville, he would always go to the sculpture room. So I gave him a set of sculpture tools and balsa wood and we had a good time working in wood. Barbara did get a little upset, however, when she found out I had given Robert dangerous tools.

Nancy would also take the children to the grocery store with her and let them put any package of cookies they wanted into the cart.

Later, when the family celebrated one of Nancy's milestone birthdays, granddaughter Allison wrote and delivered a beautiful poem describing how each of the grandchildren felt that he or she was the "favorite." In many families, there are rivalries between offspring. Not only was there never a question of favoritism in the minds of Alan, Barbara, and Carolyn, but none of the seven grand-children felt any rivalry either. They each felt a closeness to their grandmother that was so warmed by her generous spirit that they could only smile with recognition as Allison detailed how Grand-mother Roles supported and affirmed their individual personalities. Nancy may have hated teaching in a classroom, but her study of educational theory had taught her how to engage children, foster their relationships, and empower them to grow independent and confident.

EIGHTEEN

TO INTERPRET AND CREATE

"WHEN IT WAS FINISHED, HE DIDN'T WANT TO

LET THEM HAVE IT." (LATE 1980s)

It was time for Nancy to follow her heart and fulfill, in a manner discernible to the eye, the last of Dr. Alexander's "persistent problems of living," that of "interpreting and creating art and beauty."

Art truly was a passion for Nancy. She had played at sketching and painting all her life. By 1967, she was ready to devote serious time to learning her craft. That July, she and another member had an exhibition at The Arts Club that made the newspaper. During the next decade Nancy was a featured artist at The Arts Club, the Crit Club (part of the Art Center Association), and at the local colleges. She won award after award. Five of her works were hung in a single Crit Club exhibit one year. One of her works caused the *Courier-Journal* art reporter to write, "A bright, moist-seeming abstract landscape by Nancy Roles, 'Fossil Lake,' was the winner of the first award." This was in 1968 before she began taking classes.

She studied at the University of Louisville School of Fine Arts with Charles Wright. She went on to take classes at Jefferson Community College where one of her professors was Lennox Allen. As she studied under them and several other professors, she expanded her repertoire to include not just charcoal and oil-based (later acrylic-based) landscapes, but pen-and-inks, collages, and watercolors. The artist's outlook that she had retained and sustained from her youth was finally finding expression not just in her poetry but also in the creation of works on canvas and paper.

It has been said that a true poem draws the reader through the poem into his or her own personal experience; Nancy's poetry and art exhibited that quality. The art trends of the twentieth century—Fauvism, Cubism, Surrealism, Pop Art—may have met that criterion for some. Nancy's goal in her art was to bring order out of chaos, to create a timeless atmosphere that invited the viewer to contemplation, one that might lead towards a sense of peace.

She could best be described as primarily a plein air landscape painter and was influenced more by the great artists of the Renaissance than by the modernists. She dipped her toe into the pool of abstract art successfully as well, though that didn't please her as much. When one looks at the works of Giorgio de Chirico, considered by many to be the godfather of Surrealism, and places Nancy's "modern" pieces next to his, the resemblance in theme, mathematical precision, and ability is evident. Even Nancy's more avant-garde works, however, retained a sense of enigmatic and spiritual power. When she turned from oil to watercolor, she tended towards the Georgia O'Keeffe school, as many who have seen her paintings of flowers have observed.

Nancy was dedicated to her art. She once recalled:

> Mama gave me a box of family materials late in her life and I made a collage out of some of it. One of the items in the collage was a stamp. Later, I learned that the stamp was very valuable, but I didn't take it out of the collage.

She would get so caught up in the artistic realm that hours would pass without her being aware of the time. Earl learned to go to bed alone at night when she was painting because it might be three in the morning before she came out of her spell. Her explanation:

I'm kind of a night owl. I don't mind staying up all night and working. It's quiet, with no phone calls or anything else to distract.

Nancy's children and close relatives eventually owned approximately 160 of her works, accounting for only a small fraction of her finished pieces.

In 1977, The Arts Club awarded Nancy the Bernheim Memorial Competition Award for Excellence, recognizing her contributions to the club and her talent as an artist. She later shared:

> While all that was going on, I had a lot of private exhibits—at the Women's Club, the St. Matthew's Women's Club, et cetera. There was a show down in Owensboro where I won the $750 prize one year, and that painting is now hanging in its county courthouse. It is called Tied Up. I won some prizes for work at the Jefferson Community College during the time I took courses there, and some of my paintings were bought by the University of Louisville from different shows I was in. The first piece that I ever won a prize for was a collage.
>
> Grady Roundtree, the head of the U of L Medical School, came to me to do his portrait. The school wanted a picture of him for their library. He came out and sat for it. Then, when it was finished, he didn't want to let them have it, and he kept it at his home for a whole year. Then he went down and had a photographer make a picture of it for himself before he gave the portrait to the school. Of course, he was forever being honored, and whenever they were naming some hall or building for him, the honoring group would try to get that portrait. After Grady died, one of the organizations did get the photograph he had had made, but the painting I did stays in the medical school library.
>
> At some point, Carolyn gave me a box entitled "Nancy's Creations." I was to photograph everything I had done and write the work's name and history on the back. I have

done so, but I have too many pictures of my work and
need a bigger box. There are fewer than 1,000 finished
paintings, but I have a lot of original sketches and a lot of
the time I made four or five paintings on the same subject
until I got what I wanted, so that makes the number even
higher. I still have one of the very first pieces I did. It is
a charcoal of a swamp that I did when I was teaching in
Raleigh. I've always loved it, and it is the very first piece
that I put in a frame. It was done before I ever had any
training at all.

Nancy probably "finished," in the sense that they could be framed
and hung, over 2,000 and maybe closer to 3,000 works; because
she gave many away, the number cannot be determined. Perhaps
because she was so prolific and spent from the mid-1960s to the
1990s devoting much of her time to her painting, she also learned
how to mat and frame her work. The cost of framing was high, and
her frames were not good ones, but she became quite an expert in
matting.

In addition to the Roundtree portrait, she listed under "Works
Hung" the cover design of *Confederate Cross Roads*, a book by Frank
Rankin; a portrait of Leah Wolford (her friend Evelyn's mother-in-
law) in the permanent collection of Franklin College in Franklin,
Indiana; a pencil drawing in the permanent collection of Jefferson
Community College; a seascape at Cotswold Industries in New
York City; and a painting hung at Connell, Foley and Geiser law
firm in Newark. She was modest; several of her works are also
hung in bank lobbies and at insurance companies. That does not
cover the number of paintings hung in private homes, nor does
it encompass her one-woman shows and the exhibitions in which
she participated. Later on, Colonel Sanders, of Kentucky Fried
Chicken fame, asked her to do a painting of his childhood home.
Colonel Sanders saw the initial watercolor sketches and selected
the one he preferred, but he died before the final acrylic painting
was complete. The painting now hangs in the Louisville museum
devoted to that company's history. At one point in 1973, a young
man in town came to her saying that an historic stone house built in

1785 by Patrick Henry's sister was in danger of being demolished. He wondered if Nancy would do a pen-and-ink of it. He would, he said, have it reproduced and sell copies to raise money for historic preservation in Louisville. She did so, and all her children have prints of *Eight Mile House*. It is unknown how much money was raised, but the prints were sold and became a part of Louisville's heritage of art and history.

Nancy's interest in art also included the promotion of art in Louisville. For her, advocacy of community-wide artistic engagement was not only a vehicle for bringing people together and including them in the narrative of society's complex ensemble but also a means of bringing order out of chaos and peace out of fraction. Her membership in The Arts Club and the leadership positions she took there had not only contributed to the club's prestige but had also assisted in the survival of visual arts as a force in the community. Still, she saw a need for a more significant commitment. As she had done in all her years serving in medical and educational organizations, she addressed the situation and pushed The Arts Club to become proactive in the broader field of visual arts in Louisville:

> Time went on, and several of the prominent people died. After about ten years, the membership went down. They stopped doing a lot of things they used to do. I was on the board for a good many years and, at one of the meetings I suggested that they put on an Arts Club competition and invite all the people in the southern region to compete. They decided to do so, and they made me the head of it.

The new show was named the Bluegrass Art Exhibition.

> We only had it every other year. I think we had seven shows. Ray Kinstler, who painted a portrait of one of the US presidents, was a judge at one of them.

After the exhibition's first year, the City of Louisville approached Nancy and asked if they could link her event to a program the city

held annually called "A Salute to the Arts." With the approval of
The Arts Club board, this association took place.

> After that, each year, the prizes got better and larger. The
> first year the top prize was $1,000. Later we gave a lot of
> prizes, and several were in the $2,000 to $3,000 category.
> Interesting part was that the city used to have art shows
> itself. Louisville had always been famous in its cultural
> arts—music, dance. Yet they had stopped having any
> kind of interest in the fine arts (painting, sculpture, et cet-
> era). Our Arts Club Bluegrass Art Exhibition got the city
> started again. As it went along, Charles Wright got inter-
> ested in working with us, and at one point the Speed Art
> Museum thought they might. But they didn't want to put
> up any money, and the biggest job was raising the money
> for prizes. It wasn't difficult to raise money for the local
> Watercolor Society, which had an open membership, but
> The Arts Club was a private club, so that made it difficult.
> Fortunately, I had Frank Rankin, an extremely influential
> Louisvillian, to help me get the needed funds.

The Bluegrass Art Exhibitions were a highlight of the art scene
in Louisville for fifteen years. Nancy changed the focus every so
often, sometimes inviting regional artists whose primary focus was
on modern art, sometimes inviting artists who were in a particular
age category. On occasion she invited entrants from a larger geo-
graphical area. Part of the planning involved locating exhibition
halls and working with Louisville government entities to get the
arrangements made. Most of the time the artists' entries were sent
to her home and she stockpiled them until a few days before the
show, at which point she had to take charge of their transportation
to the chosen arena and the substantial task of getting them hung.

It was a labor of love; the pride on her face when she talked
about this achievement testified to her enjoyment and her pleasure
in helping other artists. Unfortunately, when the time came to stop
being chair of this event, Nancy and the board of The Arts Club

disagreed about the disbursement of the funds remaining in the Exhibition account. She explained:

> As time went on, I approached the Kentucky Colonels, which was a well-known and well-funded statewide philanthropic organization. Frank was on the board and he supported me. So, every year the Kentucky Colonels gave me $1,000 to $2,000 for a prize. There was a stipulation that I had to let them know who had won it and how much the person got. I had to show that the money was spent for nothing but prizes. That's where my trouble with The Arts Club started.
>
> After so many years, I couldn't be the chairman of the exhibition, and the president couldn't get anyone else to do it, so there was no show. Yet I had a little over $2,000 in my arts account, which was money from the Kentucky Colonels. The board of The Arts Club wanted to take the money. When the club didn't have the show, the Kentucky Colonels wrote to ask about their money. The board asked me to deal with it. I asked the Kentucky Colonels what they wanted me to do, and they asked me for my suggestion. I said that, if they didn't want it returned, that I thought it should be put in an endowment fund. Then, in future years, if the Arts Cub started to support the arts again, the money could be used for that.
>
> In the meantime, some of the members of the board got furious with me, accusing me of keeping the money from them. When I got the letter from the Kentucky Colonels, I called the president and told her what had happened. The money went into an endowment fund; it is still there, and it can only be used for a prize of some sort. There were people mad at me for doing this, and I was upset that they wanted to take the money.

Nancy would often become exercised when she saw something happen that she thought was wrong. This, however, was the only time that her children were made fully aware of her anger. She felt that her integrity had been questioned and she resigned from the club.

> At the last Bluegrass Art Exhibition, members of the Kentucky Watercolor Society approached me. They told me how much they had enjoyed the shows and, since The Arts Club wasn't going to do it anymore, they wanted to take it over, and wanted my advice on how to do it. Now the Kentucky Watercolor Society Show is one of the biggest in the nation. All I did was help them get started, but I am a member of that society. They did ask me to come in and work on that show, but I've done my work and it is enough.

"Enough" didn't happen until 1988, when she was eighty years old.

The years 1974–1987 were fruitful for Nancy, with painting and the Bluegrass Art Exhibition taking up much of her time. Both her poetry and her art were gaining recognition. The Kentucky Federation of Women's Clubs published some of her poetry; Ray Kinstler proposed her for the National Arts Club, the premier arts society in the United States, where a painting of hers was exhibited the following year; and people (some of whom she knew but many she didn't) started buying her paintings.

These were also the years when she was honored for all the work she had done for others. She was named a Kentucky Colonel (the first of two times); the mayor of Louisville recognized her as a Distinguished Citizen and the following year awarded her the title "Honorary Citizen"; and she was given an award by the state medical auxiliary and an honorary life membership "for her numerous innovative contributions."

....

You can see the breadth of Nancy's work on the next few pages.

Nancy with her art at an exhibition, 1991

Indiana Shore, Ohio River / watercolor, 1986

Leah Jackson Wolford / oil, 1970

North Carolina Pinecones / watercolor, c. 1991

Purple Orchid / watercolor, 1986

Flowers / watercolor, 1991

The Farm / acrylic, 1980

Little Goose Creek / acrylic, 1972

Town Square / acrylic, 1976

Chair Study / acrylic, 1982

© Nancy Evans Roles

Self-portrait / acrylic, c. 1982

NINETEEN

SPIRITUAL MEDITATIONS

"GOD IS THE ETERNAL PROGRESSIVE CREATIVE FORCE

OR ENERGY WE CALL LIFE." (1985)

An artist's faith is the crucial beginning point for all creativity, and the true basis for all creative activity whatever the undertaking. If there is no faith of any kind, there is no center or ground from which to proceed. The questions of what constituted ultimate reality and what was the meaning of life were metaphysical subjects that fascinated Nancy. Most important was the integration of the personal and interpersonal with the cosmos. When Nancy was eighty-five, she articulated her approach to the Divine in a letter to Barbara:

> To me, judgment, discipline, and love are human rela-
> tionships. To me, God is the eternal progressive creative
> force or energy we call life, that force found in all nature,
> organic and inorganic—that force which is continually
> revolving in cycles, changing and expanding. Within the
> eons of time, with the revolving and expanding of organic
> and inorganic matter, that which has not been "fruitful"

is slowly but gradually dried up and cast away, while the life force (energy) within all organic and inorganic matter continues creatively, i.e., the "fruitful" evolutionary processes wherein scientists observe mutations (and improved results) evidence a constant move toward perfection. As matter in either form is more "fruitful," the life within (energy) becomes more closely unified with the creative force from which it sprang. Nature, as we know it from studying our planet and our specific universe through space explorations, continually moves in orderly evolutionary patterns through expanding cycles toward perfection. This system, which to me includes the human being, is a natural process that pertains to matter and has nothing to do with God as judge but everything to do with God (Creativity), the driving force within. (Above, I use the word "fruitful" in the sense that Jesus did when he spoke to the fig tree.)

Later in the letter she went on to say:

If we conceive of God as Unconditional Love, there can be no judgment. . . . I am optimistic enough to believe that someday "living" will embrace the human relationships of the command "Love one another."

That conclusion was the direct result of her understanding of God as creative force, as energy, as life itself (in Hebrew scripture, "I am that I am" or the verb "to be"). For Nancy, to be creative was to grow towards perfection; to love unconditionally amounted to the same thing because it was completely and totally creative. To many, this would seem to negate the idea of a personal god. Yet Nancy's response would have been to state that there could be nothing more personal than the creative force that is at the seat of our animation, or, as Paul Tillich said, the "ground of our being."

She also never quit believing, as she had stated at her childhood confession, that Jesus was the son of God and her personal savior, the one through whom she could discern and cherish life's meaning, could perceive God . . . and her daily life of prayer, study, and action reflected this commitment. As she had stated in one of her Sunday school lessons, honest prayer began with the heart's yearning to be in communion with God, and to align one's priorities, desires, and relationships with the creative force. For her, this gave prayer its substance, its strength, and its resultant peace. In 1995, Nancy wrote a prayer for the Thanksgiving meal that reflected this theology:

> Almighty God, our Father,
> We thank you for the gift of life and this beautiful and bounteous world wherein we spend the days of our years. Grant us the wisdom and courage to live, expressing in word and deed a love that is continually expanding and changing to encompass the new cultures and new civilizations of present and future generations.
> As we celebrate today, may we recall the love of our forefathers, who gave thanks for their blessings, in a new world and with a new culture, on a special day set for mass celebration of love for you and mankind.
> Bless this food and all present, that each one may grow as Jesus the Christ taught us to live and love our God and Brother. In Jesus's name, Amen.

While Nancy's faith had immediacy and she was a firm believer in the passage from the biblical Letter of James that said "I by my works will show you my faith," by the closing years of her life she had become convinced that eternal life existed for all souls. She would have defined "soul" as the living creative force, the spirit that is immortal and a part of God. She wrote:

> It is my opinion that when you die, your body, of course, is ashes to ashes, but your spirit lives on. I know that is true. About two or three years ago, I dreamed about my mother. I hadn't dreamed about her since she died, and this was the only time that I did dream about her. In the dream, a very vivid dream, I was going somewhere, and went to a filling station. I couldn't get to the pumps, so I drove to where I could park. I walked around to the front

of the station. I looked up, and who was coming towards me but my mother. She looked like she did before she had wrinkles, and she had on a dress that I recognized. She looked at me and smiled. She recognized me. I was right ready to give her a kiss on her cheek when she walked right past me and disappeared right in front of my eyes.

I couldn't understand that dream for a while. I finally figured it out. Previous to that dream there had been some times that I hadn't been feeling very well, and had thought that it might be that my time to go was near. I figured that Mama passed me by because there was still work I had to do.

Had Mama not been a living spirit I would never have dreamed that. It isn't the whole reason I believe that the spirit continues after someone dies, but it certainly is a strong one. We have a brain; it is the organ through which the mind works. The mind is not located and centered in any one person but is all around you. All that is around you formulates the thinking of the mind.

When you die, your spirit is reunited with the spirit of the universe and only takes a form when it wants to perform some function. For example, I have looked at friends at different times of my life and felt I saw Christ in them. As far as taking form, no, but Christ was there. At times, this spirit that has gone on enters into someone. To me, this universe is continually being created. To me, this is the way the spirit is. When you die, you become a part of the creative movement.

For Nancy, life could be lived on moral grounds and pleasure could be experienced. However, joy, fulfillment, and peace rested on the knowledge that one's place in the universe was a part of something bigger. Without that, a time would come when the party ended and only sadness or anger remained. God had not failed; God's love was unconditional or, to phrase it in Nancy's terms, the creative force continued unabated. But the individual who denied unconditional love's reality—the understanding that we are all a part of the procession towards perfection—and thus did not experience it, lost what life is about.

To her, real true joy is found in the peace that ensues from recognizing with wonder and thankfulness our communion with all that creates. Nancy believed that with all her heart.

TWENTY

HER FAMILY CALLS

"OUR NATURAL RESPONSE IS UNDERSTANDING AND

KINDNESS, WHICH LOVE DICTATES, BUT WISDOM REQUIRES

THE EXERCISE OF CAUTION AND RESERVE." (1975)

After living her faith, Nancy's next priority was her family. From 1969 until the early 1990s, Nancy and Earl spent a good deal of their time traveling to see their daughters and their families. (Alan and his family remained in Louisville—no travel required.) They journeyed east about four times a year to celebrate holidays and marriages, births and graduations—and sometimes "just because." All the trips were by car, which entailed a fifteen-hour ride, often driven straight through in one day. When Barbara once suggested her parents fly, Earl responded that it was too expensive and that he was saving the money for her inheritance. Barbara's riposte: "Go head and fly, Dad; I can afford it." They drove.

One of the trips east, however, and one Nancy took alone, was to Lancaster, Pennsylvania, where her sister, Mattie, lived. Mattie's husband, John, had retired from his profession as an architect, and the couple's days were slow. After losing much of her hearing in college, Mattie struggled for twenty years, then had an operation that improved her hearing for a while, but it had deteriorated again by this point. John had suffered from polio as a youth and was having a hard time walking. Both had chronic pain. Then, one morning in 1975, when Mattie woke up, John was not there. She dozed a bit and then went looking. When she found him, it was too late. He had had a heart attack and had been dead for about an hour.

Nancy's attitude towards her sister was loving, even though the two had strong personalities that sometimes clashed. In writing about John's death in a letter to Carolyn, Nancy said:

> None can know the anxieties and fears that accompany loneliness, caused by death or otherwise, unless we experience the same or similar jolts. But it is heartbreaking to those who listen and love. We try, but cannot express the depth of sympathy we feel, and our anxious concern, our desire to help. Our natural response is understanding and kindness, which love dictates, but wisdom requires the exercise of caution and reserve.

It was not easy for Nancy to comfort Mattie; her sister's sensibilities were prickly. Ever since her hearing loss in college, Mattie had felt that Nancy had "stepped into her footsteps," and that feeling continued throughout her life. Still, they were sisters, they loved each other, and Nancy tried to be present and tender.

Her transition from parenting and community service to focusing more time on developing her artistic skill had to be set aside again in the fall of 1977 due to another crisis. Because of Earl's position as an industrial surgeon, his patients were usually from blue-collar backgrounds, and he often treated people of limited means. Some paid five dollars; some gave him goods in lieu of payment; even if they couldn't pay, he'd always treat them because of his kindness and fatherly nature.

One of his patients, however, concocted a scheme to defraud insurance companies through arranged automobile accidents. This man referred the "victims" to Earl with their rehearsed complaints because he knew of Earl's sympathetic approach. The insurance payout was dependent on the victims' "suffering," which had to be documented by a physician. This, however, was dependent on the patient's verbal recitation to the physician and, unfortunately, Earl believed what he was told.

As a favor to Alan, who was practicing law in Louisville, Earl then sent these patients to Alan for legal help with their insurance claims. As far as Earl was concerned, he was helping those in his care. But because insurance cases sometimes involved going to court, Alan referred these people to other lawyers, fearing that there might be a negative impression were the doctor and the lawyer for these clients related. Later, Earl recalled:

> Alan came out one night and asked, "What's all this about one of your patients being held for fraud in insurance?" I didn't know what he was talking about. Alan mentioned the man's name, and I did know him. He was a patient of mine and I had operated on him, thought a lot of him. The whole business came as a surprise to me. Within a couple of weeks, both Alan and I were indicted as co-conspirators in this man's insurance fraud. . . .
>
> Of course, we were both falsely accused and were acquitted. I got a letter from one of the female jurors later, which said that she saw no evidence at all and she had sat there wondering why there was a trial. The chairwoman of the jury said the same thing. I was seventy-two at the time, and after the trial was over, I went back to my practice and continued in medicine for another six years before I retired.

Earl saw this as an "incident." Because of his position in industrial medicine, he had acted as an expert witness for many years, and he was not intimidated by a courtroom or testifying in front of a jury. When he was on the stand, he faced the jury and proceeded to educate them in a fatherly way and won them all.

For the family, it was a serious situation and a tense time. The newspaper accounts were prejudicial, and Alan's reputation was damaged by the mere fact that he was indicted, even though the judge dismissed the case against him after the assistant DA made his presentation. However, the judge did allow Earl's case to go to trial.

Barbara and Carolyn came down for the trial and the family drew
together and gave their father and brother full-fledged support. At
no time did anyone in the family doubt Alan's or Earl's innocence;
they were ethical men and had always been so. Earl was acquitted
December 22, 1977.

Nancy never wrote about this experience, although she did
comment once:

> After the acquittal, we all walked down the street and there
> was a cathedral there and we all went inside and knelt in
> prayer for a few minutes. Then we went over to the Pen-
> dennis Club and were guests of the Wolfords for lunch.

Nancy's dear friend Evelyn Wolford said that Nancy backed Earl
completely when he was indicted and tried. As Evelyn remembered
it, some people had their doubts, and Nancy and Earl lost some
friends. Evelyn said that Nancy was hurt, but she would only express
that by commenting, when the name of a person who'd hurt her
came up, that the person was "someone she used to know." After
the trial was over, Earl said, "We have to have a party." He wanted
to show everyone that everything was OK. Earl made up the guest
list with the regular standbys. Evelyn thought it worked. Nancy and
Earl visited Barbara for Christmas that year and put the experience
behind them.

The years after the trial included many occasions and activities
during which Nancy's focus was on her children's lives. She bolstered Alan's comeback from the trial with counsel and aid, and he
welcomed it. When Barbara pursued a master's degree in religion,
Nancy constructed and sent her daughter several long letters discussing various aspects of religion and faith. Carolyn had married
in 1967, but the couple divorced after only a few years. Nancy was
just a phone call away during that difficult period, and she celebrated Carolyn's new life and eventual marriage to Mark Fleder.
She continued her habit of sending "care packages" to her children
just as she had done when they were in college (for their birthdays,
Barbara and Alan always received a yellow cake with freshly shred-
ded coconut in the icing while Carolyn got a derby pie).

Her unconditional love was also given to her brother. From the time Bill and his wife, Adele Wiley Evans, were married in the late 1920s, Adele had kept Bill from having virtually any relationship with his sisters. Nancy had adored her brother in their youth, and the pain of not knowing anything about his life was deep:

> Bill always took his wife's side. In later years, when I went down to Greensboro with my children on our way to Greenville, we would meet Bill downtown, not at his house. He didn't pursue any relationship between himself and the family outside of a yearly Christmas card with a note. The last time I saw Adele in Greensboro was rough. She was on a tear. I was with both Mattie and Mama, and Mama was very old and not well. We went into the living room after Bill opened the door, and Bill said that Adele was very sick and that we couldn't stay. Mattie couldn't be around Adele without the sparks flying and she went into the other room to see Adele. Shortly afterwards Bill told us to go into town. He was supposed to join us for dinner that night, but he called and said he couldn't come. He told us to call before we came out the next day, but we were afraid he would say not to come, so we just went. Bill came out of the house and we stayed in the front yard talking. Mama wanted to go in, but Bill said no. We stayed a few minutes more and then left.
>
> About six weeks before Mama died, Bill did come to Louisville to see her, and I believe she knew that he was there. Other than what I've related, I didn't have any contact with my brother for over forty years. The night Adele died, he called me in Louisville. I literally had to ask him if he wanted me to come down. He said yes. Mattie came too. I stayed several days and Mattie stayed a week.

With Adele's death in 1972, Bill became interested in rejoining the family and assuming his position as brother and uncle. He eventually moved to Louisville, and Nancy endorsed this decision. They did become close again; he did not, however, ever discuss the forty-two years that he had practically shunned his sisters. Perhaps it was his faithfulness to his marriage vows that had kept him away, but it was a testament to Nancy's faith that she opened her arms to him.

Earl retired in 1983 and immediately recreated his office in one of the ground-floor rooms in his home. He then sought out opportunities for intellectual growth—Russian classes, law school courses, and computer literacy classes. Nancy's response to Earl's retirement was pointed: she would not do the same. She had made him brown bag lunches for the last several years of his office practice and she continued doing so, putting his lunch in the refrigerator so he could retrieve it whenever he chose. They laughed about it, saying marriage was "for better or for worse, but not for lunch." It was obvious to both of them that these golden years would not be spent idly.

Their continued involvements in their community and, for Nancy, with her art, were interrupted frequently by visits from both Barbara's and Carolyn's families. A surprise party at Big Spring Country Club given by the children and their spouses commemorated Earl's eightieth birthday. There were about fifty people there for the dinner. In a booklet with some written toasts, there is the following:

> May the memory of the love and joy expressed in word and deed during the several days of celebration on the occasion of your 80th birthday remain in your heart till the end of time. Love, Nancy.

Again, in 1988, the children gave a party for Nancy and Earl's fiftieth anniversary. This one was at The Arts Club. There were over ninety guests at the event, and there were another twenty-six who sent either flowers or cards. In addition, Nancy and Earl went to Scarsdale to attend their granddaughter Sarah's debut that same year. (True throughout his life to his thrifty ways, Earl wore the same tuxedo with tails he had used when he was "on the boards" in his twenties. Nancy did make him buy a new shirt—and got him to refrain from bringing the top hat and spats.)

When Nancy reached her eightieth birthday, she didn't want another party. She instructed Carolyn to find a place on the Carolina coast where everyone could gather for a family celebration. The site chosen was Ocean Isle Beach, just north of the South Carolina line. Memories of Nancy's youth on the beach with friends and dinners of Southern barbecue and hush puppies were intertwined with joyous days with her husband, children, and grandchildren. The weeklong visit was such a success for all that it was repeated several times in subsequent years. Nannie Evans would have smiled, as Nancy did, to see the interplay of a close family at the beach in her home state and the bantering among the thirteen who embraced these vacations as the normal consequence of love.

Nancy and Earl Roles, 1988

TWENTY-ONE

THE FINAL YEARS TOGETHER

"MARRIAGE IS SOMETHING WE ALL MUST WORK TO REALIZE,

NOT ONLY AN EMOTIONAL LIFE TOGETHER, BUT, EVEN MORE

IMPORTANT, A GROWING SPIRITUAL RELATIONSHIP." (C. 1998)

Broadening one's vision through international travel was one of the Dewey prerequisites for teaching well and living a successful life. Until she was in her fifties, Nancy's foreign travel had included only her trips to Germany and England and the one cruise to Bermuda. When the time finally came that she could see the world, from the late 1960s on, Nancy made it a habit to study the history and the art of the countries on her itinerary. She kept five-subject notebooks on her investigations and on her return was able to discuss her opinions about these countries and even, on occasion, give lectures about them.

The records show that not only did Nancy and Earl visit the United Kingdom several times, but they also visited all the European countries including Turkey, made trips to the Mediterranean islands, Japan, and China, and traveled several times to Canada and the Caribbean. One of their journeys was even on the world-famous Concorde.

Their trip to Russia was perhaps the most intriguing to her:

We went to Russia between our trips to Japan and to China. Of course, it was the Soviet Union when we were there. When you went from one section of Russia to another, you encountered different-looking people. But the Russians were just like us, and I loved it. There are three palaces we visited around St. Petersburg, which was called Leningrad when we were there. We spent the whole day there in one of the palaces and it was beautiful. But you couldn't help but think of all the money that was spent on the palaces when so many were poor. No wonder they had a revolution. Ninety percent of the people at the time of the revolution were illiterate. After that, under Communism, everyone had to go to school, free of charge.

We took a trip down the Volga for eight days. One of the professors who was with us was a professor of Russian at the University of Georgia (USA). He was invited to come to lecture, and there was a Russian who was part of the KGB who was along. Fascinating to hear. I really thought I learned quite a bit from them. When we hear so much about people going to Siberia, maybe, instead of putting people in prison, we should have a place like Siberia. The coldest place in the Soviet Union, but you are paid and given a place to live. If you do what you are supposed to do, become a good citizen, then your time is reduced and you get to come back home. Gorbachev was president while we were there. The KGB man kept telling us about the wonderful things Gorbachev was doing.

After we returned from Russia and people asked me about my trip, I told them how wonderful I thought it was, and my opinion about what good I thought the government under Gorbachev was doing. Nobody believed me, thought I had been brainwashed. I got to the point I wouldn't talk about it. Then, about six months later everybody heard the news about the wonderful things the Premier was doing, and everyone started calling me and asking me to make speeches.

To show you how people see things differently: the

same summer I went to Russia, the head of the Louisville
Orchestra got invited to go there to conduct. He was a
celebrity, so someone was with him all the time. He stayed
in the same hotel we did, and he came back saying that
his room was bugged and that he couldn't go out without
people following him. Our rooms weren't bugged, and I
went where I wanted to. He couldn't seem to understand
that it was his position that made it important that he be
kept safe.

Even later, with failing health, Nancy and Earl continued to
explore. They cruised in the Caribbean as late as 1993. Nancy did
not go on the islands because she could not climb rocks, but that
didn't dim her pleasure; she was at heart an adventurer. The imprint
from her time with Dr. Alexander, who maintained that the truly
educated person was one who traveled and thus garnered a broader
perspective, was permanent. Travel was also an opportunity for the
artist to gather new impressions of nature and new understandings
of life's rhythms, her desire to interpret and create art and beauty
an ever-present yearning.

·······

Interspersed with these trips, however, were periods when the
couple's advancing age brought health issues that needed attention,
and each of these was accompanied by increasing fragility.

Nancy had to have an appendectomy in 1979. It was perhaps the
start of her not having a great deal of confidence in doctors, even
though, with her involvement in the medical world, some cynicism
must have been in place well before that:

When I had appendicitis, they did a certain kind of blood
test that told them if you had it. Mine was normal. And
there I lay all day long so hurting I couldn't see straight. I
finally said, "I don't care what you do, but do something."
They went in to see what was wrong; they couldn't find
my appendix. It was buried behind my kidney. They had

to move my intestines aside, bit by bit. Right then the appendix burst.

There were accidents, perhaps not unexpected given Nancy's activity level. She broke her leg, her back, and her wrist; she ended up having to have both hips replaced; she began having some kind of muscle pain that was later diagnosed as polymyalgia rheumatica, although she was convinced that she had come down with Lyme disease during a visit to Barbara's. She became increasingly angry with the doctors because they treated her like an old lady, who therefore couldn't know what she was talking about. They just didn't know Nancy.

Earl started having difficulties as well. He had always been somewhat passionate about "physical culture." Once the children were gone, he turned one of the bedrooms on the lower level into a gym and exercised on most days. However, at eighty-five he began to have symptoms that sent him in for a rare physical examination; the diagnosis was colon cancer. An operation removed the malignancy, but he had to have two others to treat complications from the first. The pain of these procedures convinced him that at his age he would rather die than go through any of that again. This orthopedic surgeon, who had performed countless operations and whose own medical history was clean and suitable for his age, could not tolerate pain and thus refused to acknowledge the cancer when it returned three years later.

....

Because of Earl's frugality, the couple was in the financial position of being able not only to make all these trips but also to handle the fiscal challenges of their later years. They had decided that they wanted to remain in their home, which meant that the expense of maintaining the property would continue and that they'd need to acquire equipment to make them more comfortable: Nancy required a health monitoring system; Earl needed oxygen; they both began to wear hearing aids; and they purchased a bed that could have its head electronically raised or lowered. They also had a security system installed and got a black Labrador retriever for additional peace of mind.

When it became necessary, they hired a caregiver. While Earl was initially reluctant to have anyone routinely in the house, he quickly changed that attitude once Geri Bell was hired. She had been of considerable help to the daughter of one of their lifelong friends, and Earl felt she was trustworthy. They eventually needed 24/7 care, and Geri helped manage the flow of daily aides. She remained a part of their lives not only through Earl's death but until Nancy herself was gone. Alan was in charge of the day-to-day decisions by that time, but both Nancy and Earl fully appreciated Geri's care and loyalty.

Even as his health declined, Earl could not seem to release control of decision-making about money or other significant issues. He did not sign over his power of attorney to Nancy until the spring of 1996, two weeks before he died. By that time, Nancy had accrued some money of her own and was not totally dependent on Earl financially. As early as the 1960s she had managed to start squirreling away some cash. It is interesting to note that both Earl's mother and his wife had to secrete money, though for opposite reasons (his father being too generous, and Earl too tight). Perhaps Nancy's funds came from gifts from her mother; later, the money must have come out of profits from the Greenville farm. While never wanting to rebel against her husband's wishes—her understanding of marriage meant that she would always support him in every way she could—at that time Nancy did start to make some of her own decisions and carry them through. Wherever she got the funds, Nancy began buying stock. She explained:

> I paid for it in cash. Earl didn't know until the following year when he had to pay income tax. He said, "What's this? You can't buy stock." He always reminded me that he had to pay taxes on it. I would say, "If you didn't, you'd have to pay me that much extra money!"

Alan later related that Earl was always of the opinion that women couldn't participate intelligently in matters involving money. Earl probably knew better, but he wanted to remain the one who handled all the finances, and Nancy's branching out definitely bothered him.

Nancy progressed from using various stockbrokers whenever she decided to purchase a particular stock to, in the 1980s, considering the use of an investment counselor. During her conversation with John Gordinier, a counselor at a highly respected Louisville investment firm, she learned that he was the grandson of someone she had known and liked, so she opened an account with him. Dividends came regularly and were her primary source of independent income until 1997. Nancy did like "safe bets" in her investments, and she directed John to only offer her stock that paid a dividend of at least 5 percent.

Nancy had always been generous. She helped out her children when she felt they needed it. By 1995, her personal annual income exceeded her own needs and desires, and she gave a large percentage to the church and to various charities.

....

As their parents aged, Carolyn and Barbara increased the frequency of their visits to Louisville, and they were both there on April 30, 1996, when Earl died. He was twelve days short of his ninety-first birthday. He was cremated, and a celebration of life was held at the funeral home. Alan videotaped the service because he was sensitive to the effect death could have on a spouse's attention and knew his mother would want to remember the details of the service. The funeral and the days surrounding it were a tender family occasion for her.

When Nancy wrote about Earl's death, she said:

> A few weeks before he died, he was conscious that he would not be here very much longer. He got to the point that he wouldn't eat. He did the best he could.
>
> I asked him two or three times about his thoughts, but he never talked about being sick. I also tried to get his thoughts about his dying, but while he asked me many times to give him my thoughts about life after death, he

wouldn't give me his own. He believed in God. He never
went to bed at night without getting down on his knees
and saying his prayers. He carried a New Testament
around in his pocket and he read it. He believed in Jesus,
but in a different way than the churches say. He didn't go
in for the virgin birth and the stuff that comes down from
the church. Thought it was completely foolish.

Both Nancy and Earl had previously faced the death of loved
ones. They believed in an afterlife of some sort, although Nancy's
attitude was that she would "cross that bridge" when she came to it.
They were pragmatic, believing that cremation was the only logical
decision since cemeteries took up a lot of land, and tombstones
and grave upkeep required financial resources that neither thought
appropriate.

Earl's death was expected, and Nancy dealt with it the way she
dealt with all the sad events in her life: following the Brown family
motto, she accepted the inevitable and was thankful for her blessings. Nancy and Earl had been married for such a long time that
the emptiness was very much present:

> I miss him mostly at meals. He is often right there. I feel
> him sitting over there, and I'm pretty sure he is present . . .
> but while he lived, we both agreed that life is for the living,
> not the dead. I therefore do not go around grieving over
> my loss.

When Barbara asked Nancy to comment on her relationship
with Earl, she wrote about it, then put her writings in a folder that
was only opened some years after she died.

> You asked about Dad and our relationship. Before we
> were married, we talked about many different subjects.
> Usually we saw things quite differently and therefore had
> some very interesting discussions. This type of conversa-
> tion continued throughout our fifty-eight years together.
> They were different but friendly, and I expect we both

profited by hearing the sometimes-opposite views. Only when the subjects dealt with personal plans or actions already taken did emotions enter the picture.

Earl often came in and told me of some experience of the day at the office or hospital and related how he had acted or reacted, then waited to see what I thought about it. If I said nothing, he would ask me. When I hesitated to answer because my thinking was not in sync with his, he would not rest until I did answer. As a rule, my answers irritated him, and he would respond by saying, "You never agree with me. Why do you always take the other side?" He then generally left the room emotionally angry or upset. Nevertheless, before the evening was over, he would again bring up the subject and defend his point of view but also ask questions in detail respecting my view. Maybe days later he would inadvertently say something that indicated he had accepted my comments and acted upon them, though he never came to the point of admitting it.

One thing seemed impossible for him: to say "I'm sorry." I think he was remembering seeing his mother more or less rule over his father, and he was determined no female was ever going to have that status with him. This for a long time bothered me, but I learned to toss it aside.

I did not talk about my husband and our relationship to my friends (only Evelyn sometimes sensed my problems or concerns). As I came to know the husbands of my friends, I always reminded myself of how lucky I was. I never met one I thought was anywhere near as tolerant and understanding as Earl. Earl had a hot temper and often lost it and really fussed. I hated a fuss and usually kept quiet. When he finished fussing, he immediately forgot about it and, if reminded of what he had said, he swore he never said such a thing. When I realized this, his fussing no longer bothered me.

I think our differences were often healthy and held us together. Truly, he was a good man with very high moral standards. Overlooking those points, our life together was very good. . . . I think Earl and I had good reason to count our many blessings.

All married people have differences and problems. We simply have to live with them and work them out. Marriage is something we all must work to realize, not only an emotional life together, but, even more important, a growing spiritual relationship. As Earl and I grew old together, we both came to know this spiritual unity and were very comfortable with it.

It seems that the New College precept of "searching for guiding principles and ultimate values" was an acknowledged part not only of Nancy's life but of Earl's as well.

TWENTY-TWO

FINISHING UP

"LET US FEEL THE RHYTHMIC PULSE OF LIFE ETERNAL.

WE HAVE NO TIME FOR TEARS." (LATE 1960s)

Nancy had always been a practical woman; after Earl's death, her practical side came out even more strongly. The mural she had been painting with her life, which she hoped would be a creditable work product, was just about finished. But details remained—modification of parts that had been left slightly undone, the matting and the framing of her accomplishment—and then the workspace must be cleared.

With the children, she spread Earl's ashes over the property he had so loved. She then took account of what needed to be done to go forward. Earl's estate was legally settled in 1998. He had promised his Nancy that she would be able to live at Woodhill Valley for the rest of her life, and probate validated this.

Nancy donated Earl's medical equipment to the Supplies Overseas program of the medical society and his clothing and accessories to Goodwill and other charities. She then proceeded to look at the house and determine what was needed to put it in good shape. The residence had been neglected during Earl's illness, and considerable repairs needed to be made. Over the next three years, Nancy had the interior of the house painted, put in new carpeting, bought several new appliances, repaired the roof, and made an unsuccessful attempt to solve the problem of rainwater gouging out the front hillside. She also bought a new Oldsmobile 88 and, on top of it all, became involved in neighborhood association meetings.

With Alan as her attorney, Nancy made sure her legal, financial, and end-of-life affairs were in order. Upon death, her body was to be donated to the University of Louisville medical school because she felt this was the most efficient use of a death. (As it turned out, her teeth were the donation they found most useful.)

From 1997 on, Nancy began actively distributing her wealth. She gave regular financial and nonfinancial gifts to family and continued her philanthropic giving, donating money to more than twenty charitable organizations in 1997 alone.

In 1994, Nancy had gone to North Carolina with her brother and daughter Barbara to do genealogical research, and all through the 1990s she continued to examine her family's history. "Getting back to her roots" was an occupation that vied with her determination to continue to paint. In the early 1990s, Barbara worked with Bill to write a partial history of his life. This history motivated Nancy and Earl to tell Barbara their stories, and talking about her life encouraged Nancy to trace her family's lines.

Nancy's health continued to decline. She had to get a brace for her right hand so that the almost claw-shaped configuration resulting from her arthritis would not be a deterrent to her holding a brush. In addition, standing for long periods had become difficult. There was a generalized pain that would not abate; she resisted talking about it, and her children understood that she would prefer to ignore it as much as possible.

In May 1997, Nancy grew short of breath to the extent that her doctor did a heart catheterization. He found that she had 80–85 percent occlusion of her right coronary artery, 40–50 percent occlusion of her left main coronary artery, and 80–90 percent occlusion of one of her carotid arteries. By November she was using oxygen at home. She refused to be sidelined, however, and continued with her social life and her art.

That same year, Nancy's brother had had some health issues while living at his retirement center. The center moved Bill to the nursing facility and put him on medications that made him hallucinate. When Nancy and Alan objected, the staff said Bill would die without them. Nancy told them that he was going to die someday anyway and that she felt he would prefer that to happen while lucid. Nancy then invited Bill to live with her. The children had no objection; not only did Nancy and Bill want it, but the arrangement provided them with each other's company and a more secure environment. As it turned out, Bill lived another five years in complete control of his physical and mental functions.

....

When people reach an advanced age, their interests often become more circumscribed. Nancy, at eighty-nine, continued to be interested in external affairs. She continued to watch the news and maintained her subscriptions to *Time* magazine and the *Courier-Journal* (Louisville's morning paper). Nevertheless, she did begin to withdraw from activities outside of her personal relationships. When she was asked to give a speech to the local medical society about her involvement over the years, she declined, giving as her reasons having the care of her brother, her age, and, while still driving, not driving in the inner city.

In 1998 and 1999, Nancy made many trips to doctors and several trips to the hospital, and the year 2000 brought ever-increasing compromises to her health. She had been a caregiver for so long that relinquishing control of her own life was difficult. She fussed for about six months before she began to deal with being elderly. Besides her hearing loss, her eyesight began to fail, and her muscle pain was significant enough that she needed a walker.

However, this did not preclude Nancy's wanting to stay active as long as possible. She took two final trips. The first was a return to Ocean Isle, North Carolina, for her ninetieth birthday celebration with her family. Her family knew it would be her last time at the shore, and they treated it as a festive experience with her at the center.

The second trip was to New York to see her oldest grandchild, James, get married. She took her aide Geri Bell with her and went to every function. She entered into the celebration with a glad heart and during the reception danced with Alan by putting her feet on his and letting him guide her around the room. Barbara and Carolyn watched with tears in their eyes at the fulsome delight of the moment. Nancy was as beautiful looking up into Alan's face as she had been when she made young men's hearts race all those years ago. The trip to New York wasn't easy at her age, but the "come hell or high water" part of her family motto strengthened her resolve to complete it.

By the summer of 2000, Alan was in charge of everything that went on at the Woodhill Valley home, and Barbara and Carolyn were flying to Louisville every few weeks. Besides wanting to spend time with their mother, they thought it was important to give Alan some relief. He had to work hard to keep good caregivers for around-the-clock support.

In addition, Nancy's mind had begun to wander, and she sometimes seemed to inhabit another time and space. Her most common hallucinations were about children; she kept seeing them in danger and would cry out to try to get them help. When she regained her senses, she would comment, "That didn't happen, did it?" One of the many friends who would visit during those last two years commented that she felt Nancy was bigger than her body, bigger than what was happening to her. Her opinion was that Nancy had "higher truths, a higher vision than most people."

Nancy had had the pleasure of watching her mother bless her first great-grandchild in 1969. The significance of this event seemed especially important to Nancy as she grew older and, when she knew her days were numbered, she told her family that she wanted to have the joy of both giving that blessing and spending a final Christmas with them. These wishes were fulfilled in the winter of 2001. Her oldest grandchild, James, brought his son to her in the fall, and the family gathered that December. On Christmas night she was wheeled to the expanded dinner table and given some spiked eggnog along with her meal. Perhaps due to the partial surcease from constant pain, or perhaps due to a gift from God, at the conclusion of the meal she indicated she had something to say. With her aide's help, she rose and welcomed everyone. She thanked her family for decorating the house and preparing the meal. She then paused and added with the saucy smile that so characterized her, "But I think I can take some credit, too, because they are my children and I raised them."

When the holiday was over and all her guests had left, Nancy turned to Geri Bell and said, "My whole body hurts, and it is from the inside out. Don't worry; it's almost over. God takes care of his own. Nothing you can do."

On Saturday night, January 4, 2002, Geri was asleep in her own home when she heard Nancy calling and it woke her up. She called the house, and the caregiver told her that Mrs. Roles was unresponsive. Geri went over to the house, dismissed the caregiver, and called Alan. Alan came immediately, and Barbara and Carolyn booked flights to get there as soon as possible. Geri sat with Nancy all night, holding her hand, rubbing her shoulders and arms, talking to her, saying prayers for her.

Nancy died in the front bedroom of Woodhill Valley at approximately 10:30 a.m. on Sunday, January 5, 2002. She was ninety-three years and four months old. Her death came when she decreed it, after she felt she had done all she could for her family and her community.

For all who knew her, Nancy's life had been a blessing. Because of her advanced age when she died, the memorial service was attended for the most part by individuals of the succeeding generation. They came not only because their own lives had been touched but also to give respect to one whose life had been important to their parents.

A year later, the U of L medical school, having done their work, returned Nancy's ashes to Alan. On May 31, 2003, Alan and Pat, Barbara and Wink, Carolyn and Mark, and Alan's children, Liz and Robert, said brief prayers together on the patio of the Woodhill Valley home and then spread Nancy's ashes over the property.

Nancy had led a memorial service at the annual convention of one of her organizations in the 1960s and had told the gathering:

> The absence of beloved friends on any memorable oc-
> casion is cause for sadness, except our hearts rejoice in

the knowledge of their elevation to positions of honor in another environment. Their vision, devotion, and service, touching God and man, is justly rewarded. Their love, their responsibilities, and their good records are ours to cherish, to shoulder, and to increase. We understand the finality of death when it visits one we love, but we see its significant beauty only with the passage of time. We forget the departure, as our sorrow is quieted by sweet memories. In faith we look forward to a future reunion. Death is not sleep. It is the final miracle of birth. Our departed friends bequeath us a noble heritage. Let us preserve and enhance it. From new frontiers, let us view the infinite beauty of God's creation—the joyous dawn of far horizons. Let us feel the rhythmic pulse of life eternal. We have no time for tears.

....

The mural that Nancy envisioned in her journal when she arrived in England in 1935 began in her imagination with the contemplation of ideas and then the sketching of a theoretical composition. She wrote that she hoped there would be a series of progressive steps taken, each step examined, studied critically, and constructed to incorporate the disparate elements of the adventure into a painting that was a "creditable, worthwhile, interesting, and meaningful accomplishment."

If Nancy's life is viewed as a mural, her finished work reflects a richly colored painting of a twentieth-century woman's journey, the development of a spiritually backdropped, active, compassionate, loving, and creative existence enlivened by sparkle, vitality, enthusiasm, and an always-charitable heart. When she died, Nancy's eternal spirit was absorbed into the evolutionary pattern of all life, the creative movement of God. Her mural was finished, and, as her daughter Carolyn said, "She went home."

AFTERWORD

My mother was not perfect. She was generally late to most social engagements (I used to tease her that she thought it was all right to start getting ready at the time the event itself was to begin); she was frequently impatient with others' lack of perception regarding the issues she considered vital to social progress (her fatigue and frustration were discernible when she returned from meetings she considered frivolous); she was not always able to banish the negative thoughts she was having (I can still see her tightening her lips to hold in a spontaneous adverse reaction); and she was a competent but not meticulous housekeeper (she had better things to do). However, when I look back at her challenges, these faults seem inconsequential. She had to grow up without a father; she had to take up a career that she disliked; she had to deal with a husband she loved but who was determined to control every aspect of their relationship; she had to deal with a child who was severely handicapped and then come to grips with his death; and she had to spend the last couple of years of her life without the use of most of her faculties.

Many people today seem to live in a world where nobility is dismissed and heroes are examined minutely in an effort to find clay feet, where historical fact is trivialized and made subject to interpretation in order to espouse a particular perspective. If my mother's story helps others to investigate issues thoughtfully before advocating any viewpoint or helps them to set and pursue creative goals, or if her journey can be used as a guide for how to live a productive, valuable life, then the creditable work that she accomplished in her own life will continue.

ACKNOWLEDGMENTS

Three people came into my life at just the right time and encouraged me to undertake this venture. Don Mazzella offered to read the record I had compiled for my family and soon came back with "there's a book here," saying that I should write a biography of my mother. During the subsequent years, he continued to support my efforts and agreed to be a beta reader. It is hard to ask someone to judge something you have written, but he made it easy—taking the time to meet with me even when his own writing demanded his full attention. He also introduced me to Ann Marie Sabath, my mentor in this effort, an author whose philosophy of "paying it forward" meant that she was always available at the other end of the phone. She made me set deadlines, bolstered me in every decision I made, and told me I was "doing it right" whenever I felt like it was all too much. Through her I met my editor, Karin Wiberg, whose sagacious advice and expertise tightened my more loquacious inclusive style and made the manuscript much more readable. Karin's comfortable personality, sympathetic guidance, and frequent reassuring comments helped me feel that I was not an outsider in the writing community.

In addition to these three, there were three others whose constant support was significant. My son Robert always remembered what I was doing and frequently asked for updates. His encouragement, quickly voiced, comforted me with his love. My dear friend Edith Hanley read the first draft and told me to keep going, that I had a worthwhile story to tell. That independent encouragement came at a pivotable time, and her continued emotional support has been precious to me.

The last of those without whom I could not have completed this project is my beloved husband, Wink. While he always insisted that it was my book and I should do what I wanted, on many occasions he helped me determine what that actually was.

These six have my deep gratitude for their unwavering confidence in me and my writing, and I want my readers to know what incredible people they are.

Barbara McKinnon's career in social justice and ministry spans more than forty years and began with involvement in community mental health programs. Through her leadership in committee work, fundraising, and direct ministry, her advocacy has supported social services programs for cancer patients as well as for people experiencing domestic violence and/or homelessness. She earned her undergraduate degree in history at Randolph-Macon Woman's College and her master of divinity at General Theological Seminary.